The use of myth in modern literature is a misleadingly familiar theme. Behind Joyce's appropriation of Homer's *Odyssey*, Lawrence's interest in 'primitive' cultures, and Yeats' nationalist folklore, lies a common metaphysical concern with the inhabiting of consciously relative world views. Understood in this way, myth is inherently flexible. It underpinned both Pound's totalised vision of society, which eventually descended into fascism, and the liberal ironic vision of Joyce and Mann. Those critics who see myth only as a form of mystification, or as an illusory search for origins, miss its use by modernists writers to highlight the ultimate contingency of all values even as they are affirmed.

In *Literature, Modernism and Myth*, Michael Bell also considers the relation of modernist myth to 'postmodernity'. The anti-foundational consciousness in such a use of myth enables it to act as a corrective to dogmatic claims, of the right or the left, including those of ideological critique. Bell shows how recent concerns with political and social responsibility, and the role of literature in formulating this, have been inherited from a number of modern writers whose very complexity in this regard has continued to obscure their significance.

This wide-ranging study is not only a comprehensive treatment of a crucial theme in modern literature; it also offers a fresh reading of the relationship between modernity and contemporary concepts of the postmodern, and makes an original contribution to the continuing debate on literature, political responsibility and ethical value.

LITERATURE, MODERNISM AND MYTH

LITERATURE, MODERNISM AND MYTH

Belief and responsibility in the twentieth century

MICHAEL BELL

Professor of English Literature,
University of Warwick

CAMBRIDGE
UNIVERSITY PRESS

Published by the Press Syndicate of the University of Cambridge
The Pitt Building, Trumpington Street, Cambridge CB2 1RP
40 West 20th Street, New York, NY 10011-4211, USA
10 Stamford Road, Oakleigh, Melbourne 3166, Australia

© Cambridge University Press 1997

First published 1997

Printed in Great Britain at the University Press, Cambridge

A catalogue record for this book is available from the British Library

Library of Congress cataloguing in publication data

Bell, Michael, 1941–
Literature, modernism and myth: belief and responsibility in the
twentieth century / Michael Bell.
p.   cm.
Includes bibliographical references and index.
ISBN 0 521 58016 1
1. Literature, Modern – 20th century – History and criticism.
2. Myth in literature.   I. Title.
PN771.B35 1997
809'.915 – dc20   96 14205 CIP

ISBN 0 521 558016 1 hardback

Contents

Contents

IV

Introduction

[F]or although in the life of the human race the mythic is an early
and primitive stage, in the life of the individual it is a late and
mature one.

(Thomas Mann)

The word 'myth' inhabits a twilight zone between literature, philosophy
and anthropology. It means both a supremely significant foundational
story and a falsehood. We therefore use it relationally; one person's belief
is another's myth. But, much as Freud argued that the word *Unheimlich*
(uncanny) *combines* the 'hidden' and the 'familiar', the word 'myth'
superimposes two meanings to reflect a cardinal recognition implicit in
the modern literary use of myth.[1] Stated as a proposition, this is simply
the fact that fully conscious citizens of the twentieth century are aware
that their deepest commitments and beliefs are part of a world view,
whether individual or collective, which cannot be transcendentally
grounded or privileged over other possible world views. The interest lies
not in the proposition itself, but in how it is lived, individually and
collectively. Taken separately, the awareness of differing world views, on
the one hand, and the question of belief or evaluative commitment on
the other, are familiar and comprehensible, whatever internal difficulties
they may each present. My concern is with their combination, which
came to a crucial point of awareness in the modernist decades, roughly
1910 to 1930, and was reflected in the formal modes of modern literature.
This has implications for the present, but it is necessary to revisit the
early decades of the century when these questions were given a decisively
influential, but still misappreciated, formulation.

The double consciousness of living a world view *as* a world view is
importantly encapsulated in modern literary mythopoeia as it unfolds
over the course of the century. I emphasise the term 'mythopoeia', or
mythmaking, rather than 'myth', since my concern is not with myth as a
traditional content or as a means of literary organisation. It is rather with

the underlying outlook that creates myth; or, more precisely again, sees the world in mythic terms. Mythopoeia is the underlying metaphysic of much modernist literature, and a way of approaching vital problems that constantly present themselves reductively. Too often, the discussion of myth is philosophical, literary or political, and fails to grasp the complete problematic that is at stake.

Self-conscious mythopoeia, recognising a world view as such while living it as conviction, is a paradox succinctly formulated by Thomas Mann: 'although in the life of the human race the mythic is indeed an early and primitive stage, in the life of the individual it is a late and mature one'.[2] The magisterial simplicity of the remark begins to dissolve if we try to assess its more specific cash-value. Is there some sleight of hand in the syntax of the sentence, a kind of zeugma, as the term 'mythic' is attributed at once to the earliest and the latest stages of culture? Or, if the term can be applied to both, does it keep the same meaning? And, if the meanings are different, what is the value of superimposing them so as to make them appear the same? What relationship is being suggested between ancient and modern? This positive formulation grew from the pre-Second World War period when Mann was still working on the affirmative mythopoeia of his Joseph novels. And if there is a single work which most summatively agonises over the darker ambivalence and the paradox of myth in relation to modernity, it is Thomas Mann's *Doctor Faustus* looking back from the catastrophe of the Second World War to consider the modern abuses of myth against the backdrop of romantic aestheticism from which, he thought, fascist ideology partly arose. Yet even his 'rejection' of myth is setting myth against myth, accepting that the sinister appeal of regressive political mythologies is to be overcome by a recognition of the mythopoeic basis of his own humanism. As the humanist schoolteacher narrator, Zeitblom, says:

school interests bound the horizon that every life needs in order to develop values, through which, however relative they are, the character and the capacities are sustained. They can, however, do that, humanly speaking, only if the relativeness remains unrecognised. Belief in absolute values, illusory as always it is, seems to me a condition of life.[3]

This is the cardinal recognition of the present book too, and yet, as stated here, its import is ambiguous. Zeitblom's last sentence states a universal need to live convictions in the absolute spirit of belief, but it is unclear whether this applies just to the pupils, in the spirit of Plato's 'great lie', or whether Zeitblom includes himself.[4] If he includes himself, his position is a logical conundrum like the Cretan liar in reverse: he affirms what he knows to be untrue. The reference to the school world already points to the ostrich-like narrowness of Zeitblom's own political horizon, but, by putting this central thought into the mouth of Zeitblom, Mann suggests more than a possible irony at the expense of the character. He also implies that the problem cannot be encompassed at the purely propositional level. The ability truly to live the implications of Zeitblom's statement, to live in the gap between its meanings, is the literary, and therefore the *critical*, dimension of conscious mythopoeia.

Criticism is particularly needful, as most of the great modern writers had powerful, in some cases notorious, convictions; Ezra Pound was nearly convicted of treason for acting on his convictions.[5] Yet they are also obliged to meditate closely on what it meant to have a conviction, since, in the cultural fragmentation of modernity, any belief inevitably became more arbitrary, relative and self-conscious. Sometimes, of course, the word 'myth' has been used to justify totalised and authoritarian convictions, but the word encompasses the whole problematic belief within which convictions are held. That doubleness is the special quality of modernist mythopoeia; sometimes felt as a running conflict between the spirit of dogmatic authority and the relativity of values and convictions. It is present in most of the great writers of the period, albeit in different ways, while the individual ambivalence is further adumbrated by the whole spectrum of writers for whom myth was an important term. The liberal and deconstructive ironies of Mann and Joyce are at one end, the fascist sympathy of Pound at the other, with Eliot, Lawrence and Yeats ambivalently between them. The term 'myth' links these figures into a common problematic whereby each sheds light on the others. All are involved in the problem of what it might now mean to live a conviction, what it is to inhabit a belief.

Being inescapably critical, the topic cannot be approached simply through the semantics of the term 'myth'. It is the development of an elusive meaning inseparable from the self-consciousness of the literary imagination itself. In fact, it is effectively a definition of imaginative literature as an important truth value peculiar to modernity. In the modernist decades, the mythopoeic model, precisely in its elusiveness, its simultaneous reference to belief and to falsehood, made an important contribution to a modern understanding of belief and conviction. Recent attempts to engage the same set of questions in other terms have unwittingly vindicated this point. On one side lies the supplanting of 'myth' by 'ideology' as the common term for describing a world view.

This is an important development to be considered over the course of the present argument. On the other side, seeking to continue the mythic project by other means, lies the school of thought, notably represented by Alasdair MacIntyre, which has tried to base the ethical life on the literary model of narrative, while the philosopher, Richard Rorty, has spelled out an inescapable irony underlying all conviction and, once again, with a strong appeal to literature for his examples.[6]

I sympathise with MacIntyre's invoking of narrative as a way of dealing with the moral life at an adequate level of complexity, but, as I have argued elsewhere, narrative offers only an illusory solution to the problem of grounding.[7] To put the point briefly, there have to be values prior to narrative as the condition of its existence; values which are implicit in the language from which narrative is created. What is largely missing from Rorty is an appreciation of conviction itself. He talks about conviction, and, more troublingly for some readers, he has strong convictions of his own on particular topics, but as a philosopher he feels no obligation to justify these in any transcendent, uncontingent sense. I find a refreshing clarity about this. In the nature of their activity, philosophers will be strong on relativity and weak on conviction. Not weak *in* conviction necessarily, just weak *on* it. In his account of moral convictions as ultimately ungroundable, contingent and to be held in a spirit of irony, Rorty effectively expresses the intellectual structure of modernist mythopoeia, but his way of doing so reinforces the pertinence of the term 'myth' in mediating between the philosophical realm on the one hand and the poetic or pragmatic realms on the other. For modernist mythopoeia is a way of combining radical relativity with the apodictic nature of conviction. And, since we continue to live in the aftermath of this period, in a curious state of having imbibed its meaning without yet consciously understanding it, I believe it is still timely, or in Nietzsche's sense 'untimely', to set out what I actually consider to be a belated argument.[8] MacIntyre and Rorty may stand as a synecdoche for the now vast secondary literature on aesthetics, ethics, anthropology, ethnology, literary and social theory touching on my theme. Much of this discussion is valuable and is part of a necessary process of cultural assimilation. I refer to it parenthetically, but concentrate on my own exposition which is conceived in rather different terms. Since much public debate is both belated, and too abstract to engage the experience in question, my purpose is to show the imaginative experience of which much recent discussion is actually a product.[9]

My approach is not opposed, but complementary. Mythopoeia has to be understood through an evaluative study of its specific instantiations; and reading around the problems central to this study brings home time and again, if not the poverty, then the limits, of theory. The questions of conviction and relativism central to this study have to be posed, but art not so usefully answered, in the abstract. The attempt to do so leads to an ideological jockeying for the purest stance. But, once you have seen the problem of cultural relativism, there is a limit to what can usefully be said at the level of theory. Furthermore, the ideologically unassailable viewpoint is a chimera whose pursuit can be actively damaging. The present study seeks to throw light on the substantive questions through texts in which they have been treated in complex and telling ways, and it also indicates the kind of knowledge it is possible, and desirable, to have of these questions. It therefore examines a series of specific instances while keeping the general question of myth in view. Crucial essays of Nietzsche hold the material within a common analytic purview, as the quotation from *Doctor Faustus* already hints in the 'horizon' image and the emphasis on necessary illusion. Accordingly, an opening, historical section summarises the essential background of German post-romantic thought and its transposition in Nietzsche. The next section considers several different writers creating a composite sense of mythopoeic self-awareness in early twentieth-century literature. Yeats, Joyce and Lawrence are the representative instances, followed by Pound and Eliot whose invoking of myth falls significantly outside this conception. In falling outside it, and in Eliot's case actively resisting it, they help to clarify it while also showing its significance as a critical point of reference. Conrad and Thomas Mann then provide a more general overview of the period leading into the second half of the century through Primo Levi. The third section briefly traces the fortunes, or misfortunes, of myth from the mid-century onwards. It concentrates entirely on narrative fiction since that is the genre most evidently concerned with the creation of collective worlds. These latter authors thematise, as well as exemplify, the central questions as the mythic undergoes new transformations over the period and is increasingly, but problematically, discarded.

PART I

CHAPTER I

Myth in the age of the world view

Martin Heidegger described modernity as the 'age of the world picture':

The expressions 'world picture of the modern age' and 'modern world picture' both mean the same thing and both assume something that never could have been before, namely, a medieval world picture and an ancient world picture. The world picture does not change from an earlier medieval one into a modern one, but rather the fact that the world becomes picture at all is what distinguishes the essence of the modern age.[1]

He claims not just that there is a distinctively modern world picture, but that the characteristic feature of modernity is to be aware of this relativity. The general recognition Heidegger defines came crucially into consciousness in the teens and twenties of the century when the consciousness of living a world view as a world view was instantiated in a number of literary and philosophical works. The present chapter retraces some of the essential movements of thought that led up to this recognition, and their relation to the term 'myth', while subsequent chapters will show in turn something of its reflection in the literary texts of the teens and then of its aftermath throughout the century.

Immanuel Kant's *Critique of Pure Reason* (1781) answered the idealism of Berkeley and the scepticism of Hume by showing how the world is a construction of the human mind according to necessary categories of thought.[2] This universalistic recognition was given a subjectivising reversal by J. G. Fichte who influenced, by his lectures at the University of Jena in the seventeen-nineties, the generation of German romantic thinkers including Friedrich Schlegel and Friedrich von Schelling.[3] Meanwhile a further potential for a relativistic inflection of Kant came from two other important lines of thought over the same period. One was the idea, especially developed by J. G. Herder, that individual peoples have their own particular identity and character expressed in their cultures.[4] The other was the recognition, notably by G. W. F.

Hegel, that all culture develops historically so that the past is also, in the words of the adage, another country.[5] Hegel's Idealist philosophy, however, still saw history as a universal process, and for a long time these potentially relativising recognitions coexisted with nationalistic, Euro-centric and scientistic habits of thought. Anthropological study in the nineteenth century, for example, although it was part of a growing interest in radically other cultural possibilities, still generally thought of 'primitive' peoples as intrinsically inferior; as indeed were the 'working' and 'criminal' classes of European nations.[6]

Only in the second decade of the twentieth century did these relativistic implications begin to touch the cultural foundations, to disturb the living and working premises. The process was still only partial even then, and is far from universal now. Most of the population anywhere continues to live in an older moral universe, just as it inhabits a Newtonian physical world, and maybe, as Thomas Mann suggested, this is no bad thing.[7] But key artists and thinkers were receptive to such seismic shifts in culture. The philosopher Karl Jaspers, in *The Psychology of World Views* (1919), wrote from his original professional standpoint of a psychologist to explain how different temperaments express themselves in different philosophical outlooks, and he assumed a relativistic expla-nation of the 'choice' of world views.[8] You can argue about all kinds of questions from within the shared premises of a world outlook, but you cannot ground such an outlook itself by argument, nor in adopting it do you exercise anything that could really be called choice, since the process of its adoption is largely unconscious. It is properly the psychologist's as much as the philosoper's province.

A comparable recognition underlies Oswald Spengler's *The Decline of the West* (1918) which traced the rise and decline of successive civilisations including his own.[9] Whereas influential nineteenth-century models of historical process, such as Auguste Comte's positivism, proposed a universal linear progress of culture, Spengler's was one of several mod-ern conceptions of cyclic rise and fall reflected in modern writers.[10] Once again, the implicit assumptions are of interest. Most evidently, Spengler expresses a widespread turn of the century pessimism of which Max Nordau's *Degeneration* (1892) was a more crude expression. And the Great War clearly gave a further edge to this interpretation of history. Yet underlying Spengler's cyclic conception is a relativistic belief that the decline of the present civilisation is far from the end of the human story, and through such cyclic conceptions several modern writers were to bounce a more open-minded implication off the emotional weight of the previous generation's pessimism. But the crucial point here is that this reading of history depends on the ability to stand mentally and emotionally outside one's own world of culture. Of course, Spengler's theory may be only a pessimistic projection from within his own cultural moment, but that does not deny its significance as a position in thought. It is the capacity to recognise one's own world view *as* a world view that is crucial to an understanding of the creative literature of the period. And this applies not just at the level of a culture, but also at the level of the individual, although few individuals could articulate such a distinctive vision as to be considered in this light. One such individual was Arthur Schopenhauer whose pessimistic, anti-idealist philosophy Nietzsche recognised as essentially a projected world view rather than an argument.[11] It is close to Joseph Conrad's definition of fiction as reality seen through temperament, or 'a passing phase of life' seen 'in the light of a sincere mood'.[12] Conrad's model is impressionistic rather than metaphysical, but with a shift in emphasis literary mimesis can become not so much an imitation of the world as an imitation of the process of inhabiting a 'world'. Or, otherwise expressed, literature is less a description than an example of what the world, humanly speaking, is.

It is worth pausing on the notion of fiction, since different terms, while seeming to deal with the same questions, often fail to get the same purchase. Wolfgang Iser, for example, has recently discussed the question of 'world making' by following the rising philosophical fortunes of the term 'fiction' since the renaissance.[13] In doing so he compares two figures who bracket the central decades of the present study. Hans Vaihinger's *The Philosophy of 'As If'* (1911) developed, or rather perhaps reduced, Nietzschean insights to argue that our whole engagement with reality occurs under the sign of hypothesis, while Nelson Goodman's *Ways of Worldmaking* (1978) argued, more radically again, that we inevitably create a multiplicity of possible worlds with no definitive way of determining between them.[14] Goodman's model offers only a weak relativism in which Iser's use of fiction as a generalised category seems to acquiesce. 'Fiction', even more than 'narrative', is a category that lends itself to a bland evasion of the truth claims, and the corresponding human commitments, which are actually involved. By contrast, Conrad's formulation, even when speaking of fiction, stresses that it is a view of *life* seen with *sincerity*. It will become evident that 'fiction' is a rival term to myth which does indeed, as Iser says, become dominant by the end of the century but only by losing its grasp on the complex of questions encompassed by 'myth'.

Modernist myth, on the other hand, focused the whole complex which is in question. Since archaic myth was foundational, holistic and inarguable, yet was from a later, scientific viewpoint clearly not 'objectively' true, it eventually provided the basis of a compelling analogy for what it might mean to inhabit as conviction a world view which is also known to be ultimately relative. The anthropological study of 'primitive' myths in the nineteenth century eventually produced a cultural reflector by which Europeans could recognise their own world view as having an ultimately similar status. As science sought to understand myth, it increasingly found itself understood *as* myth. Later in the same lecture, Heidegger identifies anthropology and modern humanism as aspects of the recognition of inhabiting a world picture rather than simply a world.[15] But this recognition could only occur if one was prepared for the double consciousness suggested in Thomas Mann's elusive formulae. It became possible in the modernist decades because of philosophical developments partly focused in the term 'myth' and arising from changes in the truth claims of some closely related areas of thought. The crucial areas are religion, science, aesthetics and history. Since all these played an important part in the construction of modern mythopoeic consciousness, and continued to be significant elements in the different world projections that followed in the wake of modernism, a brief resumé is necessary. In the nineteenth century, religion and physical science were notoriously in competition for authority, but this apparent antinomy was increasingly dissolved by another order of significance, the realm of the 'aesthetic', which, in a major line of thought passing through Nietzsche, eventually dislodged the hegemonic claims of both religion and science. Myth, too, was able to do this because of its own transformation into an aesthetic category, rather than a social, philosophical or anthropological, one. Its truth value, that is to say, increasingly incorporated the claims of poetry, religion and even science, while such a metaphysically transformed, aestheticised conception of myth affected in turn the idea of history. Since the role of the aesthetic is the crucial, and most commonly misunderstood part of this story, it is best approached through the changing truth claims of religion and science.

Myth, religion and science

The European Enlightenment attacked religion as a mixture of primitive superstition and exploitative priestly power. Constantin François Volney's tract *Les Ruines, or Meditations sur les révolutions des Empires* (1802) was narrowly rationalistic but provided a spirited and telling polemic in its historical moment.[16] It also treated religious belief in a dramatic, rather than discursive, fashion catching the sense of finally awakening from a collective illusion rather than responding to a force of pure argument. While Volney exemplifies the hostility to Christianity which was a progressive necessity of the period, the great romantic writers were generally more complex in their perception of religion even when strongly affected by this de-mythologising vision. For them, any merely rationalistic outlook was as great a mischief as the myths and superstitions it sought to dispel. Between the Scylla and Charybdis of rationalism and superstition, therefore, Christianity in particular was variously interpreted. Coleridge and Wordsworth kept faith with traditional pieties while mediating religion through their more general conceptions of the creative function of the human mind. Shelley was a militant atheist and iconoclast whose Platonism challenged both rationalism and religion. In Germany, Schlegel and Schelling wanted a new mythology not to replace religion, but to give a new appreciation of religion in the context of philosophical Idealism; and Schlegel became a Catholic following a major conversion experience. Blake anticipated the insights of Freud and Nietzsche into the processes of sublimation and repression and, with equal precocity, he also sought to create a mythology out of traditional elements including Christianity.

Hence, for many educated persons, an essential ambivalence surrounded Christian belief through much of the nineteenth century. While it was being exploded at the level of its literal historical claims, and its associated institutional authority, it retained its power as a source of ethical understanding and as a social cultural form. On this view, the discarding of its literal claims was precisely what might have given Christianity its proper truth value, although that was hardly a recognition that Christians could be expected to embrace. It was, however, the basis for more sympathetic readings of Christianity than Volney's in the course of the nineteenth century. David Strauss' *The Life of Jesus* (1835), which was translated by George Eliot, was the classic nineteenth-century critique of the historical basis of Christianity, while Matthew Arnold's essay 'Literature and Dogma' (1873) spelled out the ambivalent consequences. For Arnold, the Bible expressed a profound, collective moral experience arising from a specific history. The Bible, read as literature, gives access to this; as does all great literature. Literature becomes a fundamental mode of cultural understanding and authority. By the early twentieth century, such an interpretation might be defined as mythic, and there is a significant difference in emphasis in thinking of it as literature rather than myth. Literature, for Arnold, was to be interpreted and judged by external and rational criteria. Although it is not the product of reason, it can, and must, be rationally understood. Great poetry is the best that has been thought and said. As a mode of sense-making, therefore, literature might be seen as primordial in so far as it was not dependent on another order of meaning for its creation, yet this made it only equi-primordial with the processes of human reason. To that extent, literature was a protective category into which to place Christian belief, and this indeed reflects the attitude of much nineteenth-century thought. But a more decisive shift into myth occurs with two factors. First, when there is no other means of recognition, no other route to the truth in question. Myth, in so far as it represents an interpretation of life, reflects the enigmatic visage of life itself and increasingly the true meaning of myth seemed to lie at a more unconscious level, and even perhaps to be the opposite of its apparent significance. This leads to the second factor: a shift in evaluation. Nietzsche attacked Christianity, not just as a means of priestly or establishment power, but as a monumental unconscious fraud perpetrated by the psyche on itself; a diagnosis which was to be echoed by many in the modernist generation.[17] Christianity was now not merely a life-enhancing fiction, something to enrich the Arnoldian cultural shock, but a damaging collective illusion throwing the very basis of the culture into question. As the value sign changed, so the question of truth status became newly urgent and myth became an active, rather than an inert, category.

Romanticism also had an impact on the natural sciences. The philo-sophical belief in an ultimate unity of life, and the emphasis on organicist rather than mechanistic conceptions, led to some anti-scientific reaction resisting science with poetic Luddism. But in so far as it attacked a too mechanistic understanding of science, this was rather part of a second scientific revolution and major romantic writers saw the need to accom-modate science to poetry if the truth claims of poetry were to be sustained.[18] Although Blake attacked what he saw as the single-visioned Baconian heritage of science, Wordsworth sought to accommodate contemporary science to his conception of poetry. In his Preface to the *Lyrical Ballads* (1798) he affirmed that the poetic imagination must follow the 'man of science' in his investigations, although the claim is directed unspecifically to the future. In Germany, Schlegel and Schelling rather assimilated science to poetry and emphasised how contemporary physics already supported their Idealist metaphysics. As Schlegel put it:

All disciplines and all arts will be seized by the great revolution. You can see it already at work in physics where idealism erupted of its own even before it was touched by the magic wand of philosophy.[19]

Wordsworth's ambition to include natural science within his poetic and philosophical purview proved to be a place-holder indicating business to be done, while the German romantic conception was deeply committed to an Idealist philosophy which was increasingly discredited over the course of the following century. These ambitions were eventually to be fulfilled when natural science itself changed around the turn of the next century. Only then could it be fully assimilated into a mythopoeic holism.

For towards the end of the nineteenth century the metaphysical premises of natural science underwent a change every bit as radical as the Enlightenment's transformation of religion into myth. The assumption underlying post-Baconian science was that the underlying laws of the world could be deduced through observation and measurement. In the later decades of the nineteenth century, however, even before quantum or relativity theory, the notion of observation had become problematic. Understanding micro and macro processes, such as involved in electricity and astronomy, depended on speculative calculations going beyond what could be, in any ordinary sense, observed and, at the same time, it became evident that the universe at these levels behaved in a radically different way from the world of common-sense observation. Attempts to determine whether the fundamental constitution of matter was waves or particles yielded both answers depending on how the experiment was set up. The modern physicist was now in the position of a telephone caller to an unseen alien. The unknown being may be assumed to answer truthfully, but will not volunteer the information that it has three heads if one does not think to ask, while the posing of the 'questions' is itself a matter of highly abstract theory. Fundamental knowledge of the universe thus came to be a matter of speculative interpretation yielding possibly competing accounts with no direct observation by which to decide between them.

Karl Pearson's *The Grammar of Science* (1892), which explained this for a lay readership, had several reprintings over the next two decades.[20] Pearson argued that science does not 'explain' the workings of nature: it records what happens under particular conditions, but this is strictly a *description* not an *explanation*. This recognition caused something of a metaphysical wobble in the first three decades or so of the new century as mathematicians and physicists from Poincaré to Eddington digested these philosophical issues arising from the inner logic of the scientific disciplines. I say a wobble rather than a crisis since not all scientists felt this way and scientific business was not impeded by it. Indeed, the greatest period of expanding scientific knowledge, and subsequent technological power, rested on a shrinkage of its metaphysical premisses; progress was partly by freedom from common sense. The vast and solid pyramid of scientific knowledge was still there, but instead of being built up stone by stone on the basis of observation it was inverted to become a wide platform balancing on a fine metaphysical point. Science ceased to be the paradigmatic form of truth statement and became one of the possible human constructions. This was clearly recognised by Nietzsche and, without their always having a close technical understanding of what was involved, modern writers picked up this metaphysical implication and invoked science in their work in a spirit diametrically opposed to that of nineteenth-century realism and naturalism. Summarising this period for the lay reader in 1928, Arthur Eddington opened with a striking image.[21] The modern physicist, he says, writes on the same common-sense table as the layman, while knowing it to be in reality not a solid plane, but a conglomeration of particles which, given the right technique, can be penetrated without disturbance. Thomas Mann had used the X-ray in *The Magic Mountain* (1924) and it is a precise analogy for the double consciousness of modernist mythopoeia to which Mann's transcendence of realism and science was already leading him.[22] By 1926 he had begun working on the mythopoeic sequence of the Joseph novels to be discussed in a later chapter.

Science, then, like religion, lost a certain literalism, and assumed objectivity in its truth value. Both religion and science had now to be understood as active creations of human culture rather than as direct accounts of external reality. This is the sense in which they each took a step towards myth. Mythopoeia, without losing its archaic overtones, became the paradigmatic capacity of the human mind. On this view, instead of myth being the early stage out of which the sophisticated intellectual disciplines of modern culture developed, it is rather the permanent ground on which they rest, or even the soil in which their roots are invisibly nourished. An idea long ago propounded by Gianbattista Vico in his *The New Science* (1725), and rehearsed in much romantic thought, came fully into its own with the new science of the twentieth century.[23] Vico, whom Joyce so admired, was, like Blake, a modern before his time. Of course, this all applies only at a certain level of interpretation. Religion and science concern discrete domains and maintained their internal disciplinary criteria. There is no simple collapsing of terms involved and the internal meanings of each realm are not simply transposable. It is rather that the internal criteria of scientific disciplines are themselves contained within a larger language and culture whose nature is seen to be ultimately mythopoeic. The knowledge or insight made possible by these fields of inquiry now functioned, one might say, under a different sign; a sign perhaps of responsibility, as even the objectivity of scientific knowledge was sustained by a committed activity of the mind. After all, if most of the scientists who have ever lived are alive now, this is a broader cultural fact, a commitment of values, as well as an internal fact about science itself. A complementary point is that the growth of modern science had been partly a matter of beating the bounds of what is properly scientific. Mesmerism and phrenology, for example, did not make it into the twentieth century as sciences, but two important revolutions in human self-understanding occurred over the same period with a troubling ambiguity as to their scientific status.

The revolutions in thought associated with Sigmund Freud and Karl Marx covered respectively the internal domain of the psyche and the external domain of economic and social process.[24] They shared the view that conscious and apparent meanings are often an unwitting mask for a true state of affairs which has to be raised to consciousness. Each developed for this purpose a powerful hermeneutic method with ambiguous claims to scientific status. Freud sought the rigour of science, and his conviction that in a scientific purview everything must be explicable was a powerful aid to inquiry, but his methods could not be submitted to the scientific criterion of disproof. In this respect, his readiness to claim the poets as his predecessors, and his use of a mythic nomenclature for psychological complexes, rightly suggest that his influential mapping of the human psyche as conscious, unconscious and superego was essentially mythic; something more than an heuristic fiction or hypothesis, yet less than a scientifically verifiable truth. In Marx, likewise, there was a notorious ambiguity as to whether the historical process he described, the gradual replacement of the bourgeois order by socialism, was a scientific prediction or a utopian call to revolutionary action. Doubtless much of the power of his thought arose from the ambiguous combination and, although the mixture was seized on by his critics as a weakness, it is not self-evident that it is so. Maybe it is just in the nature of the case. On this kind of reading, Marx and Freud were dealing with the very substance of myth, of collective beliefs hermeneutically won from experience and then projected on to the world as motives for action.

If Marx and Freud were mythopoeic de-mythologisers, they had, like the physicist, urgent tasks to achieve and they wished to be as authoritative as possible. They did not advertise their mythopoeic bases. Nietzsche, by contrast, seized on the recognition that the element of myth, which was usually an embarassment within these individual disciplines, was a cardinal and potentially positive aspect of modern culture: 'great men, universally gifted, have contrived, with an incredible amount of thought, to make use of the paraphernalia of science itself, to point out the limits and the relativity of knowledge generally, and thus to deny decisively the claim of science to universal validity and universal aims'.[25] To appreciate fully what this meant for Nietzsche, and for the modern period more generally, it will be necessary to outline some crucial elements in his thought, for, while most of his insights can be found elsewhere and earlier, he uniquely combined them. His mythopoeic vision encompassed religion, science and psychology focused in a changing meaning of the 'aesthetic' which is to be understood in the context of German romantic and Idealist thought about myth.

Myth: romantic to modern

Literary modernism was a further expression of the romantic impulse complicated, among other things, by the assimilation of much anti-romantic reaction. Burton Feldman and Robert D. Richardson in their survey of uses of the term 'myth' from early Enlightenment to modern times note that the romantic and modern periods are the twin peaks of its positive ambition.[26] In this respect, the Victorian period was a second phase of Enlightenment when myth became once again an object of rationalistic scepticism albeit in the apparently more appreciative mode of scholarly investigation. Despite their mutual differences, Max Müller, E. B. Tylor and Andrew Lang all placed myth at a 'primitive' distance.[27] Yet this very distance became invested with nostalgia, and by the early years of the next century the pendulum swung again. Frazer's *The Golden Bough* embodied a turn of the century ambivalence by being at once the classic product of the Victorian period and also marking its end.[28] As John Vickery has pointed out in detail, despite being a work of Victorian scepticism, it awakened in the modernist generation a sympathy for its vanished myths.[29] But, just as the preceding context of Victorian historicism differed from Enlightenment universalism, so the modernist appreciation of myth differed from the romantic.

A general difference can be felt in the rhetorical aura of the appeal to myth in the modern period; it is often darker and more ambivalent; as in Yeats' 'rough beast' slouching 'towards Bethlehem'.[30] Although the romantic appreciation of myth was importantly a critique of Enlightenment, it was also largely a self-corrective impulse from within the Enlightenment itself. The rationalistic aspect of the Enlightenment had called up counterbalancing movements such as the cult of sentiment; the taste for the gothic or the sublime; the idealisation of 'primitive' man as the 'noble savage'; and an appreciative regionalism of nature and culture. But, by the turn of the twentieth century, the whole enterprise of European civilisation was under a newly radical scrutiny. The French Revolution and the Great War have a certain homology as epochal events throwing into question the civilisation that produced them. Where the bloody development of the French Revolution came as a shock and disillusion to many of the romantic generation, and was often laid at the door of French rationalism, the Great War was more frequently absorbed, at least with hindsight, as a bitter confirmation of fundamental errors within Western culture at large. Ezra Pound's reference to the whole Western tradition as 'an old bitch gone in the teeth . . . a botched civilization . . . a few thousand battered books' catches the point with complex irony.[31] Likewise, Thomas Mann's *The Magic Mountain* (1924) and D. H. Lawrence's *Women in Love* (1921) were conceived before the war, yet both absorbed the war into their darker final versions as confirming their pan-European readings of the culture. Of course, the story is more complicated and individual cases do not conform to this generalisation, but there is a shift, and, whatever his actual influence may have been, Nietzsche's critique of the Western tradition represents a radical turning-point and a dilemma with which we are still coming to terms. On such a view, neither Enlightenment nor its alternatives are viable.

But, apart from changes in historical mood and circumstances, and the drift towards a mythopoeic understanding of religion and science, there is something more philosophically specific. The romantic era anticipated much twentieth-century thought about myth without sharing the same world picture or the philosophical premises. Romantic mythopoeia was conceived not just in the afterglow of the Enlightenment belief in the goodness of sentiment, but in the fullest flowering of German philosophical Idealism. Modernist mythopoeia, by contrast, grew out of the reaction against a debased sentimentalism and accompanied the collapse of the whole Idealist tradition. If romantic interest in myth was partly a reaction against the narrower kind of Enlightenment rationalism, for the German Idealists it was most importantly a way of rethinking difficulties within the Enlightenment order inherited from Kant. Where Fichte gave Kant a subjectivist inflection, seeing the world as an aspect of the mind, Schelling responded in turn by seeing mind as an aspect of the world. It therefore became necessary to posit an original unity beyond either condition. Myth provided a model for conceiving the Absolute, or unconditioned; a unity which must underlie the relation of the I to the not I. This concern was reflected in all intellectual disciplines, and Friedrich Schlegel, for example, emphasised how his conception of poetry rested on the 'great phenomenon of our age . . . Idealism'.[32]

In his *Dialogue on Poetry* (1800), one of Schlegel's interlocutors, Ludoviko, gives an extended 'Discourse on Mythology' arguing that, since poetry and mythology are inseparable, the revival of modern poetry depends on the creation of a 'new mythology'. The notion of a 'new mythology' started a hare that has run and run in German debate right down to the late twentieth century, and it has distracted attention from the more subtle reformulation by which myth was eventually to fulfil this ambition in an unexpected way. The modernist generation of the early twentieth century was effectively to reinvent in its own terms Ludoviko's proposition that the inextricability of poetry and mythology made poetry itself the mythopoeic or primordial faculty. As 'Ludoviko' puts it:

Neither this wit nor a mythology can exist without something original and inimitable which is absolutely irreducible, and in which after all the transformations its original character and creative energy are still dimly visible, where the naive profundity permits the semblance of the absurd and of madness, of simplicity and foolishness, to shimmer through. For this is the beginning of all poetry, to cancel the progression and laws of rationally thinking reason, and to transplant us once again into the beautiful confusion of imagination, into the original chaos of human nature, for which I know as yet no more beautiful symbol than the motley throng of the ancient gods.[33]

Schlegel's enthusiastic tone, and the conception of the primitive as classical, or the classical as primitive, to which he appeals here, encapsulate the high point of romantic Idealism. Whereas in the mid-eighteenth century J. J. Winkelmann had spoken of the 'noble simplicity and quiet grandeur' of ancient Greek statuary, Schlegel now sees in early Greek culture rather an originary and creative chaos, yet he is still some way from Nietzsche's later vision, in *The Birth of Tragedy*, of primordial destruction represented by the god Dionysos.[34] But what most relates this idealist model to modernist mythopoeia is the recognition that the ultimate truth to which Schlegel and Schelling, in their early thought, were striving, was not philosophically expressible or derivable. That is the force of 'simplicity and foolishness' in the passage just quoted. And so Schelling argued in his *System of Transcendental Idealism*:

if it is art alone that can succeed in making objective with universal validity what the philosopher can only represent subjectively, then it is to be expected . . . that as philosophy, and with it all the sciences that were brought to perfection by it, was born and nurtured by poetry in the childhood of science, so now after their completion they will return as just so many individual streams to the universal ocean of poetry from which they started out. On the whole it is not difficult to say what will be the intermediate stage in the return of science to poetry, since one such intermediate stage existed in mythology before this seemingly irresolvable breach occurred. But how a new mythology (which cannot be the invention of an individual poet but only of a new generation that represents things as if it were a single poet) can itself arise, is a problem for whose solution we must look to the future destiny of the world and further course of history alone.[35]

Poetry is the only means of representing the Absolute, which cannot be philosophically grounded, yet it is not merely a subjective creation of the poet. Schelling was prescient in leaving the realisation of his project to a future generation, since modernist mythopoeia is the recreation of this model without the Idealist foundation. In turning against the Idealist tradition, these modernist writers turned away from the metaphysical problem of grounding, and sought in myth a mode of self-grounding. The turn to myth was part of a larger rejection of metaphysics which can be seen in Heidegger and Wittgenstein.

I have emphasised the darkening and oppositional aspect of modern mythopoeia, but when its philosophical ambition is understood it becomes clear why it does not have to be simply iconoclastic or primitivist. Indeed, the ideological thrust of works conceived on this basis could also be highly conservative with respect to Enlightenment values. Whereas romantic writers often valued myth from within Enlightenment, in the modern period it was often Enlightenment values which were sustained by a self-conscious mythopoeia. The difference would be, for example, to recognise the principle of reason as a universal value without necessarily accepting it as a supreme one. Nietzsche's 'genealogical' exposure of reason, and even of grammar, did not mean that he could not use them.[36] The kind and degree of significance accorded to rationality is itself a matter of choice. And if one *adopts* it as a supreme value, that means it is not really one although the difference might not be apparent from the outside. The effective conduct might be the same while being open to a different internal potential. More importantly, this is not just a possible position but an inevitable one. Lezsek Kolakowski, Peter Sloterdijk and Charles Taylor are among the many who have pointed out that rationality is always in the service of an implicit world of background values and commitments which reason itself cannot encompass.[37] Mythopoeia is not the arbitrary creation of these, but a recognition of their inevitability. It follows, therefore, that the new anti-metaphysic could be used to 'save the appearances' of a traditional order, much as historic buildings are sometimes internally reconstructed with modern materials and techniques so as to preserve their historical character and appearance.[38]

But the architect, of course, seeks to hide the handiwork; the building should seem as far as possible unchanged, and in that respect the image seems not to translate into a literary analogy, for in literature and thought the philosophical substructure is part of the meaning and needs to be in some way visible. Yet, in the case of modernist mythopoeia, or the world view consciously lived as such, the architectural analogy is apt since the imaginative experience must not be so self-conscious as to undermine the intuitive spontaneity of the represented world. As Mann's Zeitblom said, the relative nature of truth has somehow to remain known and yet hidden. This points to a central and delicate aspect of the whole topic: the three modern writers who open this study, Yeats, Joyce and Lawrence, are all, despite their mutual differences, remarkable examples of this implicitness. Their 'metaphysic', to use Lawrence's term, is not worn on the sleeve or made to be the overt point of the whole. They all have urgent and substantial things to say and do not dwell too self-consciously on the medium in which these things are constituted; or if, as in Joyce's case, the medium is highlighted it is still within this broader spirit. The nature of this half-concealed metaphysic is best understood through Nietzsche's transformation of the notion of the aesthetic.

Nietzsche and the aesthetic turn

If the mythopoeic ambitions of Schlegel and Schelling were the product of metaphysical Idealism, then the crucial question for modernist mythopoeia is how it could have survived the general collapse of philosophical idealism in the modern period. The rhetoric of the German Idealists invests the term 'myth' with the optimistic vagueness of a summative gesture, but the notion of the aesthetic is truly central to this tradition of thought. In the immediate post-Kantian tradition culminating in Hegel, a fundamental significance is accorded to the realm of art, and the period as a whole produced what are still some of the finest treatises ever written on aesthetic questions, such as Schiller's letters *On the Aesthetic Education of Man* (1796) and Hegel's own *Lectures on the Aesthetic* (pub. 1835–8). Idealism saw poetry as the only expression of supremely important philosophical truth, and we might add that its preoccupations with the relation between the real and the ideal, or between the individual and the universal, are as much aesthetic as philosophical concerns. The close interdependence of the aesthetic and the metaphysical, and their equivocal primacy, set the stage for a gradual reversal of their relation. As the Idealist tradition came under critical pressure in the course of the nineteenth century, the realm of the aesthetic gained an increasingly independent importance. It was the realm of art which, like Queequeg's life-saving coffin after the wreck of the *Pequod* in *Moby Dick*, was to survive the wreck of idealism by an unexpected change of function. Instead of a metaphysic sustaining the realm of the aesthetic, the aesthetic now contained a metaphysic, and it was by a gradual assimilation to an aesthetic significance that myth was able to assume the philosophical weight it was to carry in post-Nietzschean modernity. But this has often proved difficult to grasp in practice, just as it is difficult to see a coffin as a boat. The important line of thought in question here passes through Schopenhauer and Nietzsche, and, since it is often misappreciated, it needs to be looked at in detail.

In his still early *The Birth of Tragedy out of the Spirit of Music* (1872) Nietzsche was explicit about how his thinking on the nature of the aesthetic had grown out of a sympathetic but critical reading of Schopenhauer. Meanwhile Schopenhauer himself was a reversal of Hegel whose optimistic vision of a world spirit to be realised in history became the blind will of nature in Schopenhauer's pessimistic counter argument. Nietzsche was later to look back ruefully on *The Birth of Tragedy*, deprecating the Wagnerian enthusiasm of its prose and its use of Kantian and Schopenhauerian terms.[39] But this means that the work provides an early, yet already distinctive, version of Nietzsche's understanding of the aesthetic while at the same time, because its influences are still evident, revealing his longer-term place in the transposition of post-Kantian thought.

In *The Birth of Tragedy*, Nietzsche repeats three times the formula that 'Only as an *aesthetic phenomenon* are human existence and the world eternally *justified*.' The claim that the aesthetic could 'justify' human existence was eventually to require a full-scale reversal of Schopenhauer's pessimism, but one reason the reversal could not be immediate was that its significance depended in the first instance on an inward assimilation of Schopenhauer's metaphysics of illusion. While seeing tragedy as ultimately affirmative, which is his point of resistance to Schopenhauer, Nietzsche is still placing this affirmation within a nihilistic conception and, furthermore, one for which the modality of dream is essential: 'Let us imagine the dreamer: in the midst of the illusion of the dream world and without disturbing it, he calls out to himself: "It is a dream. I will dream on"' (*Birth of Tragedy* p. 44). But what for Schopenhauer was a scandalised and tragic vision of human being in a world of Darwinian process *avant la lettre* became for Nietzsche a working conception of the human psyche. Nietzsche's proto-modernist metaphysic was a fully digested and transformed Schopenhauer. He assimilated the dualistic elements of life and art so completely that they ceased to be separably apparent, and this is an important clue to the metaphysics of literary modernism at large. In the great works of modernism, as has already been noted, the mythopoeic metaphysic disappears into the texture of the living experience, or of the text, achieving very often a naturalness which has effectively disguised the metaphysical implication of its aesthetic forms. The same process is foreshadowed in Nietzsche's thought by the gradual, apparent disappearance of the separable category of the aesthetic as he inherited it from Schopenhauer. The shift can be seen by comparing his treatments of Schopenhauer in *The Birth of Tragedy* and in one of his very last works, *Twilight of the Idols* (1888).

Schopenhauer's metaphysic might be seen in retrospect as the internal correlative of the Darwinism he actually antedated. He saw human consciousness as a function produced by natural evolution as part of its blind, inhuman process. But the irony of consciousness is that it fulfils its function so effectively by imagining itself to be independent and purposive. It is as if nature would endow a billiard-ball with consciousness so that it moves itself across the table by its own desire when the appropriate moment comes. For Schopenhauer, all human purposes and meanings are illusions, and hence the supreme importance of the aesthetic domain is that it is a conscious illusion. Art is the realm in which human beings can escape, albeit only mentally and momentarily, from the blind process of nature which consciousness otherwise serves. On this model, the realm of the aesthetic stands in absolute contradistinction to nature by setting the conscious illusion of art against the compelling and unconscious illusions of life. This is the model that Nietzsche would both use and invert.

In *The Birth of Tragedy* the first occurrence of the aphorism on the aesthetic justification of existence arises from an argument about the aesthetics of the lyric in which Nietzsche seeks to improve Schopenhauer's account using Schopenhauer's own metaphysic. The problem was that if the lyric is an expression of personal feeling, and is therefore part of the illusory compulsion of all emotional life, how could it be artistic? Schopenhauer's solution, Nietzsche says, was to see the lyric as a hybrid form in which the power of the whole lay in its constant crossing back and forth from the expression of the feeling to an artistic awareness of the feeling self as a dramatic entity. Nietzsche's own solution to this dilemma is rather to deny Schopenhauer's dualistic terms, and that in turn leads him to the summative vision of the metaphysical significance of art at large with which he ends that section of *Birth of Tragedy*.

Who could fail to recognise in this description that lyric poetry is here characterised as an incompletely attained art that arrives at its goal infrequently and only, as it were, by leaps? Indeed, it is describd as a semi art whose *essence* is said to consist in this, that willing and pur contemplation, i.e., the unaesthetic and the aesthetic condition, are wonderfully mingled with each other. We contend, on the contrary, that the whole opposition between subjective and objective, which Schopenhauer still uses as a measure of value in classifying the arts, is altogether irrelevant in aesthetics, since the subject, the willing individual that furthers his own egoistic ends, can be conceived of only as the antagonist, not as the origin of art. Insofar as the subject is the artist, however, he has already been released from his individual will, and has become, as it were, the medium through which the one truly existent subject celebrates his release in appearance. For to our humiliation *and* exultation, one thing above all must be clear to us. The entire comedy of art is neither performed for our betterment or education nor are we the true authors of this art world. On the contrary, we may assume that we are merely images and artistic projections for the true author, and that we have our highest dignity in our significance as works of art – for it is only as an *aesthetic phenomenon* that existence and the world are eternally *justified* – while of course our consciousness of our own significance hardly differs from that which the soldiers painted on the canvas have of the battle represented on it. Thus all our knowledge of art is basically quite illusory, because as knowing beings we are not one and identical with that being which, as the sole author and spectator of this comedy of art, prepares a perpetual entertainment for itself. Only in so far as the genius in the act of artistic creation coalesces with this primordial artist of the world, does he know anything of the eternal essence of art; for in this state he is, in a marvellous manner, like the weird image of the fairy tale which can turn its eyes at will and behold itself; he is at once subject and object, at once poet, actor, and spectator. (*Birth of Tragedy* pp. 51–2)

The argument is as much metaphysical as aesthetic. The *image* of god is kept as demiurge, creative artist and spectator, while the *reality* of god becomes merely a function, an imagined standpoint, played over the Schopenhauerian Will or Darwinian process. The standpoint proposed for the artist so interweaves the categories of life and art that the distinction seems almost to dissolve. And, indeed, the elaborated aesthetic structure which was necessary to the formulation of this standpoint was to drop away in Nietzsche's thinking; or apparently so, since the aesthetic condition was to remain an intrinsic part of his meaning. This raises a vital feature of Nietzsche's mode of thinking, and a recurrent difficulty in understanding him, that in his mature thought his aesthetic terms are importantly there and not there at the same time. They are the only way to define his metaphysical, or anti-metaphysical, vision, yet this has to be understood as a vision of life not just of art. This becomes more evident in comparing his later formulation in *Twilight of the Idols*.

By the time of *Twilight of the Idols*, Nietzsche is much more dismissive of Schopenhauer and, at first glance, the complex metaphysics of illusion and art in *Birth of Tragedy* seem to have been abandoned for a simpler vitalism. Schopenhauer is now dismissed as yet another idealist, a secularised 'Christian', providing merely a further metaphysical alibi for flinching away from life. He is a 'singular saint' whose metaphysical explanation of aesthetic beauty is belied by life itself. For rather than aesthetic beauty being born of the contemplative escape from natural process, Nietzsche now sees beauty, whether in art or in life, as that which draws us to the affirmation and continuation of life, most notably in the expression and celebration of sexuality, while ugliness is what make us turn in disgust from degeneration and decay, from all forms of life in decline (*Twilight* pp. 78–80). So too, the earlier polarity of Dionysian and Apollonian has been replaced by what is now called simply Dionysian affirmation (*Twilight* pp. 108–11). The Apollonian dream of civilised order seems no longer the necessary counter-principle to the primal Dionysian energy.

But this shift in emphasis assimilates rather than rejects his earlier aestheticised terms. His later Dionysian affirmation is not of primal chaos, but of internally organised instinct; it incorporates the Apollonian principle of order: 'To *have* to combat one's instincts – that is the formula for *décadence*: as long as life is ascending, happiness and instinct are one' (*Twilight* p. 34). So too, when Nietzsche now affirms an attitude of 'joyful and trusting fatalism', he is implicitly invoking the former standpoint of the demiurge as author and spectator (*Twilight* p. 103). 'Character' in a play or a painting takes its meaning from the complete work. Such a meaning is not available either to the character or, by analogy, to individuals in life, but Nietzsche now attributes this perspective to the Nietzschean subject rather than to the primordial artist/creator. Strictly speaking, of course, although the individual subject in *The Birth of Tragedy* was said to know no more of the complete work, or even that there *is* a work, than the soldiers painted on the canvas, this statement was already a way of affirming a possible, if imaginary, viewpoint of the subject. The whole comedy of art which is not played for the benefit of the subject represents none the less a standpoint created within and by the Nietzschean subject itself. In other words, the whole reference to the 'soldiers in the painting' and 'the weird image of the fairy tale' has to be understood as an example of Nietzsche's characteristic device of the thought experiment. This may be impossible in reality or in logic while making a serious point. There is a related thought experiment in his early essay on *The Uses and Disadvantages of History for Life* when he suggests that the reader ask his friends if they would be willing to relive the last ten years of their lives. (*Untimely Meditations* p. 65). The unreal question has a diagnostic purpose in that anyone living properly in the moment, Nietzsche suggests, could accept the thought of endless repetition since the felt value of their momentary existence would not be governed by nostalgia or hope. We could gloss this point once again by analogy with art in that we do watch over and again the action of a play because it has an intrinsic value, to be experienced moment by moment and as a whole, rather than simply as an outcome to be reached. In such ways, Nietzsche typically creates a position in thought which has no equivalent in reality, but which is then applied as a model of life; or more precisely as a psychological posture for living.

When the passage from *The Birth of Tragedy* is understood in this spirit Nietzsche's later 'position' in *Twilight* is not really so different. He now emphasises the living attitude, the outcome, rather that the play of aesthetic analogies by which this attitude is defined or reached. The important point, however, is not so much the underlying continuity between the two works, but that, when the aesthetic becomes a life model, its force lies in its being almost elided. Having inherited Schopenhauer's use of the aesthetic as a counter-term to life, Nietzsche gradually assimilated the one realm to the other while keeping a sense of their contrastive meanings. This is not aestheticism. Aestheticism is the adoption of art as an order opposed to life. Nietzsche did something quite different. He affirmed life on the model of art. The separate realm of the aesthetic retains its meaning as a position in thought in order to define a living posture. Kant's formula of 'purposiveness without purpose' now applies not just to the aesthetic, but to the human, realm.[40] This is the essential shift by which modernist writers, such as Joyce, were to assimilate naturalism to aestheticism. Nietzsche stands to modernism as Schopenhauer stood to the aestheticist and symbolist movements.

At first glance this may seem a distinction without a difference: if art and life are merged what does it matter which of them is the model? Or if the categories are dissolved, how can their meanings persist? The present study seeks to show that it is indeed a definitive difference for twentieth-century literature and thought, and Nietzsche remains important to the argument in several ways. Two aspects of his thought are relevant here. First there is the abstract elusiveness, the sense of intellectual sleight of hand, in maintaining the contrastive meaning of the aesthetic while dissolving it into a life term. This is reminiscent of Thomas Mann's juggling with the word 'mythic'. And secondly there is the question of the cash value of this model as enshrining any possible form of life. It is necessary, in other words, both to identify a metaphysical posture and to see what weight of experience it can actually bear. Both these aspects have proved a troubling legacy, but the first point perhaps depends in practice on the second. Only by seeing the metaphysic in action can one properly understand and assess it. What it is and what it is worth are closely linked. Such a critical assessment will be attempted through the close discussion of literary texts in later chapters, but it is vital to clarify how this aestheticised model of human existence differs from aestheticism.

Philosophical discussions of the 'aesthetic' tend to be focused primarily on its metaphysical aspect and often miss what is at least equally important, namely the critical. Even such excellent recent treatments as those of Peter Alan Dale, Alan Megill and Robert Pippin seem to understand the aesthetic only in its aspect of separation as enshrined in the word 'aesthetic*ism*'.[41] But it is an important difference between life and art that art, precisely because it is a human product, is inescapably an object of judgement in a way that objects in reality are not. Trees, or even people, are not good or bad in the sense that poems or cooking are, and seeing life under an aesthetic sign, as Nietzsche suggested, does not

put it outside the realm of ethical judgement, or relegate it to some
specially aesthetic domain. On the contrary, the implicit process of
judgement, which is the inescapable condition of conscious being, comes
more sharply and urgently into focus in the response to a work of art. As
F. R. Leavis used to say, adapting T. S. Eliot, we have to respond to
literature as literature and not another thing, but there are no specifically
literary values. Literary criticism is never merely 'literary' any more than
it is simply ethical or political. Likewise Arnold's rather jaded formula
that literature is a 'criticism of life' has to be understood not in the sense
that literature of itself offers such a criticism, but in the sense that it
cannot be read uncritically; without, that is to say, exercising the critical
faculty; if only in the negative mode of boredom.[42] And, precisely
because there is no instrumental purpose being served, the critical
function may be unusually conscious and focused; indeed it *is* the
internal telos. Values are considered *per se*. Imaginative literature is a
specific organisation of values to which one responds, to be sure, in an
intrinsic or contemplative rather than an immediately practical mode,
but to which one cannot respond neutrally. That is the full sense in which
it provides a model for the Nietzschean conception of life understood
aesthetically. Life is lived *as* an intrinsic, rather than *for* an instrumental
or teleological, value, and, this being the case, it involves a rigorously
intrinsic self-critique.

   Philosophical commentators often read Nietzsche's aphorism about
the aesthetic justification of human existence and the world as if existence itself were at stake; as if Nietzsche had said that the *world* is an
aesthetic phenomenon.[43] But existence is his premiss; his theme is the
evaluative question of *justification*. Likewise, Wolfgang Iser, pursuing the
theme of philosophical fiction, almost ignores Nietzsche while concentrating on his more two-dimensional academic disciple Hans Vaihinger.
He then passes to Nelson Goodman as if showing progress, rather than
the splintering and diminution, of this line of thought, and at one point
he approvingly quotes Goodman affirming that his relativistic account of
world-making is one that, in so far as it involves an aesthetic model, must
refrain from making judgements of quality.[44] Goodman is speaking here
as a narrowly conventional philosopher; as a frequenter of the arts he
would know that the question of quality is of the essence. This was the
dimension that Nietzsche never slighted and, whatever problems his
own writings raise, he remains invaluable for the present theme.

   In effect, the Nietzschean aesthetic model, which is the prototype for
much modern literature, proposes the intolerable enterprise of living

with the complete responsibility required for the production of any real poem; including the responsibility for its unconscious or inspired aspects. Much as Borges' story of 'Funes the Memorious' offered the philosophically pregnant fantasy of a stupendous feat of perception and memory, so Nietzsche proposes that another quite normal and necessary capacity for living, namely the constant critical negotiation of myriad implicit responses and choices, be conducted at an unimaginably high level of responsible organisation.[45] Self-conscious mythopoeia is responsibility raised, holistically, to the highest power. The meaning of responsibility is exemplified in his early essay on 'The Uses and Disadvantages of History for Life'. In attacking nineteenth-century scientific historicism it was not unique, even in the 1870s, but Nietzsche's way of linking this critique to the realms of the aesthetic and the mythopoeic gave it a positive inflection anticipating some of the crucial techniques of modern literature. The essay is about responsibility in the communal, as well as the personal, sphere, and, since its formulations were to prove central to several key modern writers, and went on to provide a significant frame of reference throughout the century, it is worth briefly rehearsing its terms.

Myth and history

The development of historical consciousness over the nineteenth century transformed the self-perception of humanity. The newly recognised scale of evolutionary and geological time relativised human 'nature' as radically subject to evolutionary change, and the same general truth had to apply in the more immediate domain of history. Historical process, as in Marx, came to supplant fixed essence in the understanding of humanity. The nineteenth-century novel was an obvious expression of this consciousness. Many of the great novelists of the period wrote at least one historical novel in the sense of the sub-genre generated by Walter Scott. More significantly, the historical novel was a formative principle within nineteenth-century realist fiction at large. Historical causality and change were central to its philosophical rationale and narrative method. But by the end of the century the very power of the historical mode of understanding was coming to seem problematic to some observers.[46] Since history involves human purposes and values not just in subject-matter, but in the historian too, it cannot be studied on the model of the natural sciences. The word 'history', indeed, means two quite different things which may be fatally confused. It can mean the unimaginably vast series of events and processes making up collective human life, or it can mean the intellectual discipline by which we attempt to understand this. The latter is always a human construction put over the former; a necessary act fraught with danger. One danger is that historical projections may serve dubious or unconscious purposes even irrespective of their truth value. The most effective lies, after all, are those which use the truth, or which the liar has come to believe. Yet there is no alternative to historical understanding, and Nietzsche attempts to acknowledge both sides of this dilemma. Indeed, his essay is itself something of an imaginative flight anticipating later departures from historical realism in fiction.

The essay is anti-historicist in its overall polemical thrust because, for Nietzsche, this was the necessary diagnostic emphasis for his own historical moment in which, as he saw it, the culture was overburdened with the weight of historical consciousness. But the very writing of such a polemical essay is an historical act, and his overall attitude is more even-handed in both undercutting historical consciousness and affirming historical action. There are positive uses of history to be disentangled from the disadvantages. Nietzsche attempts to make these discriminations by categorising a number of ways of viewing history which effectively criticise each other while each having its own internal uses and disadvantages for life.

He first divides his subject into three large categories: the unhistorical, the historical and the superhistorical consciousness. To be unhistorical is to have no historical consciousness at all. A pure case of this would be animals, whose past appears to live in them as instinct and habit rather than as a consciousness of time as such. Such an existence may have the advantage in wholeness and spontaneity of being, but it is hardly possible or desirable as a human aspiration. Again, it is a deliberate extreme, a thought experiment, to provide an analytic purchase on the normal state. Nietzsche's true subject is a diagnostic examination of the historical consciousness taken for granted by educated people of his own time, and to complete his focus on this he sets up a further speculative extreme on the other side of it which he calls the superhistorical consciousness. Initially this seems to be presented as a desirable state, a position of ultimate wisdom.

> If . . . one could scent out and retrospectively breathe this unhistorical atmosphere within which every great historical event has taken place, he might . . . raise himself to a *superhistorical* vantage point such as Niebuhr once described as the possible outcome of historical reflection. 'History, grasped clearly and in detail', he says, 'is useful in one way at least: it enables us to recognise how unaware even the greatest and highest spirits of our human race have been of

the chance nature of the form assumed by the eyes through which they see and through which they compel everyone to see – compel, that is, because the intensity of their consciousness is exceptionally great. He who has not grasped this quite definitely and in many instances will be subjugated by the appearance of a powerful spirit who brings to a given form the most impassioned commitment.' We may use the word 'superhistorical' because the viewer from this vantage point could no longer feel any temptation to go on living or to take part in history; he would have recognized the essential condition of all happenings – this blindness and injustice in the soul of him who acts; he would, indeed, be cured for ever of taking history too seriously, for he would have learned from all men and all experiences, whether among the Greeks or Turks, from a single hour of the first or of the nineteenth century, to answer his own question as to how or to what end life is lived.[47]

Yet, even as he defines this superior wisdom, Nietzsche's praise is qualified: the superhistorical man can no longer 'take part in history', and Nietzsche subsequently leaves the superhistorical men to 'their nausea and their wisdom'.[48] The work of the world needs to be done. The ambivalence of the superhistorical spirit was to prove a central problem in modern literature and the ambivalence is identified by Nietzsche as being in the object itself rather than reflecting merely some uncertainty on his own part. He is seeking to identify both its positive value and its dangers. Furthermore, like the unhistorical spirit, it is a rare and transient perception even for highly gifted and cultured individuals. It is another of Nietzsche's speculative extremes, but a contemplation of what he means by the unhistorical and the superhistorical states, even though they are unsatisfactory or impossible in themselves, has a transformative effect on the historical consciousness which becomes more relative and conditional, more open to an awareness of its hidden motives, its evasions and its self-projections. The unhistorical and the superhistorical are inextricable aspects of a truly vital, self-critical historical consciousness.

   He goes on, therefore, to focus on the historical consciousness proper, setting out once again three categories, each of which has its true uses and its advantages. These he calls the monumental, the antiquarian and the critical spirits. The significance of these will be developed later in relation to specific literary texts. Nietzsche's apparent imposition of a rather arbitrary grid on his subject is not a way of imposing a fixed order, but the reverse. It is a structural device by which to express the alert, responsible relativity that is required for living with the historical sense. There is no golden rule that is not contradicted by another equally golden. In this spirit, for example, Nietzsche later returns to the superhistorical state which he had earlier seemed to reject. Attacking the supposed objectivity of the scientist as a model for the historian, he proposes instead the impersonal vision of the artist: 'the outwardly tranquil but inwardly flashing eye of the artist.'[49] Only when conceived as a work of art is history truly impersonal, and this involves some superhistorical detachment, the capacity to stand outside the motivating passions while understanding them with dramatic inwardness, and also a touch of unhistorical commitment. The importance of this account for later chapters of the present study lies not just in Nietzsche's articulation of these questions, but in his critical problematising of them. The upshot of Nietzsche's conception with its conscious mixture of naivety and sophistication, its active commitment within a necessary relativism, its sense of historical 'truth' as a permanently moveable feast, and its appeal to an aesthetic model, is that all these recognitions are gathered into the standpoint of what is best called a self-conscious mythopoeia. The deliberately oxymoronic phrase holds together all the aspects which otherwise collapse into reductive half truths.

Nietzsche speaks of the artist or historian, but his most telling image is of the individual as acting within an horizon, and, since this image will continue to haunt many of the texts to be discussed in later chapters, it is as well to pause on its precise formulation.

And this is a universal law: a living thing can be healthy, strong and fruitful only when bounded by a horizon; if it is incapable of drawing a horizon around itself, and at the same time too self-centred to enclose its own view within that of another, it will pine away slowly or hasten to its timely end. Cheerfulness, the good conscience, the joyful deed, confidence in the future – all of them depend, in the case of the individual as of a nation, on the existence of a line dividing the bright and discernible from the unilluminable and dark; on one's being just as able to forget at the right time as to remember at the right time; on the possession of a powerful instinct for sensing when it is necessary to feel historically and when unhistorically. This, precisely, is the proposition the reader is invited to meditate upon: *the unhistorical and the historical are necessary in equal measure for the health of an individual, of a people and of a culture.*[50]

The horizon image avoids both solipsistic subjectivity and any claims to a privileged or objective viewpoint. In order to act cogently it is necessary to know your own world and its limits. On this view, it is as important to forget as to remember, although there are no general rules to tell you what and when. Or rather there are only general rules which therefore cannot tell you. Furthermore, the horizon image encompasses not just what can be seen, but what can be thought; it is the limit of what reason or consciousness can reach against the background of the implicit. You can be conscious of *having* a world view, but not *of* the world view itself. Funes the Memorious, when endowed with total consciousness, was paralysed. Also an horizon is mobile. Few individuals keep the same horizon throughout a lifetime, nor can anyone absolutely share the horizon of another being. All this is stated early on in the essay as a general truth which pertains whether individuals are conscious of it or not. But Nietzsche proposes to make it self-conscious. He would have us live with the overarching awareness that our world is essentially an horizon. This double consciousness of sustaining, while acting within, a world view is the essential posture of modernist mythopoeia whose tranformations can be seen in the voluminous literature of the twentieth century which has continued to explore the problematics of history under the sign of myth.

Why Nietzsche?

Nietzsche has become a much discussed, indeed a fashionable, figure in the last few decades. Among the reasons for making central use of him here is the fact that his recent popularity is part of an, often unwitting, rediscovery of modernism. He also represents an important point of connection between German philosophical thought and modern literature in English.[51] It is useful to look at this literature through a German philosophical lens, but only when it is understood that the traditions are very different. For present purposes, the invaluable feature of German thought is its sustained theorising of myth in relation to metaphysical and aesthetic questions, but, in distinguishing the ambitions of the German romantics from modern literary mythopoeia in English, I was making a national cultural, as well as an historical, contrast. For the concern with creating a 'new mythology' has persisted till the present as a peculiarly German theme.[52] That is partly because the foundational ambition of myth is linked to the question of the legitimacy of the national state which has remained, for obvious historical reasons, a special concern for German intellectuals. The modern British writers, on the other hand, were characteristically opposite to this. They tended to *use* the mythopoeic standpoint rather than very overtly to *thematise* it. This reflects their understanding that one does not really choose to create myth, but rather one inevitably lives within a mythic horizon by the sheer fact of conscious and responsive being in the world. For these writers, therefore, the literary choice of specific myths is ultimately only an *emblem* of this underlying condition. By this imaginative device, the mythic basis is raised to consciousness without being separated as a complete idea and thereby losing its holistic meaning. To thematise the question too directly would be to falsify or kill it.

Yet Nietzsche's impact on the modernist generation is such that something must be said about the question of 'influence'. It is often remarked, disapprovingly, that there are almost as many Nietzsches as there are readers of him, but perhaps this fact has to be more clearly recognised as *part* of the package rather than as a problem *of* the package. In contrast to Swift's view of satire as a glass in which the reader sees everyone's face but his own, Nietzsche presents readers with a glass in which they cannot but create their own images. He sees himself as psychologist as much as philosopher, and practising psychologists wish clients to discover themselves and live the discovery. There is a certain legitimacy, therefore, in the way individuals create their own Nietzsche, and my analysis of modernist assimilations of him is conducted in that spirit. If Thomas Mann, in the Joseph novels, sifts out the darker side of Nietzsche's thought for the sake of its life-affirming and diagnostic insights, I take this to be a properly creative, Nietzschean reading rather than a simply myopic or suppressive one. Such a reading is not disguising some unconscious fascism. Of course, if you are a fascist and you want to draw on Nietzsche for support then, by the same logic, no one can gainsay you, but it is *you* who are the fascist and it is a Nietzschean point to insist on this responsibility. For present purposes, then, the pursuit of a 'true' Nietzsche is not strictly to the point, although his example remains prescient and not least in relation to the two final modernist themes to be touched on here: language and the self.

Nietzsche's aesthetic turn was followed in the next generation by a linguistic turn to which he had already given a memorable expression in his remark that 'truth is a mobile army of metaphors'.[53] Typically, however, the vertiginously deconstructive impact of that recognition contains a creative growing point in the very word 'metaphor'; and, of course, in the actual metaphor of the moving army in which he encapsulates the point. Theoretical accounts of language over the course of the century have increasingly tended towards a deconstructive emphasis and what Paul Ricoeur has called the 'hermeneutics of suspicion'.[54] Modern literature, on the other hand, covers the spectrum of these possibilities, and many of the greatest works are those which follow Nietzsche's example in using the deconstructive insight in a creative

spirit. His recognition of radical metaphoricity is a definition of modernist mythopoeia at the level of language.

This creative inflection of deconstructive consciousness with respect
to language is bound up with the notion of subjectivity. Stable identity
dissolves into linguistic process, but what truly disappears is the Cartesian ego. As Heidegger and Wittgenstein were to emphasise, meditation on language brings home the illusion of the isolated subject. This
means that the modernist self persists but is lived as myth, as consciously ungroundable. An emblem of this recognition can be seen in the
recurrent recourse to the figure of Odysseus. In several major writers
Odysseus, the wandering sailor, is the archetypal figure, rather than
Prometheus who was central to romantic mythopoeia. In fact, Odysseus had a Promethean or Faustian aspect as the figure who sailed
through the Pillars of Hercules to discover the world beyond, but,
whereas Tennyson's Ulysses still trailed such romantic ambitions, his
modern descendents, in Joyce, Pound or Theodor Adorno have more
practical concerns. Odysseus has courage, sometimes a foolhardy courage, but his worldly shrewdness prefers, as far as possible, to avoid
disturbing the gods. There is, furthermore, an important generic implication to this difference, since Prometheus is a figure from primary
myth while Odysseus, a legendary hero, belongs to the incipiently
realist world of epic and his character traits reflect this generic difference which Adorno and Horkheimer make central to their analysis of
Odysseus in relation to myth and modernity.[55] For them, the epic
provenance of the figure, in a narrative form midway between myth
and realism, represents the ambiguous relation between myth and
modernity: Odysseus embodies a cultural moment in which the very
sustaining of an individual self is still fragile, and the temptation to
dissolve it in the mythical appeal of the Sirens can only be resisted by
external force. I have reservations about this reading to take up later,
but it provides a suggestive model for the use of Odysseus as a figure of
modernity, since this was a time when the individual self was once
again becoming fragile. In the Cyclops episode, with a wit much
appreciated by Joyce and Pound, Odysseus secures his personal survival by a pun on his own name as meaning 'no man'. Emblematically,
the self survives by its conscious implosion at the level of idea or
essence. The question of identity, and the recognition that it may have
no essential centre, lies at the heart of modernism, and indeed it follows
inescapably that the mythopoeic horizon of modern consciousness
would entail an equally mythopoeic conception of the self. The

mythopoeic awareness inevitably encompasses the self as well as the world. Charles Taylor's *Sources of the Self* has traced very amply the background to that question.[56] What needs to be emphasised is that the modern dissolution of the idea of the individual is not merely destructive. In so far as it is the dissolution of the Cartesian ego, it opens up different modes of relation to the world and different ways of conceiving, and therefore perhaps of experiencing, the self. As with conceptions of language, modern literature provides examples across the spectrum of possible views and evaluations, but the emphasis of the present study falls on those complex cases in which theoretically opposed conceptions combine in self-conscious myth.

How the true world became myth

The posture of modernist mythopoeia might be summed up in the following fable. Plato thought that reality was outside the cave of the phenomenal world in which humanity is imprisoned. Aristotle, followed by many natural scientists, saw this cave as the extent of reality. For them, there is no world beyond. Kant came to see that whatever there might be beyond the cave, the cave itself was not simply a given environment, but a human construction. We live in a humanly constructed edifice, and for Kant this was a large house in which all humanity dwelt. Modernist mythopoeia is the recognition that this edifice of the human world is not a building resting on the ground, but a boat; and if all men dwell in one it is not necessarily the same one. There is a multiplicity of possible human worlds. Furthermore, if a boat is more fragile than a house, and depends on certain internal orderings to keep it afloat, it has the advantage of not being fixed within a single horizon. Its relative fragility may be more a gain than a loss. At the same time, sailing and navigation are special arts requiring a high level of internal discipline and attention, just as the inhabiting of a self-conscious mythopoeia requires a constant self-critique. This internal demand affects in turn the relation to the outside world. The sailor's Odyssean life has traditionally required courage as well as expertise. Apart from the danger of sinking if the boat is not well-constructed and maintained, there is the possibility of encountering the radically new and foreign. Much of the finest literature of the twentieth century has developed the equivalent capacity to encounter the foreign and to inhabit one's own culture as a provisional and shifting horizon whose form is, in many respects, quite arbitrary yet which hangs together by its own internal coherence. Appropriately, over the course of the century, there is a gradual shift of emphasis from the metaphysical to the political aspect of myth, since myth is not just a subjective projection, or an 'internal coherence theory', it is a way of getting truly to see the world.

PART 2

CHAPTER 2

Varieties of modernist mythopoeia

W. B. YEATS: 'IN DREAMS BEGIN RESPONSIBILITIES'

William Butler Yeats (1865–1939) was a mature poet in a late romantic mode before he remade himself into a modern one. He was also an influential figure whose political beliefs, particularly in his later years, were disturbing. Yeats often presented himself as a poet rather than a man of truly political interests, as in his poem 'Politics' responding to a remark of Thomas Mann.

'In our time the destiny of man presents its meaning in political terms' – Thomas Mann

> How can I, that girl standing there,
> My attention fix
> On Roman or on Russian
> Or on Spanish politics?[1]

In the context of the thirties, this treads a dubious line between honesty to mood and a would-be seductive fecklessness, and Conor Cruise O'Brien has shown that Yeats was highly, if not consistently, political.[2] As O'Brien says, it is not enough to accept Yeats's own statement by detaching the poetry from the politics, and, he concludes, the power of Yeats' poetry derives precisely from the darker elements on which it draws.

Yeats' poetic career remains open to different interpretations, especially on the question of whether his transformation from ' romantic' to 'modern' was really a radical change or rather a way of keeping faith with an old conception in a new world. Even now, he preserves a cunning elusiveness, and not least at the moments in which he may seem most unambiguously accessible. His gift for resonant, memorable phrases and broad rhetorical questions at once disguises and exacerbates the underlying elusiveness, since these ringing moments are often subtly qualified by their contexts. In Yeats, scepticism went as far down as belief itself. A certain mental reservation was not opposed to belief, but was a function of it. This is partly the traditional posture of the artist, as when Yeats says:

The artist who permits opinion to master his work is always insincere, always what Balzac calls an unconscious comedian, a man playing to a public for an end, or a philanthropist who has made the most tragic and useless of sacrifices.[3]

And a few lines earlier in the same piece Yeats has reinforced the art/life dichotomy by remarking 'I do not mean that the artist should not as a man be a good citizen and hold opinions like another'. But there is an ambiguity here as to whether the philanthropist is another image for the 'unconscious comedian' as *artist*, or an alternative to him drawn from the sphere of life. The ambiguity is suggestive, for the dangers of mere opinion apply not just to artists, but to all citizens, and we may recollect that 'tragic' and possibly 'useless' sacrifice was the question thrown up by the rebel nationalists whom he celebrated, however reservedly, in 'Easter 1916'. The artist's philosophic reserve was the model for a relation to belief at large, and in being so it threatens to dissolve the very distinction of art and life on which the statement is based, as indeed happens in 'Easter 1916'.

Significantly, Yeats uses here the dismissive term 'opinion' rather than 'belief'. 'Belief' in Yeats could never have the externally conceived, merely mastering power of 'opinion'. It is rather the soil out of which the individual poem grows and is perhaps only knowable through the poem with which it is none the less never completely identical. For Yeats, many poems, and different inflections of belief, could grow from the same soil. Yeats' 'saint', perhaps, located at the most 'primary' point of Yeats' visionary system, is one who achieves a direct 'unity with the source of his being' through a selfless submission, and would be incapable of anything so personal as opinion. A poem, by contrast, is rather a personal assertion, an 'antithetical' growth upwards to the light, yet it too must have its root in the same darkness. Myth for Yeats is the recognition that the roots of belief are always underground; unearthed they wither. There is an important point here quite distinct from a sentimentally uncritical refusal to inspect one's own beliefs. It is the recognition that the ultimate sources of belief are not open to complete inspection, and another set of dangers, or inauthenticities, arises from supposing that they are. Yeats' best poems have elaborate internal structures to recognise the necessary horizon of darkness that for him surrounds all belief. That is his way of being authentic. Only as Yeats matured did these dramatic techniques come fully into play, but the early poetry provided the groundwork. Two aspects are important here: his interest in Celtic and folk material and the studied indeterminacy of meaning in his verse. He initially collected folklore and belief as a parallel, or alternative, interest to political nationalism. But by the turn of the century, as Mary Ellen Thuente has shown, it had taken on for him a more universal aspect.[4] He reversed Arnold's account of the Celtic as especially poetic and imaginative.[5] He did not deny these qualities, but saw them as features of all early cultures which had been preserved more fully in the Celtic traditions.[6] On this view, of course, the importance of the Celt was even greater in giving access to a universally human origin and showing it to be a still active psychic possibility.

The doubleness of the local and the universal is clear in his poem 'The Valley of the Black Pig'; especially when read in conjunction with the later note printed in the *Collected Poems*:

> The dews drop slowly and dreams gather: unknown spears
> Suddenly hurtle before my dream-awakened eyes,
> And then the clash of fallen horsemen and the cries
> Of unknown perishing armies beat about my ears.
>
> *(Collected Poems* p. 73)

The poem has a characteristic sense of both precision and mystery. The precision is partly musical, in the rhythmic cadences and in the internal echoings of words and sounds, and it is dramatically convincing in conjuring what Yeats would call a 'mood'. Its studied indeterminacy takes on a further interest in the light of Yeats' note added around the turn of the century. He first comments on the prevalence of the legend of the Black Pig all over Ireland, and the expectation that the battle would one day see the 'rout of the enemies of Ireland'. In this interpretation the legend has been, and continues to be, a political force. But Yeats concludes:

If one reads Rhys' *Celtic Heathendom* by the light of Frazer's *Golden Bough* . . . one sees that the Battle is mythological, and that the Pig it is named from must be a type of cold and winter doing battle with the summer, or of death battling with life. 1899–1906. (*Collected Poems* p. 527)

This is not just a different meaning, but a different order of meaning. The use of Frazer takes him from a local, political meaning to a universal, seasonal one. The shift is significant for the whole modernist period. Frazer, along with Freud, offered universalist explanations of myth which were peculiarly sympathetic to the modernist generation as part of its progressive continuity with the Enlightenment. Furthermore, the Frazerian explanation recognises the myth more clearly *as* myth, whereas the common people who speak of the coming battle are assumed to be accepting it at the level of belief. The myth provides the poet with some common ground with folk belief while inhabiting it on different terms.

The indeterminate meaning of the legend is reflected in the manner of the poem which exemplifies a widespread late nineteenth-century, broadly symbolist, poetic creating mood through the sounds and associations of words with as open a reference as possible. Such a poetic works in happy combination with the poem's legendary subject-matter. The poetic manner reflects the openness of meaning that characterises myth, while the mythic subject gives point to a poetic principle which can otherwise seem merely empty or precious. The central vision of the battle remains ambiguous, particularly as focused in the phrase 'dream-awakened eyes'. The speaker could be awakened *from* dream by the vision; or awakened *into* a visionary dream, or awakened *by* it to a new knowledge in the waking world. All three meanings lurk in the phrase to give the visionary insight its indeterminate location. 'Dream' is a key Yeatsian term which frequently introduces a radical ambiguity of status into the dramatic situation of a poem. It is able to do in homely and subliminal ways what would not be possible for a more overtly problematic term like 'myth'. The Concordance to Yeats' poems gives no entries for 'myth' as against several pages for 'dream'. 'Myth' enforces the distinction of belief and non-belief, whereas the function of the word 'dream' is most characteristically to dissolve these categories.[7] Here, the poem uses the word 'dream' while the analytic note uses 'myth'. To appreciate this it is helpful to compare a poem from Yeats' very first volume, Crossways (1889), with a mature poem whose title proclaims its inextricably mythic and historical significance, 'Easter 1916'.

In 'The Stolen Child' Irish folk legend again combines in a peculiarly fruitful way with Yeats' early poetic. While much of his early poetry expresses a late romantic nostalgia for a dream world, this poem offers a critique of that very nostalgia. But the full force of the critique lies in the way it arises from inside the nostalgia itself. The first three stanzas sing the attraction of the faery world followed by a hypnotically repeated refrain inviting the 'human child' to 'come away' with the faery.

Where dips the rocky highland
Of Sleuth Wood in the lake,
There lies a leafy island
Where flapping herons wake
The drowsy water-rats;
There we've hid our faery vats,

Full of berries
And of reddest stolen cherries.
Come away, O human child!
To the waters and the wild
With a faery hand in hand,
For the world's more full of weeping than you
can understand. *(Collected Poems p. 20)*

Yet even from the first stanza some of the faery expressions jar in a slightly ominous way. The 'drowsy water rats' have a lotos-like suggestion, although the 'reddest stolen cherries' allow us to take this as something merely childish and mischievous, and at this point unease is outweighed by the aura of innocence. Similarly, in the next stanza 'mingling hands and mingling glances' may have a furtive undertone, while chasing 'frothy bubbles' suggests something frivolous and deceptive, but still there is an uncertainty as to how seriously we should take this. In the dramatic context, the cause of the unease is still only a hint. The third stanza, without breaking the overall spell, makes the stronger suggestion that the faery themselves give 'unquiet dreams' and are thus the source of the dissatisfaction with the natural world upon which the attraction of their own world is predicated. Only in the fourth and final stanza is the trap sprung as the child leaves with the faery while they sing of the common world he is leaving forever.

Away with us he's going,
The solemn-eyed:
He'll hear no more the lowing
Of the calves on the warm hillside . . .
For he comes, the human child . . .
From a world more full of weeping than he
can understand.

Typically, the refrain changes its implication and compresses the articulated structure of the poem into a single ambivalent formula. The poem makes us feel the hypnotic seduction of the faery, while being uncertain till the end what weight to give to the resulting unease. And in so far as the seduction is in the very language of the poem, its sinister attraction is that of the poetry itself. The faery world is not just an emblem, but an

example, of the empty seduction of poetry when conceived as the
indulgence of a post-romantic dream world. The legendary folk motif of
the stolen child focuses the note of danger from the outside, while the
language of the poem makes us experience the attraction from within.
The overall effect is a double ambivalence: even when we have absorbed
the ambivalence of desire and loss packed into the faery refrain, the
underlying premiss that the natural world is 'full of weeping' is never
actually gainsaid. Yet this multiple ambivalence reinforces the dualistic
premiss of the poem. Overall, the poem continues to assume the
fundamental post-romantic dualism of a dream world even while sub-
jecting its emotional consequences to an intimate critique.

Before comparing this poem with 'Easter 1916', it should be noted that
in 1902 Yeats first read a one-volume selection of Nietzsche and continued to read him passionately for several years.[8] The direct impact of
Nietzsche on any of the modernist writers is difficult to determine
because several of them were already primed to recognise his major
insights in their own terms. Yeats had already learned a lot from Blake,
and, although the 'influence' of Nietzsche on Yeats has been the object of
several extended studies, I wish only to stress the 'confluence'.[9] For the
historical vision of the poem, as well as the larger Yeatsian *A Vision* to
which it was already an approach, are broadly consonant with the
Nietzschean conception of history, and the parallel is useful in comparing Yeats to later writers. I am thinking not just of the affirmative
sense of tragedy in each of them, but of the implied metaphysical
premisses. This is the aspect which is developed with minute and subtle
care, and in entirely Yeatsian terms, in 'Easter 1916', and which hinges,
once again, on the use of dream; albeit a dream now more evidently
cognate with trauma.

'Easter 1916' is a world away from 'The Stolen Child'. It addresses a
contemporary political question in a comparatively realistic idiom. Yet
both poems are concerned with a powerful enchantment which troubles
the stream of natural life, and each turns on the dangerous choice of a
dream world articulated through four stanzas developing an ambivalent
refrain. Like many of Yeats' greatest poems, it is a dramatic self-
communing to create a final affirmation out of radical uncertainty. The
speaker initially presents himself as clubman and littérateur in a prosaic
but cosy Dublin. His prosaic language is embodied in the studied
looseness of the repeated phrase 'polite meaningless words' (Collected
Poems p. 202). Yet the remark is that of a conscious stylist, and at the end
of the section he has come up with the striking formula 'a terrible beauty

is born'. The phrase already stands above the grey Dublin world, yet it retains some sense of being possibly one of the speaker's striking phrases, his admitted habit of talking for effect. Only by the end does a more exalted idiom provide the phrase with a fully appropriate setting.

The second stanza invokes four unnamed figures associated with the uprising, as in:

> That woman's days were spent
> In ignorant goodwill . . .

At this point the absence of names enhances the sense of the speaker's former intimacy, albeit as it now turns out an illusory intimacy, with the figures concerned. We do not, after all, need to name our friends to ourselves. At the end of the poem he will name four executed rebels, although these are not quite the same people. Keeping the same number is part of the structural control of the poem's argument, for we think of the comments on the first four when the final four are named, and MacBride is the crucial figure linking and reversing the two moments. But the detail is more complex. The mention of Constance Markiewicz, the only woman and not one of those actually executed, introduces a major Yeatsian theme which is itself of mythic proportions. The description of Constance Markiewicz has behind it the figure of Maud Gonne who represented for Yeats the tragic waste of beauty and personality in the shrillness of politics. The enumeration of these four figures therefore begins with the most fundamental Yeatsian criticism and ends with the most personal bitterness. Yet once again, as with the opening section, a theatrical image is finally used to lead into the ambivalently affirmative formula of the poem's refrain. A typical pattern of Yeats' reverie poems is becoming evident. At the beginnning of the poem the speaker intuits a truth which he still cannot fully grasp or justify. Over the course of the poem, the truth becomes an authentic one and we come to understand what 'authentic' might mean for Yeats.

In the third section, the Yeatsian critique already raised in connection with Constance Markiewicz, becomes central:

> Hearts with one purpose alone
> Through summer and winter seem
> Enchanted to a stone
> To trouble the living stream.

Yeats' radical objection to the rebels is not to their violence or their political judgement. He is concerned with the damage done to the human psyche by the narrow concentration on a single purpose which is,

as Nietzsche suggested, the necessary basis of historical action. And so he
contrasts the continuous, procreative change of natural process to the
stony fixity of such a political goal. Yet there lurks a problem in this
apparently bold dichotomy. The stone itself is just as much a part of
nature as are the birds or the water, and, more importantly, the whole
poem is about change and transformation in a way that throws the
assumed limits of the natural into radical question. Yeats would doubtless also be aware of the references to stone in the nomenclature of
ancient Irish heroes. The stony-hearted rebels have changed everything
and been transformed themselves. As Shakespeare's Polixenes says 'art
itself is nature'.[10] What we call nature can be changed by man without
ceasing to be part of a larger natural process. Yeats puts his most serious
objection in the third section before seeking to overcome it in the
conclusion, while already in the third section he has placed a deconstructive ambiguity at the heart of his own critique.

The final stanza then plays up the speaker's bottomless uncertainties:

> O when may it suffice?
> That is Heaven's part, our part
> To murmur name upon name,
> As a mother names her child
> When sleep at last has come
> On limbs that had run wild.
> What is it but nightfall?
> No, no, not night but death:
> Was it needless death after all?

Each thought generates, as if by association, another level of question:
naming, sleep and death. Yet this apparently loose sequence is thematically pregnant. The reference to 'Heaven's part' keeps within the
theatrical image, while reminding us that the word 'Easter' in the poem's
title echoes the most distinguished instance of an apparently ignomini-
ous and futile sacrifice which proved to be of world historical import.
The mother gives a homely but relevant force to the theme of emotional
and creative naming: identity is formed by the power of love as focused
in a name. And 'limbs that had run wild' uses another key Yeatsian term
which looks back to the vitality of nature in stanza three and onwards to
the 'bewildered' of the conclusion. Yet these suggestions remain subliminal. The speaker's conscious thought, in which everything dissolves into
uncertainty, rides on an unconscious process of association whereby the
positive values of the poem are being grouped. Somewhat as Beethoven,
in the Ninth Symphony, allows words to burst from a nonverbal form
built up in the music, so Yeats' final assertion emerges with apparently

arbitrary suddenness from a process dramatised by the poem throughout but only now made available, if indeed it is fully available even now, to the consciousness of its speaker. Such a highly controlled enactment of unconscious process, and one in which the speaker is also in some sense the poet, is difficult to assess precisely as an acknowledgement of the unconscious. The unconscious or irrational element is so finely played that the distinction nearly dissolves. It embodies the Nietzschean conception of responsibility as accommodating the instinctive and the unconscious, while the act of composing of the poem, and the forming of an historical judgement, are inextricably combined.

This very precise play with the pre-rational can be seen in the word 'dream' on which the poem hinges. For the final dissolution of categories is anticipated in the earlier lines on MacBride: 'This man I had dreamed / A drunken, vainglorious lout'. This had seemed merely a dead metaphor for 'supposed him to be', but it now becomes evident that Yeats is doing something much more radical. He is counterposing two dreams. At the opening of the poem, we seemed to have a real world of historical Dublin against which the rebels' aspiration might be defined as a dream. Yet those 'grey eighteenth-century houses' already had something of the faded backdrop of a theatrical set in contrast to the vivid faces of the actors, and the speaker now recognises that there is no single standpoint from which to declare reality, there is only a choice of dreams. Whereas 'The Stolen Child' rested on a duality of worlds, this poem invokes a comparable dualism only to dissolve it. One dream is not epistemologically privileged over another; the only question is allegiance: by which dream do we wish to identify ourselves collectively? The brute reality of the event has no meaning until it is given one by collective imaginative assent. Yeats makes a bid to define this meaning through his poem, and is fully conscious of significant forebears in that much of ancient Irish history was only preserved through its poets.

And so, as a conscious act of arbitrary but considered identification, the speaker moves to the poem's final affirmation and becomes one with the poet. Yeats, the Dublin clubman and raconteur, who was identified by his speech, becomes W. B. Yeats, Irish poet, who 'writes it out in a verse'. Only now does he name the patriots as they, like the poet himself, have ceased to be their everyday selves and have become figures defining the new collective dream. For good or ill, these names will be part of Irish self-definition in the future. By an extraordinary stroke, Yeats takes these four names, in reality as arbitrary as if they were shaken from a telephone directory, and with no more than three 'ands' he arranges them in a

rhythmic order echoing the most ancient metre of the language in which
he is writing. It is the Anglo-Saxon stressed form with its overtones of
preliterate memory preserved in rhythmic structures such as survive in
'to *have* and to *hold*, to *love* and to *cherish*, till *death* do us *part*'. In a double
sense, he 'numbers' them in the song. With the further echoes of prayer
in 'Now and in time to be', and of popular patriotic song in 'Wherever
green is worn', he completes the note of traditionary collective memory
transcending the personal situation and viewpoint of the speaker.

Of course, the poem is fraught with problems. The later history of
violence in Ireland hangs darkly over its affirmation of heroism. This is
part of a larger question about the political implications of modernist
mythopoeia more generally, and one to which I will return. For the
present, I would say that it is a magnificent and truthful poem. Catching the historical moment on the wing, Yeats contributed indelibly to
its definition in the darker spirit of O'Brien's comment quoted earlier.
The title now refers to more than a poem, while the poem itself
remains to trouble the living stream. In this respect it is illuminating to
compare 'Easter 1916' with its nearest English counterpart: Marvell's
'Horatian Ode Upon Cromwell's Return from Ireland'. Although the
'Irish' question is involved in both poems, the point of comparison is
that they are meditations on the necessity of political violence and
particularly as part of the foundational myth of a state. Marvell is, or
seeks to appear, more rational and considered. The poet's voice is that
of gravely historical, classically educated judgement. Adopting the Roman form of the Horatian Ode, he weighs, in balanced rhyming
couplets, the competing imperatives and risks in the strong leadership
of Cromwell. In each poem there are two bodies of imagery, from
nature and from theatre, which are at once contrasted and subtly
interwoven. In Marvell's case, the theatre image which presents
Charles I so heroically as 'the royal actor' at his execution also suggests
a damaging artificiality, a merely theatrical mode of being, undercut by
the Roman allusion to the bloody sacrifice that inaugurated the state.
Yeats' mode of 'argument', by contrast, undermines the processes of
conscious and rational judgement. For him, the theatrical gesture lies
at the heart of historical 'truth', for in this domain truth is not just seen,
but made, and he might have applied to the 'bewildered' patriots
Jacques Derrida's remark that 'there neither can, nor should be, any
concept adequate to what we call responsibility. Responsibility carries
within it, and must do, an essential excessiveness.'[11] This Jacques is no
fatalist, but he appreciates the modern complexity of free will. So too,

Yeats' posture is troubling, but partly because, in our day, it is inescapably true. 'Easter 1916' catches the nature of contemporary historical truth as penetratingly as did Marvell in his day. Yeats knows there is no ultimate grounding beyond the consensual horizon which he defines not just *in* but *as* a poem.

In 'Easter 1916', then, Yeats' conception of history arrives at the same metaphysical recognition as Nietzsche in his horizon image. Human beings create their individual and communal horizons. Yet the metaphysical precision of the poem is so entirely at one with the political theme that it hardly attracts attention to itself, let alone suggests a Nietzschean source. The sources are rather a transformation of his earlier poetic. But this was the time at which Yeats started to develop a broader vision of history based upon a mythopoeic and cyclic conception. In 1917, Yeats' new wife, Georgie Hyde-Lees, started to produce 'automatic writings' dictated by supernatural 'instructors'. These were the eventual basis of the historical and symbolic system set out in *A Vision* (1st version, 1924). Here Yeats broadened the mythopoeic metaphysic of 'Easter 1916' into a comprehensive view of human history as a series of cycles. At this point, the echoes of Nietzsche, and an unwitting parallel with his disciple Oswald Spengler, become more marked. *A Vision* set out twenty-eight phases of the moon from darkness, to light, and to darkness again as symbols of individual psychological types and of general states through which civilisations pass in the roughly two-thousand-year cycle of their rise and decline. It was thus a mapping of human psychological types who, as individuals, might not necessarily reflect the characteristic condition of the cultural phase in which they happened to live. He took moonlight rather than sunlight as his symbolic positive because he privileged the assertion of imaginative power, which he called 'antithetical', rather than the traditional light of reason which ultimately accepts the given, or 'primary', state. All human culture was for him a creative affirmation against the primary darkness and collectivity. And so likewise he associated aristocracy with the creative affirmation and democracy with a merging into the collective. What is important for present purposes is that, like Blake's symbolic systems, it should have been written at all, and the kind of belief status Yeats accords it. For he himself felt the need to raise this question within *A Vision*. His remarks are well known. The symbolic system enabled him 'to hold in a single thought reality and justice'; it was an essentially 'aesthetic arrangement of experience like the ovoids of Brancusi or the cubes of Wyndham Lewis'; and the 'instructors' have answered his direct question about its meaning by saying they have brought him 'metaphors for poetry'.[12] Typically, Yeats goes out of his way to raise the question of belief only to dissolve it into aesthetic terms. Once again, as in Nietzsche, the aesthetic definition applies not to existence, but to justification; it is not in any simple sense a truth question.

One way of taking *A Vision* is to see it as essentially a poem, except that this only leads back to the conundrum of the belief status of poetic expression. Not, that is to say, the poetic expression of belief, but the kind of hypothetical commitment demanded by the sheer fact of the artistic frame; what Coleridge defined as a willing suspension of disbelief. Coleridge's formula handily distinguishes the truth claims of fiction because it assumes a working borderline between belief and disbelief, whereas it is precisely this borderline that Yeats constantly elides. In *A Vision*, because it is set out like a discursive treatise, the question of its truth claims necessarily comes into view, but only in a way that obliges Yeats to put us off without much illumination of them. The poetry, by contrast, handles the same question with great subtlety because it is completely absorbed into the structure and fabric of the verse. It is an inextricable aspect of the subject. If *A Vision* is a kind of poem, then it is to the poetry that we must turn to find out what this means and, in doing so, we can see why the model of poetic belief cannot be confined to poetic occasions.

The single poem which most fully elaborates the Yeatsian metaphysic of belief as it is raised in *A Vision* is 'Lapis Lazuli' from his volume *Last Poems*, and, as it happens, this poem also continues very directly the line of development seen in 'The Stolen Child' and 'Easter 1916'. Some readers find 'Lapis Lazuli' too emptily rhetorical in the manner of much of Yeats' late verse. Whether or not it is one of his greatest poems, it is a peculiarly exemplary one, and, when this latter aspect is clearly seen, the true power of the poem also becomes more evident. Its power lies in its being, in the proper sense of the word, a metaphysical poem. It is one of those moments in literature which require a precise philosophical lens. For 'Lapis Lazuli', like 'Easter 1916', is a meditation on historical violence, but considered this time as a more general and speculative question. Once again, the poem has four stanzas and turns on an equivocal distinction of worlds, although this time art, rather than dream, provides the alternative possibility. The poem sets itself the task of justifying art in the midst of historical violence. It does so by an extraordinary reformulation of the question, so that the implicit bases of the challenge to art are dissolved, while the rhetorical sweep of the poem

naturalises its intellectual subtlety so completely that readers have repeatedly missed it.

Over its four sections, the poem oscillates between history imaged as
contemporary military violence, art as in Shakespearean tragedy, history
again in the long vista of rising and falling civilisations, and finally art
once again in the Chinese carving of the title. The apparent schematism
of this structure is misleading in that its purpose is increasingly to dissolve
these categories. The challenge of the poem is focused in the word 'gay'
as Yeats sets out to justify the perennial gaiety of the artist. The word
occurs once in each section and is the final word of the poem. This
closely reasoned dialectical structure provides Yeats' own characteristic
vindication of art, although the term 'gay' signals the Nietzschean and
metaphysical provenance of his thinking. Nietzsche's 'gaiety', as in *The
Gay Science*, contrasts with the 'joy' of the romantics.[13] Where romantic
'joy' was an emotion, or a more general sense of well-being, welling up,
or not, beyond the individual's control, gaiety is a more willed posture.
Although it has an emotional and psychological dimension, it designates
a more considered and chosen outlook; a philosophical posture, or world
view, rather than a mood.

As in 'Easter 1916', the opening includes a note of stylistic parody; in
this case the language of the newspaper:

> For everybody knows or else should know
> That if nothing drastic is done
> Aeroplane and Zeppelin will come out
> Pitch like King Billy bomb-balls in
> Until the town lie beaten flat.
>
> (Collected Poems p. 338)

Yet the reference to violence preserves a detached generality. 'King Billy
bomb-balls' conflates folk memory of William of Orange with contemporary allusion to Kaiser Wilhelm to invoke a generic town as lying
'beaten flat'. The note of generality prepares for the following section
when the tragic experience is contained within an aesthetic frame
affirming the power of the human imagination to make suffering, even
the agony of its own situation, the object of ecstatic contemplation. The
full force of this idea, as it is actually embodied in the verse, derives from
Yeats sustaining the paradoxical suggestion that the ecstatic sense of
tragedy realised and contemplated in dramatic art is not simply the
imaginative creation of the artist, but is somehow the same as that of the
beaten town in the opening section.

The second section opens with the general statement 'All perform

their tragic play', as if echoing the theme of 'All the world's a stage', then
continues:

> There struts Hamlet, there is Lear,
> That's Ophelia, that Cordelia;
> Yet they, should the last scene be there,
> The great stage curtain about to drop,
> If worthy their prominent part in the play,
> Do not break up their lines to weep,
> They know that Hamlet and Lear are gay;

The generality of the opening line proves to be misleading. As so often
with Yeats' apparently casual syntax, the sentence gives the impression
of a clear line of thought while actually leaving the syntactical relations
suggestively open. This linguistic peculiarity is in itself an important
index of Yeats' cast of mind, and time and again, as in the present
instance, it plays an important poetic role. He was quite conscious of this,
as can be seen from his comment on similar technique in Blake: 'The
form of sincere poetry, unlike the form of "popular poetry", may indeed
be sometimes obscure, or ungrammatical, as in the best of the *Songs of
Innocence and Experience.*'[14] In the present case, the syntactical logic is
formally clear enough, but it only gradually asserts itself over the
rhetorical movement. Only as the sentence continues does it become
clear that the 'tragic play' of the opening line refers syntactically to the
literary tragedy of Shakespeare, contained within the artistic frame of
theatrical illusion, while its opening position, and apparent generality of
reference at that point, imply at first that it refers back to, or at least
includes, the contemporary historical tragedy, the beaten town, of the
first section. This initial flicker of ambiguity concerning the location of
the 'tragic play', whether it refers to art or life, would be only a
momentary distraction if it occurred in isolation, but, in fact, while it is
still in the course of syntactical resolution, it is reinforced and developed
throughout the second section of the poem.

In the line 'Yet they, should the last scene be there' the subject 'they'
clearly refers to the dramatic characters named in the preceding lines.
Yet when the same pronoun recurs four lines later, apparently as a mere
recapitulation, in 'They know that Hamlet and Lear are gay', its
meaning has undergone a subtle but important change. Taken in
isolation the line would be taken to mean that some other consciousness,
such as the actor's, possesses this knowledge. The earlier suggestions in
'part' and 'lines' are now picked up, and the implication is that the
dramatic characters have such a reified sense of their own roles that they

transcend them to become their own actors or authors. The two aspects of the stage figures, as real persons and as dramatic creations, are at once distinguished and yet merged. The statement that the tragic figures 'If worthy their prominent part in the play / Do not break up their lines to weep' continues to ride on this anti-logical merging. Whether we see 'worthy' as referring more to character or to actor, breaking up the lines to weep would in either case remove the existential ground of the weeping. A character who weeps is no longer the character created by those lines, while an actor's weeping would banish the whole illusion on which the suffering depends.

This delicate superimposition of the logical levels of the actor/character relation grows out of the opening line of the second section with its equivocal superimposition of tragic experience as encountered both within and outside the dramatic frame. The overall effect is to suggest that the inextricability of the agony and the transcending power of the imagination, as embodied in the inner structure of the dramatic emotion, applies universally between tragic circumstances and the human mind. Accordingly, in the latter part of this section, the line 'Blackout; Heaven blazing into the head' combines death in a bombing raid with the tragic illumination of the final curtain. The whole second section expresses in a vividly concrete, yet analytically elusive, image both the transforming power of artistic imagination and its larger relation to experience. With a deceptive simplicity of means Yeats has done something truly remarkable. He has encapsulated the complexity of art emotion created out of the conjunction of two worlds which can never directly meet; and nor can they, within that emotion, be taken apart. There is no such thing as a special 'art emotion', and the actual experience is of an intuitive emotional whole. That is why Yeats' dissolution of categories has to be subliminal. When watching a great tragic drama, we do not need consciously to unpick the abstract layers of the experience, although we are undoubtedly affected by them. It is a difficult balancing act for Yeats to make something actively part of the meaning and yet not too conscious in the reading. A failure to recognise the complex intellectual structure of the poem is what leads some readers to see it as merely empty rhetoric. Harold Bloom, for example, who is no clumsy reader of Yeats, once complained that 'the gaiety of Lear is, of course, non-existent'.[15] This is quite true, but there is gaiety, for want of a better word, certainly an elation, in the *enacting* of Lear; and this gaiety of the actor is predicated both on the suffering of the character and on the actor's knowledge of what suffering means in the world. Whether for the actor or for the artistic spectator, the mind suffering the agony is not separable from the mind that holds it in being and experiences it as ecstasy. The sheer familiarity of this experience of dramatic emotion, and the near impossibility of discussing it in the abstract without banality, tend to blind us to its extraordinary complexity and implication. Yeats' imaginative intensity in the poem is not the rhetorical overstatement of a banal theme, but the inward rediscovery of a truth so familiar and fundamental that it constantly evades recognition.

As the poem returns to an historical vista in the third section, it continues the equivocal merging of art and life. Callimachus' marble is first compared to the softer medium of bronze and ultimately resembles drapery moving in the wind. His 'long lamp chimney' is only 'shaped like the stem of a slender palm', yet the simile suggests that its transience is ultimately part of a natural process. Marble, even when shaped by Callimachus, is no less natural than the stone that troubled the living stream of 'Easter 1916'. But in truth this whole historical vista is mainly a structural shift by which to move back into, and complete, the complex intra-aesthetic argument started in the Shakespeare section. The earlier definition of aesthetic emotion is picked up in the final section of the poem which enacts a very similar process in reverse.

> Two Chinamen, behind them a third,
> Are carved in lapis lazuli,
> Over them flies a long-legged bird,
> A symbol of longevity;
> The third, doubtless a serving-man,
> Carries a musical instrument.
> Every discoloration of the stone,
>
> Every accidental crack or dent,
> Seems a water-course or an avalanche,
> Or lofty slope where it still snows
> Though doubtless plum or cherry-branch
> Sweetens the little half-way house
> Those Chinamen climb towards, and I
> Delight to imagine them seated there;
> There, on the tragic scene they stare,
> One asks for mournful melodies;
> Accomplished fingers begin to play.
> Their eyes, mid many wrinkles, their eyes,
> Their ancient, glittering eyes, are gay.

Instead of life contemplated in an artistic frame, we now have art figures contemplating the life around them: the previous movement inwards to art becomes a movement outwards to life. The central figures in this final section, the two Chinamen, are introduced with a momentary ambiguity which precisely parallels that of 'All perform their tragic play'. At first mention they seem to be real persons, until the following line specifies that they are part of a carving. Once again, this momentary ambiguity is only the first stage in the development of a subliminal, imagistic argument which, despite its continuity of thought and syntax, is also a resolution of the earlier sections of the poem; which may be why there is a typographical break separating the final affirmation.

With the line 'The third, doubtless a serving man' an intricate double action begins. The word 'doubtless' implies that the scene the poet is describing depends in part on his own imaginative interpretation of the carving. It is the beginning of a growth away from the carved scene to an independently existing realistic action; a gradual shift from the stillness of art to the movement of life. Yet at the same time the word 'doubtless', by the very fact that it implies interpretative activity, is a reminder that the scene is actually a piece of carved stone. As so often in Yeats, the word you least notice is doing the crucial work. This double suggestion is developed over the next four lines as the arbitrary imperfections of the stone are imaginatively transmuted into the details of a more and more vital natural setting: the seeming 'water-course' and 'avalanche' lead to actual movement in 'it still snows'. Once again, the word 'doubtless' introduces the next phase as the Chinamen are now seen to be in motion too. The detail of the 'little half-way house' unobtrusively merges two orders of size. It is small to the Chinamen while being for us a tiny detail on a miniature carving. The inconspicuous ambiguity of the phrase holds in simultaneous focus the disparate orders of life and art, and it is only in the last six lines that Yeats allows his imagined scene to take leave almost completely of the carving. The final moment is freely and explicitly created by the poet's imagination: the Chinamen are now seen as having actually arrived at their destination, and they are moving, speaking and smiling. It is from this vantage-point, in an ontological as well as a physical sense, that they stare upon the tragic scene. The use of the same word 'scene' focuses the parallel, and the difference, between this moment and the stage scene of section two. The Chinamen are staring at the tragic scene of life outside the boundaries of the work of art that provides their viewpoint. It is as if the Shakespearean figures, like Nietzsche's weird image from the fairy tale, were knowingly to look out at their audience. Yeats has created for his expression of tragic gaiety a standpoint that looks out on, and is continuous with, life, yet which is made possible only by a work of art. Moving from the second to the final section, therefore, the overall strategy is first to contain tragic experience within an aesthetic frame while keeping it continuous with life, and then to use the aesthetic vantage-point, the capacity for transcendence, as a way of looking on the tragedy of life. The very specific complementing of the second section by the fourth is caught in the different uses of the word 'play', which in each case help to define the crucial term 'gay'. In the second part, where 'play' is a noun, the accent falls on the containing frame of the drama. In the last section it is a verb as the wisdom or gaiety of art is, in every possible sense, brought to life.

The interweaving of life and art in the poem conditions the final affirmation and gives it a discursively elusive, although intuitively comprehensible, basis. The gaiety is directly attributed only to the Chinamen; these are not actual persons, but creatures of the poet's imagination, and are dependent in turn on the stone figures of the carving. This indirection is an important part of the affirmation. It is as if Yeats' affirmation, the very meaning of which necessitates a singleness of expression undisturbed by realistic qualification or an ironic tone, could only accommodate itself to reality by locating itself at this elusive ontological remove. But the larger point is more positive than that. The dominant impression of the poem is of a smooth surface and simple, or at least unitary, utterance. Its affirmation, whatever it yields to close analysis, does not seem qualified or elusive; and the resultant emotion is complex without seeming complicated. As Yeats himself put it in the comments already quoted on Blake's 'ungrammatical' technique, 'it must have perfections that escape analysis'. Yeats' subtlety is that he does not so much create ambiguities, as dissolve the categorial discriminations. This is his most essential link with Nietzsche. Art remains a crucial term for defining the affirmative posture within the poem, yet in the same gesture it is dissolved back into a life term. Whether or not one accepts the particular Nietzschean and Yeatsian inflection of this model towards tragic affirmation, the metaphysical and emotional complex so defined is inarguable. All the *significance* of art has to lie somewhere between art and life, and who is to say that the proposition is not reversible, that the 'significance' of life does not lie there too? There are few more clearly thematised examples of the significant elusiveness of the aesthetic as a necessary yet dissolving category.

In contrast, the immediately preceding poem in the same collection, 'The Gyres', makes a similar affirmation but with an emptily rhetorical effect (*Collected Poems* p. 337). Individual lines have the authentic Yeatsian grain, but the poem does not create its viewpoint. It does not earn its affirmation. Yeats was a great poet, but not all the time, and his social and political outlook was not always admirable either. Maybe there is a connection between the imaginative short cut of 'The Gyres' and the Yeats who, for a while, supported the fascist blueshirts. I believe the metaphysical subtlety of a poem like 'Lapis Lazuli' represented the side of Yeats which knew how to keep a distance from a reductive politics, but the case would be hard to show conclusively. What must be said is that there is no short cut, or ideological system, which can guarantee our historical, political or ethical commitments. The self-conscious mythopoeia of modernism makes this responsibility conscious, but it cannot guarantee the decent living of it, and the significance of Yeats' historical vision is that it could not survive as a simple fixture outside of its particular poetic realisations. It had to be freshly earned each time, even if this was a truth that he himself did not always recognise. In this respect, 'Lapis Lazuli' is deeply representative, but not necessarily typical. It expresses the proper complexity of his vision in a way that many poems do not.

F. R. Leavis insisted that Yeats' truly great poems were relatively few. He saw what I have described as a self-consciously metaphysical posture rather as 'posturing' in the more everyday sense of striking attitudes, and he compared him unfavourably with Blake's essential impersonality, his ability to speak simply for his subject.[16] Leavis was largely right in the critical event, but he missed the underlying motive which led Yeats to run these risks. Yeats was not just a poseur, he adopted postures because all belief for him stood under a dramatic, aesthetic or mythopoeic sign. And that means that another kind of exercise has to be done, or has also to be done, with Yeats' *œuvre* from the one Leavis sought to perform. Rather than just winnowing out the truly great poems, we have also to recognise that the careful construction of each volume, and of the *Collected Poems*, points to something significant about the relations between poems. The kind of internal elusiveness shown in 'Lapis Lazuli' is reflected in the way individual poems repeatedly qualify each other. Yeats' poems do not just refer to each other and to common themes: in doing so they radically criticise each other.

This is generally recognised, and was already evident in the way 'The Stolen Child', over and above its internal ambivalence, provided an implicit critique of the post-romantic longing for a dream world expressed in the same volume at large. Even *Crossways* had its crosscurrents. But the point needs to be emphasised that if the elusive posture of 'Lapis Lazuli' were always affirmed, then it would cease to be elusive. However internally subtle, it would become a matter of habitual faith. For the individual poem to have inner integrity, therefore, it needs to jostle with, rather than simply support, the neighbouring poems in the collection. Similarly, those readers who see 'Lapis Lazuli' as merely a piece of rhetoric do indeed have a point. The poem wears its rhetoric on its sleeve because part of what we should pick up from it is that it expresses a possible attitude, what Yeats called a 'mood', rather than a fixed dogma. Just as the poem works by a bracketed identification with the tragic characters, so Yeats' Chinamen are the equivalent of Nietzsche's 'superhistorical men' whom he left to their 'wisdom and their nausea' after expressing with sympathetic inwardness the liberating force of the superhistorical understanding. So too, Nietzsche could return, later again, to the superhistorical wisdom as an aspect of properly historical understanding, as a freedom from entrapment in historical forms and imperatives.

Yeats' self-consciously composed '*œuvre*, therefore, reinforces the dramatic relativity of individual poems. 'Among School Children' seems to me his greatest single poem; partly because it not only, like 'Lapis Lazuli', stands independently of Yeats' private symbolism, but actively leans against the whole spirit of the Yeatsian pursuit of spiritual wisdom as that is embodied in, say, the Byzantium poems; although they too, of course, have their inner ambivalence and complexity. 'Among School Children' is his prototypical reverie poem encapsulating the process of an emotional recognition, but the truth it recognises has the deeper pathos of throwing into question so much, not just of his personal life, but of his artistic creed. In that respect the poem relates to his *œuvre* as does Proust's moment of recognition at the Guermantes' ball in *Time Regained*. The elderly speaker sees the error of his previous life's work of which we also now know the inner story. Except that Yeats has no transcendent bliss to gain from this, only a passionate affirmation whose pathos lies in its being too late for him.

The poem enacts an unconsciously growing awareness opposite to that seen in 'Easter 1916'. In the earlier poem, the final recognition was stated at once in what was to become the poem's refrain. The poem then caught up, through an intensely concentrated and self-questioning reverie, with its initial intuition. In 'Among School Children', by contrast, the speaker is rather seeking to repress an emotional truth. His initial 'questioning' is merely the enactment of his expected role; little more

than 'polite meaningless words'. Then the sentence is broken off by a
hyphen three lines short of the end of the first stanza as the speaker is
made suddenly self-conscious by the children's wondering stares:

> - the children's eyes
> In momentary wonder stare upon
> A sixty-year-old smiling public man.
>   (Collected Poems pp. 242–5)

This triggers a Proustian emotional memory as the sight of one of the
children is transfigured into the imagined presence of Maud Gonne as a
child. But this thought is too painful and he seeks to suppress it with a
hyphen breaking into the syntax once again three lines before the end of
stanza five:

> - enough of that,
> Better to smile on all that smile . . .

But the emotional memory has started an ambiguous process of generalised reflection running through stanzas v to vii: this may be a way of
replacing the memory with something less painful and personal or of
unconsciously maintaining the emotional momentum. The ambiguous
emotional freight of this 'philosophical' reflection has actually been
prepared for, since the initial images of Maud as child and as adult were
already invested with Platonic imagery:

> . . . our two natures blent
> Into a sphere from youthful sympathy,
> Or else, to alter Plato's parable,
> Into the yolk and white of the one shell.

Plato is invoked in an apparently positive way to provide the image of
wholeness and complete identity in sexual love; although even here the
speaker alters Plato's abstract image of the perfect sphere into the
homely and organic, as well as Ledean, egg; and, of course, the image of
the sphere came not from Socrates, but from his unspiritual opponent
Aristophanes. The second 'Platonic' echo is more oblique, and more
damaging, as the idealism of the later European tradition combines
Plato's unreal 'shadows' on the cave wall with the biblical 'mess of
pottage'.

> Her present image floats into the mind –
> Did Quattrocento finger fashion it
> Hollow of cheek as though it drank the wind
> And took a mess of shadows for its meat?

Yeats' own Platonising tendency is casually evoked without becoming a conscious issue, or bearing on the speaker. And so he proceeds to think of the ageing son against the youthful mother's pain and hope:

> What youthful mother . . .
> Would think her son, did she but see that shape
> With sixty or more winters on its head,
> A compensation for the pang of his birth . . .

Unlike the mother's naming her child in 'Easter 1916', this mother's hopeful love is powerless to form the future identity. And he goes on to reflect on the great philosophical systems by which the human mind has sought to form its world; presenting these, not as products of argument, but mythopoeically, as so many totalising visions each encapsulated in a single compelling image. Like Stephen Dedalus, he sets Plato against Aristotle, and with similar respect for Aristotle's comparative solidity, but Yeats is not so much concerned to plot a course between them as to see them all, in varying degrees, as seductive illusions. The generalised form of moral reflection still attempts to keep personal emotional implication at a distance, but suddenly all the previous elements, the nun, the schoolroom, the mother and the philosophers, combine to represent one great error. It is an intellectual error of dualistic projection, but so emotionally compelling and habitual in our culture as to be usually unrecognisable as such. And so, for the third and last time, a hyphen breaks into the syntax of the penultimate verse at almost the same spot as on the two previous occasions, except that here the recognition floods over the stanza end to run into the last stanza with its concluding apostrophe to a different kind of 'presence', Heideggerean rather than Proustian:

> O chestnut-tree, great-rooted blossomer,
> Are you the leaf, the blossom, or the bole?
> O body swayed to music, O brightening glance,
> How can we know the dancer from the dance?

The great anti-dualist statement is not primarily philosophical. It is concerned, like Nietzsche, with the psychological origins and consequences of ideas; with genealogy and judgement rather than 'truth'. The final recognition comes from a powerful backwash of feeling in which the initial repressive habits dramatised in the early part of the poem are the pervasive impulse underlying the *œuvre*.

This is the other great motif of modernist mythopoeia. Where 'Lapis Lazuli' expressed the metaphysical elusiveness of a world view modelled on the aesthetic, 'Among School Children' expresses the need for a non-dualistic wholeness in the self, and in the relation to the world, for which the pre-Socratics were a favourite example.[17] The relation of this poem to others such as the Byzantium poems, focuses the nature of belief or truth in Yeats, for this poem does not cancel out the others, and the transcendental longing of 'Byzantium' recurs later in the *Collected Poems*. In fact, while discussing the poem, I have spoken not of 'belief' or 'truth' so much as 'recognition'. There is, in other words, a generalisable aspect, and the final statement is couched in universal terms, but the utterance is emotionally specific to its occasion. Different and conflicting truths may be appropriate to other occasions. The traditional function of philosophy is to try to disentangle general and objective truths from the mass of particulars. By contrast, Yeats' truth lies not on the horizontal and objective plane of generality, but on the vertical axis of contextual and emotional specificity. Not objectivity, but a certain impersonality, is needed to convert emotion into truth. The truths by which we live are relational, but they are not simply 'relative' in the vulgar sense of being merely arbitrary. The sense that fundamental 'truths' of value are always dynamic, specific and earned is Yeats' point of fundamental affinity with Nietzsche. Late in life, Yeats summed up as follows the Blakean spirit of contraries which was his underlying conviction, his belief about belief:

I think that two conceptions, that of reality as a congeries of beings, that of reality as a single being, alternate in our emotion and in history, and must always remain something that human reason, because subject always to one or the other, cannot reconcile. I am always, in all I do, driven to a moment which is the realisation of myself as unique and free, or to a moment which is the surrender to God of all that I am . . . Could those two impulses, one as much part of truth as the other, be reconciled, or if one or the other could prevail, all life would cease. (Explorations p. 305)

The sense of 'reality' here is emotional and historical while his final reference is to 'truth', not '*the* truth'.

The final phase

I have concentrated on poems which enact this relational recognition, although other poems seem more simply assertive of specific beliefs and the bearing of Yeats' *œuvre* as a whole has remained controversial. The highlighting of particular assertions leads some readers to see his last phase as a final rejection of myth. This is, I believe, a misreading, but it is one which, when it is understood as such, clarifies what myth essentially means in Yeats. The view that Yeats came to reject myth has a long history including Lilian Feder's *Ancient Myth in Modern Poetry* and Daniel Albright's *The Myth against Myth*.[18] Although these studies are now rather old, they usefully set out layers of the question. Feder's account is part of a general survey of modern poets on this theme, and she understands myth psychologically or emotionally rather than metaphysically. She does not, therefore, discuss how Yeats continually brackets his emotional beliefs, or expresses particular convictions within a larger relational consciousness. She is a first-level reader for whom 'The Circus Animals' Desertion' is a straightforward rejection of Yeats' successive illusions. But much earlier in his career, in 'A Coat', Yeats had claimed to be 'walking naked' (*Collected Poems* p. 142). Sure enough, he had at that point outgrown and discarded an earlier poetic manner, but 'walking naked' is itself as much a rhetorical feint as Astrophil's 'Look into thy heart and write'.[19] It is when Yeats affects to be unaccommodated man that we need to be most careful. The mythopoeia is in the man, not in the clothes.

Albright has a more subtle engagement with the poetry and he recognises that these questions are both crucial and elusive. His whole account keeps bringing them to the fore, and in his discussion of 'The Circus Animals' Desertion' he quotes a discarded concluding stanza which suggests a much more affirmative posture than the final version. Albright interprets the rejection of this stanza to mean that such a mood has no place in the poem, and this is undoubtedly right, but the thought that it might have done, or that it was part of the larger creative impulse, is open to varying interpretation. I believe the affirmation in the discarded stanza corresponds to something implicit in the final version, but which the terms of Albright's argument lead him to block out. His final summary of Yeatsian mythopoeia, arising from his discussion of 'The Circus Animals' Desertion', is worth quoting at length for the way in which he identifies the issues while missing their point.

At the end Yeats did not want the God of nowhere and nothing, a vacant transcendence, but instead was content with excremental reality; when the cannon-smoke of the cancelled stanza cleared away, only a devastated land-scape remained. Having spent his mythopoeic life exploring the desolation of unreality, Yeats was now ready to embrace the 'desolation of reality' . . . 'The Circus Animals' Desertion' is an attempt to reconcile an antinomy: 1) art is art because it is not life; 2) no poet has any myth except autobiography. The thesis derives from Goethe, but has the force of Wilde's aesthetics and de l'Isle Adam's *Axel* behind it; and the antithesis as well is curiously associated with Wilde, with his dictum in 'The Critic as Artist' that criticism, the highest form of art, is autobiography. The whole circus metaphor suggests that art has nothing to do with life, that art is so evasive that it is almost nugatory; but the end of the poem indicates that a radical breakdown in the wall between life and art is occurring. The most remarkable aspect of the poem is its suggestion that the breakdown has been struggling to occur since the beginning of Yeats' career, that it is a continuously recurring process which keeps art honest, prevents it from veering into clownish sterility.[20]

This invites an analogous comment to Nietzsche's on Schopenhauer's account of the lyric. Schopenhauer, he said, had set out all the elements while missing their relationship, because he was locked into precisely the dualistic assumptions which the work of art itself had transcended. So too, Albright sees that the mythopoeic assertion was inveterate in Yeats till the end; he sees that the poem is a breakdown of the categories of life and art; he sees the assimilated background of aestheticist thought; and he sees that what is at stake is something that has been at work from the outset of Yeats' career: but he does not see what all these things mean. Yeats has long passed from the Schopenhauerian dualism of the aesthetic movement to a Nietzschean mythopoeia which dissolves art into life particularly through the image of theatre. Yeatsian myth does not lie in any of the particular circus 'ladders', but in the ceaseless and inescapable dynamic of their creation. Is there even an echo of snakes and ladders here? At any rate, Yeats does not say he is leaving the circus, rather that he '*must* lie down where all the ladders *start*' (my emphasis).

The mood of the poem is, of course, largely bitter, which explains the excision of the more affirmative stanza quoted by Albright, but the poem does not lose touch with the metaphysic, or anti-metaphysic, that underlies Nietzsche's 'joyful and trusting fatalism'.[21] Yeats' declaration 'I must lie down' has a bottomless ambivalence of will and necessity as well as an ambiguity as to whether it is relinquishing or restarting the process. Whereas Nietzsche, faced with Schopenhauer's discursive account of the lyric, went into a play of images which drew attention to its own paradoxicality, its absolute resistance to a rationalist accounting, Albright does the opposite. Yeats' Nietzschean dissolution of the categories is rationalised back into logical antinomies. And yet he is also partly right, because if the categories were not still 'there' their significant dissolution could not occur.

A late remark of Yeats suggests the relation of different world orders within a single *œuvre*:

if I would escape from patter I must touch upon things too deep for my intellect and my knowledge, and besides I want to make my readers understand that explanations of the world lie one inside another, each complete in itself, like those perforated Chinese ivory balls.[22]

One might, on this model, be internally ignorant of a whole explanatory system and yet understand its place in the larger order of possibilities. And conversely, one could have a full internal knowledge of one system of explanation and, for that very reason, fail to see its limited nature. But having accepted this open play of systems, he continues:

The mathematician Poincaré . . . described space as the creation of our ancestors, meaning . . . that the mind split itself into mind and space. Space was to antiquity mind's inseparable 'other', coincident with objects, the table not the place it occupies. During the seventeenth century it was separated from mind and objects alike, and thought of as nothing yet a reality, the place not the table, with material objects separated from taste, smell, sound, from all the mathematician could not measure . . . Nature or reality as known to poets and tramps has no moment, no impression, no perception like another, everything is unique, and nothing is measurable.[23]

Here Yeats' Blakean objection to the dualistic and generalising tendencies of modern thought rather undercuts the openness of his initial statement on the acceptability of different orders of explanation. He is still part of the romantic critique of modernity even while opening himself to the relativist spirit which was part of modernity's transformation of romanticism. He was still caught in conservative and romantic mythologies even while having developed the critical means to deconstruct them as mythologies, and, while his self-conscious mythopoeia represents a progressive possibility, his case overall enforces the point that there are no guarantees of getting it right: conscious mythopoeia can be a sophisticated form of wilfulness.

To bring out Yeats' limitation in this regard, it is worth noting that the image of different orders of explanation fitting together like perforated ivory balls is precisely appropriate to the way the different techniques of *Ulysses* combine to suggest an image of modern thought. But Yeats was not able to appreciate this in Joyce. He saw Joyce rather as a continuation of the naturalist spirit in a more radical form, as if the materialist world were now being allowed completely to invade consciousness. As two Irishmen hovering consciously between cultures they came to similar points by different routes. Joyce was initially smothered by belief just as formatively as Yeats had been deprived of it. But part of the reason Yeats did not recognise Joyce as something importantly different from a naturalist is that Joyce's aesthetic synthesis was actually more thoroughgoing and complete than his own. And being primarily a novelist rather than a poet, Joyce had in an important sense to create a world. Where the visionary Yeats deliberately immersed himself in dream, the myopic Joyce sought to present a world open to the most objective perception.

JAMES JOYCE'S *ULYSSES*:
TRIESTE–ZURICH–PARIS 1914–1922

The shadow hanging over the notion of myth is subjectivity: that myth is merely a projection. Joyce and Lawrence grasped this nettle by questioning the Cartesian dualism on which it is based. Indeed, a radical attack on Cartesianism was central to the period, and, rather than being merely 'subjective', myth was a focus for questioning subjectivity itself. In this respect, there is a multiple significance in the bald locations and dates with which *Ulysses* concludes: 'Trieste, Zurich, Paris. 1914–1922'.[24] Joyce's narrative is anchored in history and exemplifies the characteristically modern standpoint of exile whereby the local or national is best understood by the insider who has stepped outside the local frames of understanding and feeling. The book's standpoint is cosmopolitan on a European scale, despite the localism of its setting, and the opening date of 1914 could hardly be more historically resonant for the European continent as a whole. But, underlying these political and historical overtones, the very categories of time and space are significant elements in the book's actively mythopoeic design. Richard Ellman has suggested that *Ulysses* is systematically constructed on the coordinates of space and time; the first episode being strongly spatial, the second historical and the third a combination and so on.[25] Whether or not such triadic variations do significantly run through the book, the ending undoubtedly privileges categories which have acquired, over the course of the narrative, a Kantian significance in creating the world of the book. As we leave the world of *Ulysses*, its fundamental categories are those by which our own, or any, world is created. The overt creation of a world, and the jostling of different possible worlds, is the mythopoeic dimension of *Ulysses*. Some ancient disagreements about the book are worth reviewing as a way into this.

The early reception of *Ulysses* emphasised its satiric treatment of modernity along broadly Flaubertian lines. Wyndham Lewis' attack on Joyce in *Time and Western Man* (1927) rests on this assumption, and Yeats' response to Joyce as the running to seed of naturalism was likewise formed within this period. Over the succeeding decades, the comedic

spirit came to seem dominant led partly by the cheery appreciation of
Stuart Gilbert's influential *James Joyce's 'Ulysses'* (1930). It is now evident
that these rival responses point to a deeper effect. Joyce presents the
world in a spirit of objective acceptance, but, since a world created in
words can never be neutrally represented, he continually highlights, and
then neutralises, the representations. He invokes the rival spirits of satire
and celebration with an even-handed irony which suspends them both.
It is a complex evaluative equation in which the two sides cancel each
other out to create a significant, rather than a mere, neutrality. Thomas
Mann's almost contemporary *The Magic Mountain* enacts a more overt
process of multiplying and dissolving viewpoints in the strange environment of the *Berghof* remote from the 'flatlands' of everyday existence.
'Man', he says, 'is the Lord of counterpositions'.[26] But, where Thomas
Mann is primarily concerned with defining an inner, spiritual condition,
in a highly specialised imaginative environment, Joyce wishes to reveal
and restore the ordinary world as a sufficient value in itself, and the
process of self-cancellation is not therefore so explicit. It is embedded in
the texture of the narrative presentation.

This relates to another long-running dichotomy in the reception of
Ulysses. Readers have continually disagreed as to whether the work
affirms an overall unity or whether it is an endlessly relativistic play of
discourses.[27] The ultimate effect once again is to dissolve the terms of the
dichotomy while deliberately invoking them. The terms have to be
invoked in order to be significantly transcended or cancelled out; but
here a more intrinsic kind of contradiction is involved than the balancing
of conflicting attitudes. As an opposition of logical principles, it focuses
more sharply the philosophical substructure of irresolvability, of suspended commitments, on which the work rests. *Ulysses* has a studied
metaphysical elusiveness; as Philip Herring recognises in *Joyce's Uncertainty Principle* (1987). What matters is not so much the specific provenance of the discourses invoked by the techniques of the successive
episodes, but their relativised status within the whole. To add more of
them would not expand the point 'by an inch or an ounce'. The episodic
structure of *Ulysses* recalls Yeats' interlocking ivory balls, with the
difference that his image suggests separable layers, just as Yeats saw
himself as oscillating continually between the two principles, and his
poetic *œuvre* continued to affirm and resist unity by turns. A more integral
relativity within unity is built into the single structure of *Ulysses*. To
appreciate this it is helpful to consider more closely the inner logic of the
book's structure in which single episodes represent different ways of

constructing the world. For the narrative techniques of individual episodes are successive microcosms of the whole. Each highlights a mode of
perception which can then be recognised as a governing principle of the
entire book. Furthermore, the aspects highlighted in these episodes are
the paradigmatic features of modernism at large as *Ulysses* continually
thematises its own modernity. Yet it does so in a manner which is still
very implicit, as compared with the overtly philosophical meditations to
be found in the fiction of Thomas Mann. Although the *techniques* are
highly self-conscious, their *meaning* is not directly stated, and the potentially philosophical questions embodied in the successive narrative techniques remain precisely that, embodied, and are resistant to any systematic discursive account. This is evident in several of the episodes in which
the world-creating function is focused.

Consciousness and the world

The phrase 'stream of consciousness' gave an influentially misleading
stamp to the perception of Joyce. While rightly reflecting the central
importance of personal consciousness in Joyce's fiction, it encouraged a
subjectivist inference. By contrast, Ezra Pound, commenting on Joyce's
earlier fiction, remarked on his objectivity: 'Mr. Joyce deals with subjective things but he presents them with such clarity of outline that he might
be dealing with locomotives or with builder's specifications.'[28] Pound
admired the studied objectivity of Joyce's early Flaubertian mode and
went on seeking it, for as long as possible, in the later Joyce where
'objectivity' is increasingly achieved *through* 'subjectivity'. For *Ulysses*
gave a different inflection to the Flaubertian tradition, and the shift was
ultimately metaphysical. In Flaubert, the attitude of the narrator is still
paramount, even if it is given a negative and ironic sign. Nineteenth-
century novelists, like George Eliot and Dickens, typically presented the
world as humanly meaningful, or else, like Flaubert, as shockingly
lacking in meaning, whereas Joyce presents a world quite independent of
human meaning; although not of human perception. Instead of the
Wordsworthian inflection inherited by George Eliot, which emphasised
the humanly transformative dimension of the Kantian paradigm whereby there are no neutral facts, Joyce reversed the emphasis to privilege the
objective being of the world for which consciousness is a necessary
condition. Since the world can only be known in consciousness, Joycean
objectivity is not just a reversal, it dissolves the dualistic assumptions of
the word 'consciousness' itself. *Ulysses* conveys, rather than an authorial

posture of impersonality, a world of things appreciated just for being there. Joyce expressed this underlying attitude when he wrote to ask his Aunt Josephine to check the height of the railings at 7 Eccles Street to see if Bloom could climb over them.[29] Such a joke on the extra-fictional reality indicates his preoccupation with it.

This preoccupation first emerges strongly in the 'Proteus' episode:

Ineluctable modality of the visible: at least that if no more, thought through my eyes. Signatures of all things I am here to read, seaspawn and seawrack, the nearing tide, that rusty boot. Snotgreen, bluesilver, rust: coloured signs. Limits of the diaphane. But he adds: in bodies. Then he was aware of them bodies before of them coloured. How? By knocking his sconce against them, sure. Bald he was and a millionaire, *maestro di color che sanno*. Limit of the diaphane in. Why in? Diaphane, adiaphane. Shut your eyes and see.
Stephen closed his eyes to hear his boots crush crackling wrack and shells. You are walking through it howsomever. I am, a stride at a time. A very short space of time through very short times of space. Five, six: the *Nacheinander*. Exactly: and that is the ineluctable modality of the audible. Open your eyes. No. Jesus! If I fell over a cliff that beetles o'er his base, fell through the *Nebeneinander* ineluctably! (Ulysses p. 31)

In this episode, readers first face the extreme privacy of Stephen's reflections arising from his personal memories as much as from external stimuli. The immediate impact suggests an enclosure in consciousness. Yet the subject of Stephen's meditation, and his closing his eyes to reflect on 'the ineluctable modality of the visible', enforce the inescapable existence of the external world within the modality of his consciousness and perception. The 'ineluctable modality of the visible' soon divides into the more objectified categories of time and space, the *nacheinander* and the *nebeneinander*. Whether or not Joyce had any specific reference in mind here, and Lessing's *Laocoön* (1766) has been suggested, the use of the German words points to a broadly Kantian rather than Cartesian provenance.[30] Kant's categories, including time and space, through which he saw all experience as constituted, were at once mental or logical categories and the structuring principles of the phenomenal world. World and the mind are functions of each other. Kant's philosophy was foundational to modern thought by overcoming an earlier, Cartesian dualism as well as, by the mid-eighteenth century, Hume's scepticism and Bishop Berkeley's idealism; about which Stephen ruminates later in the episode. It is typical that Stephen's overt thought should be of Aristotle, Jakob Boehme and Berkeley, and that the narrative technique should echo Descartes' systematic perceptual doubt, while the deeper implication is Kantian and ultimately post-Kantian. Joyce compresses an essential history of thought here just as he compresses a history of literature in his modern recycling of Homer. The technique of *Ulysses* is not so much subjective as a way of dissolving subjectivity.

In 'Proteus' we have still to look rather closely to see this implication, but as the book goes on we develop a more complex sense of its apparent subjectivism as not so much reversed as constantly reversible. Instead of a world sustained by a possibly solipsistic consciousness, one can see consciousness as the problematic phenomenon sustained within and by a world. The inextricablity of consciousness and world has a subjective aspect, to be sure, but equally an objective one. The late episodes, 'Circe' and 'Ithaca', are the thematic correlative of this technique as Bloom participates in his own objectification as part of his acceptance of himself in the world. 'Circe' prepares for the spirit of impersonal acceptance in 'Ithaca' by treating the inner world of the psyche in a reified, phenomenalised fashion, and suggesting the human implication of doing so. In the brothel, the 'external' world has receded before the free play of psychic fantasy. It was, of course, part of Joyce's modernity, along with Freud, to express, as part of overall psychic health, the repressed, pornographic underworld of what Stephen Marcus has called the 'other Victorians'.[31] At one level this is a matter of acknowledgement in the spirit of *nihil humanum mihi alienum est*, but the episode suggests a more fundamental condition of possibility in Bloom. As his psychic world assumes the archaic form of a psychomachia, whereby psychic elements become apparently tangible objects, the pseudo-dramatic technique takes on a symbolic force. It expresses the impersonal, phenomenal light in which Bloom, the least egotistic of men, inhabits his own psychic world. The objectifying technique underwrites the emotional detachment with which Bloom finally contemplates his own situation as summed up in the progressive formula 'Envy, Jealousy, Abnegation, Equanimity' (*Ulysses* p. 602).

At the same time, the technique by-passes Bloom's self-consciousness so that it is not merely a self-conscious posture on his part. In these later episodes, a quasi-ethical value emerges for the objectification of consciousness which has been implicit from the beginning of the book. Philosophers of being, who wish to define existential attitudes which are not in themselves ethical but which must underlie and govern the ethical, sometimes refer to this realm of underlying attitude as proto-ethical. By analogy with this, one might say that the narrative technique defines a proto-ethical outlook for which Bloom's personal consciousness provides an equivalent in the ethical sphere. The technique elaborates and endorses the meaning of his intuitive posture without creating the wrong sort of self-consciousness either for Bloom or for the reader. It presents his emotional posture as something more positive than withdrawal or indifference, and associates him with the Shakespearean acceptance of human variety as thematised in the Library episode, 'Scylla and Charybdis'.[32] But the ultimate formula for his emotional impersonality comes in 'Ithaca' where the technique is a comedic invocation of science. Since the use of science in 'Ithaca' has, once again, a microcosmic value for the book, and an exemplary significance for modernism at large, it is worth unfolding its relation to the themes of subjectivity and mythopoeia.

Modernism and science

The nineteenth-century novel commonly privileged natural science as the paradigmatic form of truth statement. In modernism, however, science became simply one of the possible world constructions open to human culture, and, in making 'science' the overtly comic technique of a single episode, Joyce expresses its relativity with respect to the whole. It is just one way of organising the world. At the immediate dramatic level, the scientific catechism of 'Ithaca' encapsulates the transformed Flaubertianism which has been developed over the course of *Ulysses*. The successive techniques of the later episodes have an increasingly impersonalising effect for which 'scientific' discourse is the culmination. From this point of view what is at stake is not science as a form of objective knowledge, but the scientific outlook as a mode of emotional impersonality; and the overtly comedic or parodic spirit of the episode enforces this by increasing the emotional distance while also preventing the science from being taken too seriously as a form of knowledge. The 'science' of the episode is an essentially literary standpoint which modulates seamlessly into frankly poetic moments, such as 'the heaventree of stars hung with humid nightblue fruit' (*Ulysses* p. 573). In this way, the nihilistic impersonality of Flaubert, which was scientifically as well as aesthetically tinged, gets turned into something genially comedic. In the Joycean context it becomes an impersonal acceptance of the world and of humanity.

Yet this literary invoking of science is also an implicit comment on the human place of science itself. To prize science for its emotional impersonality, rather than for its claims to objective knowledge, is to suggest the limits of those claims. To see the proper force of this implication, both in

Ulysses and for modernism more generally, it is necessary to recall the transformations in the perceived truth status of science in the latter part of the nineteenth century. By the turn of the century the notion of scientific observation was deeply problematic; the whole edifice of modern scientific knowledge was a human construction yet, Eddington said, the modern physicist does not inhabit a different world from the layman so much as two different world perceptions at once. There is an exactly analogous relation of modernism to realism, a simultaneous inhabiting of two apparently incommensurable orders of truth, for which science was repeatedly recognised to be the appropriate focaliser. Modernist writers were aware of the constructed nature of the world, but sought none the less to represent it truthfully in fiction, and this representation includes both the ordinary phenomenal appearances and the constructed reality of the world. The primary impulse of modernism, that is to say, was not anti-realist, which was to come later, but super-realist, and the typical quarrel with earlier fiction was not with its attempted realism, but with the inadequacy of its realist conception. In her essay on 'Modern Fiction' Woolf objects to the externality and limitation of earlier conceptions just as Lawrence does when he dismisses the 'old stable ego' of nineteenth-century fiction.[33] Indeed the modernists' acute awareness of the world as sustained by the constructions of consciousness, far from weakening the realist impulse, actually gave it an enhanced power. In many respects the modernists beat the nineteenth-century realists at their own game, and it was not totally misguided to mistake Joyce for a naturalist. Proust can describe a late summer afternoon with a sensuous immediacy and emotional precision not to be bettered by Keats or George Eliot, and yet it is the very fact that this whole world proves to have been conjured out of the narrator's emotional memory that gives it its peculiar truth. Proust's nostalgia is explicitly for an imagined, rather than a real, experience. Beneath the local quality of the episode there is an underlying recognition that this conjured world is not, as in George Eliot, a real world nostalgically remembered, so much as a world whose effective existence is a creation of the nostalgia itself. Maybe that is why there is no free-floating nostalgia in Proust as there sometimes is in Eliot. In this respect, he is actually more responsible than she.

As with the 'Proteus' episode, the recognition of subjectivity becomes a way of acknowledging the being of the world. Modernism was a moment, like that of Cervantes and Shakespeare, when fundamental changes in world view, what Thomas Kuhn called paradigm shifts, were occurring.[34] Modernism was a peculiar synthesis which preserved the realist world on the basis of a new metaphysic, and the old science is parodically presented in 'Ithaca' through a relativised, constructive consciousness which is the proper contemporary of modern science. Pound remarked that avant-garde attempts in the arts to adopt the techniques of other media or disciplines are usually false: what is consciously adopted is usually out of date in its own field while genuine contemporaneity across different fields is likely to be unconscious and will not 'seem superficially similar'.[35] The technique of 'Ithaca' makes the point demonstratively. Its contemporaneity with the new science lies not at the level of its overt imitation/parody of science, but in the awareness of its own discourse as a relative projection alongside the other discourses making up the world of *Ulysses*. Just as Stephen ruminates on Aristotle and Boehme within a Kantian narrative world, so the overt invoking of science on a reductively old-fashioned model allows the underlying implication of the narrative technique to be thoroughly modern. The real humour of the episode lies in its presenting a 'Newtonian' world through the literary equivalent of an Heisenbergian one; within a discourse that recognises its own constructive involvement in the world it 'describes'.

Having grasped the doubleness of the technique, one can appreciate how the layman's common-sense world is transformed. From the realist's point of view, it both is and is not business as usual as Joyce constructs his naturalistic texture within a symbolist metaphysic. The double consciousness in question here bears on two different levels whose relation is like what I have described as ethical and proto-ethical consciousness. The latter part of the book increasingly expresses a general attitude towards being; an attitude which will in turn affect ethical and emotional questions. Again, it is useful to compare Thomas Mann's use of science in *The Magic Mountain* as Hans Castorp initially tries to understand life and love scientifically. At this early stage in Castorp's quest, Mann uses the X-ray to show how Hans comes to see, and is of the first generation ever to see, his own skeleton.[36] A purely scientific and technological mode of vision, even in the pursuit of health and an understanding of the mystery of life, is deathly, and it appropriately reveals a *memento mori*. Modern medical science, as exemplified in the sanatorium, is commonly bound up with a cultural fear and denial of death; and the whole ambiguity of the sanatorium, of course, lies in the sinister double sense in which its regime is good for the disease. But the X-ray machine is later echoed by another piece of modern technology, the gramophone, which in the period in question has the heavy and ornate appearance of a sarcophagus. As Hans listens to music singing seductively of death he comes, through the means of art, to understand intuitively the appeal of death, and thereby to transcend it. Art, as in the Dionysian experience invoked in *The Birth of Tragedy*, is an important form of inner knowledge which neither imitates, nor offers itself for imitation. So too, modern mythopoeic writers frequently had a strategic anti-humanism, aimed not against the human, but against the limits of humanism. For Nietzsche, the loss of this mythopoeic inner negotiation under the sign of the aesthetic had already occurred within the history of Greek drama, and the ultimate decline into psychological realism and rational explanation, or into the simply human viewpoint, is what he saw in the novel.[37]

That is why Mann departs from novelistic realism in this book. A conscious contemporary of Freud, he saw the conflict of eros and thanatos as conducted beyond the purview of rational consciousness, and irrespective of the particular objects in the world through which it manifests itself. Ultimately, he suggests, and once again the thought is at a proto-ethical level, we must honour life rather than death and must therefore learn truly to distinguish between them as an attitudinal rather than as a purely physical matter. From this point of view the empirical weight of realism, like the rational processes of consciousness, may be misleading; indeed, it is almost designed to be so. And science too, while having its evident uses, has its insidious dangers when taken as a complete account of the human world. Whereas, in nineteenth-century fiction, the medical profession often represented a humanised science, and was thus even a model of the novelist, Mann enforces a dichotomy between psychological health and medical science, while Joyce similarly presents science as offering a strictly relative order of truth in a narrative form which transcends realistic mimesis. So too, Mann's use of music as an aesthetic, and ultimately mythopoeic, negotiation of psychic conflict, parallels the more homely use of music in *Ulysses*. In Joyce, the German romantically-derived conception of music, as the realm of the irrational and the primordial, dwindles to sentimental temptations in a bar.

Time, music and spatial form

The proto-ethical detachment of *Ulysses* is bound up with an intuition of the timeless. *Ulysses*, as much as *The Magic Mountain*, is a book about time or, more precisely, about the timeless within time. Joyce's remark to

Carlo Linati, that he wished to present life not *sub specie aeternitatis* but from the standpoint *temporis nostri*, still conjures up the standpoint of the eternal within human time.[38] Joseph Frank long ago identified spatial form as a defining feature of modernist narrative in contrast to the historicism of nineteenth-century fiction, and in his seminal essay he made a brief, undeveloped reference to the relation between spatialised form and myth.[39] Since Frank was not engaging the internal complexities of modernist mythopoeia as such, this relationship needs to be more fully unfolded, and, once again, the whole question of modernist spatialising is thematised within the text of *Ulysses* in a way that reveals its relation to the mythopoeic.

The 'Sirens' episode, by focusing on music, epitomises the essential questions at stake here, since music is a medium which highlights the aesthetic transposability of time and space, whereas narrative tends to disguise it. In realist narrative artistic spatialising is only half emergent from the experience, whereas in the non-referential art of music the two dimensions, and their transposability, are more sharply delineated. When music is performed, the temporality of the form is inseparable from that of the performance. But, more importantly, the momentary experience of a musical sound has no meaning without the structural whole of which it is a part, and this meaning is only present to the listener through a spatialised memory or anticipation. That is equally true for the closing note of a symphony or a beat in a rhythmic phrase, and music has been a vital metaphor and structural device for modernist writers seeking a transcendence of time. In his account of 'The Making of *The Magic Mountain*', Thomas Mann comments on the way the book needs to be read twice before it can be understood at all, because it is composed on the same principle as a symphony.[40] The classic instance is T. S. Eliot's *Four Quartets* in which a studied invocation of musical form is used to intuit a mystical experience beyond time. In a general way this spatialising of time clearly applies to *Ulysses* too, and the musical motif of the 'Sirens' episode is Joyce's way of focusing this for the book as a whole. But, to see more precisely how the spatialising is made significant within the episode, it is necessary to distinguish it from the other, rival significance that has been accorded to music in modern literature.

In German post-romantic tradition through Schopenhauer, Wagner, Nietzsche and on into Thomas Mann, music expressed the pre-verbal realm of feeling. It was associated with the primordial state which may engulf civilised and rational order. The 'Sirens' episode offers a homely equivalent of this, since, for Joyce, the enemy is rather a national proclivity for sentimentality in the sexual, artistic and political realms, and music, in this episode, expresses the seductive emotional yearnings to which other characters succumb, while Bloom is able to keep such feelings at a distance. At the same time, Bloom's control over the seductions of sentiment is expressed in the use of 'musical' form as narrative organisation. In other words, behind, or secretly within, the apparent lyricism we recognise the astringency of a formal structure. By setting out the 'motifs' of the episode as an apparently meaningless series of phrases at the beginning of the chapter, Joyce gives us something which we can only later appreciate as being a kind of overture delineating the essential thematic structure of the whole.

> Bronze by gold heard the hoofrons, steelyringing.
> Imperthnthn, thnthnthn.
> Chips, picking chips off rocky thumbnail, chips.
> Horrid! And gold flushed more.
>
> (*Ulysses* p. 210)

The initial meaninglessness focuses the spatialised form of the subsequent episode. Once again, of course, nothing of this means anything to Bloom himself. His sober avoidance of lyrical extremes is purely intuitive. None the less, with the usual double irony of *Ulysses*, it is Bloom who alerts us to the significance of the technique.

> Numbers it is. All music when you come to think. Two multiplied by two divided by half is twice one. Vibrations: chords those are. One plus two plus six is seven. Do anything you like with figures juggling. Always find out this equal to that. Symmetry under a cemetery wall. He doesn't see my mourning. Callous: all for his own gut. Musemathematics. And you think your listening to the etherial. (*Ulysses* p. 228)

While Bloom's practicality saves him from excessive sentiment, his reflections direct us towards the corresponding aspect of the narrative technique: what is perceived as an emotional or spiritual experience in time is in fact a structure of mathematical, spatialised relations.

The importance of the spatialised form is that the larger intuition of the timeless figured in the Homeric parallel is not imported as a ready-made significance somehow inherent in the mythic parallel as such, but is actually created anew within the momentary process of the narrative. In other words, the timeless order apparently enshrined in myth is the product of a secular aesthetic structure, as when Nietzsche spoke of putting 'the stamp of the eternal' on experience.[41] The aesthetic is the condition by which modern sensibility creates an *equivalent* of the mythic. The story of Odysseus, in so far as it is a cultural myth, suggests a timeless structure of experience given to the writer, but Joyce's spatialising holds the archaic structure in *counterpoint* to its modern re-enactment. As the modern *construction* of a world enfolds the older sense of a *given* form, neither has its complete meaning by itself. Mann's sense of the mythic, quoted at the outset, as being at once a primitive condition from which it is necessary to escape and the most sophisticated condition to which one should strive, is embodied in this self-conscious reconstruction of the already given. Strictly speaking, the Homeric parallel is not so much the source of the book's transcendent standpoint as an emblem of it. Equivalence, rather than identity, is the key to understanding the relation of primary to self-conscious myth as proposed by Thomas Mann's formula, and the crucial question for *Ulysses* is not the *interpretation* of the Homeric parallel, but its metaphysical *status*.

Ulysses *and Homer*

In what sense is Homer present in *Ulysses*? It is, to be sure, a 'ghostly' one, like the presence of Shakespeare in Stephen's account of *Hamlet*, but the book's technique involves something more than the fading of the author into impersonality. The whole meaning of the book is, in an important sense, a ghostly one, and Homer is a key term in defining it. Ezra Pound advised the reader to ignore the Homeric parallel which, he claimed, was merely part of Joyce's 'medievalism', his penchant for creating elaborate systems, and the reader should regard it simply as a 'scaffolding'; necessary to the construction, but not to the use, of the completed work.[42] As an antidote to the incipient Joyce industry, which immediately focused on the Homeric allusions, Pound's advice was salutary; but taken in itself it is too extreme. The book is after all called *Ulysses*, even though Joyce removed the Homeric chapter titles before publication and withdrew the Homeric scheme he had initially made available to Valéry Larbaud. These authorial equivocations have an emblematic value for the status of the Homeric allusions in the book which retains a 'now you see it now you don't' quality each time we reread the text. Either to overemphasise or to ignore the Homeric allusions is to miss the point; for the Homeric parallel provides the precise formal correlative for Thomas Mann's problematic formula, and it typifies an important generic transformation in modern fiction at large. If the history of European fiction was the slow emergence of the novel from romance and ultimately from epic, the early twentieth century saw a conscious return of the novel to the bosom of epic, and through that to myth. Of course, the novel continued throughout its history, from Cervantes, through Fielding and Tolstoy, to *contain* the epic impulse, but only in the modern period did the novel seek once again to rest itself on epic and mythopoeic bases. *Ulysses* helps to focus the paradoxical and elusive nature of this return; and to what extent it is a return at all.

Although epic remains a vital term to express the significance of the modern form, Joyce's construction is not Homer; it is a modern equivalent, and perhaps no worse for that. There is a familiar double irony in *Ulysses* whereby the normal, eighteenth-century working of the mock heroic to mock the present is reversed at the expense of the heroic itself. The 'Cyclops' episode is Joyce's classic reduction to absurdity of an anachronistic survival of the heroic in his own day. So too, on a more metaphysical level, *Ulysses* keeps Homer as a defining term while transforming his meaning: the changed attitude to the classic is suggested in the allusion to Matthew Arnold's 'Hellenising' ambition. (*Ulysses* pp. 6–7) In the Preface to his 1853 poems, Arnold spoke of the impact of Greek culture for an educated man of his day as something purely internal. The steadying and purifying effect of the classics, the capacity to see things in their proper proportions, remains a possession of the individual sensibility and has no active relation to contemporary life.

I know not how it is, but their commerce with the ancients appears to me to produce, in those who constantly practise it, a steadying and composing effect upon their judgement, not of literary works only, but of men and events in general. They are like persons who have had a very weighty and impressive experience: they are more truly than others under the empire of facts, and more independent of the language current among those with whom they live . . . If they are endeavouring to practise any art, they remember the plain and simple proceedings of the old artists, who attained their grand results by penetrating themselves with some noble and significant action, not by inflating themselves with belief in the pre-eminent importance and greatness of their own times.

· · ·

If asked to afford this by means of subjects drawn form the age itself, they ask what special fitness the present age has for supplying them. They are told that it is an era of progress, an age commissioned to carry out the great ideas of industrial development and social amelioration. They reply that with all this they can do nothing; that the elements they need for the practise of their art are great actions, calculated powerfully and delightfully to affect what is permanent in the human soul; that so far as the present age can supply such actions, they will gladly make use of them; but that an age wanting in moral grandeur can with difficulty supply such, and an age of spiritual discomfort with difficulty be powerfully and delightfully affected by them.[43]

This is Nietzsche's theme of internal culture for external barbarians, except that Arnold would himself be the object of Nietzsche's critique.[44] *Ulysses* dissolves the snobbery of the Arnoldian dilemma by incorporating both its aspects within a single viewpoint. In Joyce, the Homeric example becomes a transformative way of looking rather than the object itself and, of course, in Joyce the way of looking is everything. As Thomas Mann remarked: 'mythical knowledge resides in the gazer and not in that at which he gazes'.[45] Dublin remains what it is, 'dear' and 'dirty', while the Joycean/Homeric lens changes our view of it (*Ulysses* p. 119). The true image of the Homeric standpoint in *Ulysses*, therefore, is not Pound's scaffolding, but Wittgenstein's ladder. Towards the end of the *Tractatus*, Wittgenstein points out that his argument has undercut itself and the reader will now have to remove it like a ladder after climbing.[46] This is an apt image for the paradoxical standpoint of modernist mythopoeia; to which Wittgenstein's mature philosophical thought, with its emphasis on 'forms of life', bears a close relation.[47] Homer defines, but does not ground, the world of *Ulysses*.

In effect, Joyce has constructed, under the emblematic sign of myth, a frankly synthetic unity. Colin Falck has argued that literature is itself our modern form of myth.[48] This is true, but only by a more circuitous route than he has in mind, and the synthetic dimension is the point of difference. Rather than say literature *is* myth, as if myth were the essentially poetic form argued by much early twentieth-century anthropology, we have to say that it is an aesthetic *equivalent*. For modern mythopoeia, as seen in Joyce or Mann, is synthetic in two important and related senses. First, it effects a synthesis in bringing disparate elements together. The disciplinary discourses invoked by the different episodes are ostentatiously incommensurable, yet they form a narrative unity, and, furthermore, as I have suggested, the successive techniques highlight features of the narrative at large so that each episode affirms a unity despite the separateness of its discourse. This intuition of unity within incommensurable differences is the central project of modern mythopoeia. Primary myth, by contrast, could be defined as that stage in culture in which the disciplinary fields of a modern world view had not yet distinguished themselves. For example, an inherited ritual performed for some efficacious purpose, such as rain-making, would effectively function as religion, science, art and history, but could not do so if these functions were separably conceived in the modern sense. The term 'university', which might better be polyversity, enshrines this characteristic of modern culture. Each of the different disciplines encompasses the whole of life, but can only do so within its specific mode of enquiry. None of them can redeem the claim to overall meaning that the word university seems to make. But *Ulysses* invokes this multiplicity of discourses and treats them as if they were a unity.

The force of the 'as if' is what needs to be defined. Part of the point seems to be an equivalent of Vaihinger's universal 'As If'; in other words, the second sense of synthetic as 'artificial', or man-made, is just as crucial as the first, for the unifying synthesis can only be achieved on this condition. But to appreciate the force of this it is helpful to move from the level of disciplinary discourses to the more basic question of language in which the mythopoeic potential most crucially resides. For although discourses can be made self-conscious, they cannot be separated from the implicit collectivity of language from which they arise.

Language

Different discourses, as F. R. Leavis used to insist, are not different languages.[49] Language contains all the specialised discourses and is the condition of their coming into being. Towards the end of *Ulysses*, having established the principle of competing or complementary discourses of which the narrative is composed, Joyce considers language itself in 'Oxen of the Sun'. While the various discourses are spread out spatially and contemporaneously across the modern narrative, this episode invokes the historical development of English through a series of personal literary styles and raises a radical question about the nature of language.

Setting 'Oxen of the Sun' in the lying-in hospital, Joyce parallels the evolution of language with foetal development, but the parodic sign under which the episode is written invites us to question the suitability of the organic metaphor with respect to language. The nineteenth century had adopted the organism as a fundamental metaphor replacing the machine or clock which was the governing metaphor of the eighteenth century. By the early twentieth century, however, the organic metaphor was itself giving way, and language, in the period of Ferdinand de Saussure, was not so readily conceived on the model of an organism growing in a specific national soil. It was rather to be seen as a sign system constructed with arbitrary materials out of an intrinsic, relational logic.[50]

At this point, indeed, a complicating factor has to be noted, namely that the deep metaphor of the twentieth century was to become very largely language itself. The discovery of a genetic 'code' in the mid-century neatly encapsulates the reversal by which the act of procreation, the most fundamentally organic act, and a central metaphor in Joyce's aesthetic thought, came to be understood on a linguistic analogy. But the adoption of language as the deep metaphor of the period has also made it hard to get an analogical grip on language itself. And, in the event, twentieth-century thinking about language has remained divided between, on the one hand, scientific, or scientistic, approaches often assimilating Saussure, and, on the other hand, a more poetic and holistic understanding for which Martin Heidegger is the most philosophically prestigious example. 'Oxen of the Sun' sits right on this fault line which had opened up just before the episodes of *Ulysses* began to appear. Is language a synthetic instrument open to technical analysis, as if from outside, or is it a medium which we inhabit, and therefore can only know, partially, organically, and from within?

In going through the series of personal styles, Joyce is not parodying them in any merely debunking sense, yet there remains an inescapable implication of their effective reproducibility; the tricks of style can be learned and imitated. Underlying Dickens' self-bestowed nickname of the 'Inimitable' lies a more general claim to authorial individuality which is here put under threat. Furthermore, this technique, like all the techniques of *Ulysses*, has the effect of removing any personal style, any conscious or unwitting signature, of the author. If Joyce's style were to be added to the historical list what would it be like? What Joyce seems to be doing here is parodying the organic metaphor itself, and the related notion of the individual self, without quite discarding them. Or perhaps it is closer to the spirit of Derrida's 'deconstruction' which does not seek to expose discourse as unusable, but rather to ride, demonstratively, the process of its deconstructability. Hence, just as the different discourses of *Ulysses* are treated only 'as if' they were a unity, so language and personal identity have a similar status of being necessary terms placed under erasure.

Both the overall narrative structure of *Ulysses*, then, and its linguistic medium, are ostentatiously synthetic while behaving as if they were organic. The book creates an artistic unity as the emblem of a possible living attitude which cannot be transcendentally grounded. On the contrary, it turns consciously upon itself 'like the world, macro and microcosm, upon the void. Upon incertitude, upon unlikelihood' (*Ulysses*

p. 170). Yet, although the world of the book has no ground, there is an earth. Once again, *existence* is not at stake, only its *justification*; although that lies partly in the appreciation of existence itself, an acceptance of the being of the world. To that extent, it is a switch from Nietzschean affirmation to a Heideggerean sense of Being which is the discursive equivalent of much modernist literature. D. H. Lawrence, as will be seen, is a striking case. At one level, the self-sufficiency of *Ulysses* is created aesthetically in the transformed Nietzschean, rather than the symbolist or Schopenhauerian, sense. But the further, Heideggerean, aspect is to give back the phenomenal world with an intrinsic value. Joyce's 'railings' are a homely synecdoche for Heideggerean Being. In this way, modernist mythopoeia combines the life-enabling, unifying aspects of archaic myth with radical scepticism, and Homer remains a necessary term even while he is replaced as an aesthetically constructed equivalence. Yet the Homeric parallel, in its aspect as given legend, still suggests a hidden, transhistorical structure like the rings in a tree-trunk which will be the same at whatever point it is cut. It is necessary, therefore, to see how this metaphysical, or anti-metaphysical, model relates to the question of history, for history is lived and judged by values which are not in themselves explicable by history, and the superhistorical is partly an emblem of this recognition.

History and the superhistorical

The ghostly presence of Homer resembles a Nietzschean thought experiment; a necessary but elusive term, like the 'weird image from the fairy tale' in *The Birth of Tragedy*, or the 'aesthetic' standpoint in 'Lapis Lazuli'. The Homeric parallel encapsulates the meaning of the superhistorical as neither a possible, nor a desirable, standpoint in which to live. It is a glimpsed recognition whose meaning really lies in its bearing on historical consciousness. But where Nietzsche made this reservation explicit, Joyce does not, and in articulating what is mainly implicit in *Ulysses*, he provides an inwardly critical purchase on the transcendent stance of Joyce's novel.

The superhistorical spirit is an essentially speculative vantage-point revealing the blindness and illusion of one's contemporaries caught within the passions and urgencies of their day. This is suggested in Stephen's often quoted remark 'History . . . is a nightmare from which I am trying to awake' (*Ulysses* p. 28). Of course, Stephen himself means nothing metaphysically profound by it. It is merely one of his self-consciously striking phrases. Yet the fuller context of *Ulysses* revives a dead metaphorical suggestion in his phrase. Saying 'awake', rather than, for example 'escape', gives the remark a further edge which, like Bloom's comment on musical structure, conveys a meaning beyond what the character himself has in mind. Stephen's phrase suggests that history itself is the unreality, the sphere of illusion, which it should be possible to dispel. Indeed, the early episode 'Nestor', in which this remark occurs, takes history as its primary theme and makes clear that Stephen's problem with 'history' lies not at the level of events but in the reification of historical process for which Mr Deasy's anti-Semitic religious teleology provides a representatively crass example.

England is in the hands of the Jews. In all the highest places: her finance, her press. And they are the signs of a nation's decay. (*Ulysses* p. 28)

Historical teleology is frequently an illusion. We understand this implication through the superhistorical vantage-point of the book as a whole, while the immediate meaning of the phrase enforces the brute reality of the history in which he feels himself to be enmeshed. Whereas Yeats' Chinamen in 'Lapis Lazuli' express the superhistorical in its purity, and are then qualified by their place in his *œuvre*, *Ulysses* brings these competing attitudes together. If the superhistorical standpoint is the cardinal point of similarity with Nietzsche, the force and subtlety of his essay lies in its internal relativity by which no principle has a fixed value, either positive or negative. He goes on to divide the historical consciousness itself into the three further categories of the monumental, the antiquarian and the critical; the first two emphasising the ambivalence of the historical sense, and the third suggesting how this ambivalence should be lived. It is worth pausing briefly on their equivalents in *Ulysses*, for it also avoids any bland adoption of the superhistorical posture which is, none the less, its governing spirit.

By the monumental spirit, Nietzsche means the summative, unified perception possessed by world-historical figures such as Napoleon. This is dangerous when it outweighs other aspects of the historical consciousness. When the monumental spirit dominates, he says, history is brought damagingly close to fiction: 'there have been ages, indeed, which were quite incapable of distinguishing between a monumentalised past and a mythical fiction' (*Untimely Meditations* p. 70). In this context he is highly critical of myth and, given Nietzsche's co-option by Nazi ideologues, there is a nice irony in his effective warning of the Hitler type: 'Monumental history deceives by analogies: with seductive similarities it inspires the courageous to foolhardiness and the inspired to fanaticism; and when we go on to think of this kind of history in the hands and heads of gifted egoists and visionary scoundrels, then we see empires destroyed, princes murdered, wars and revolutions launched.'[51] Nietzsche is still close to the nineteenth-century preoccupation with Napoleon, and his term 'monumental' is the word used by Dostoevsky's Raskolnikov in his dangerous obsession with the Napoleonic model.[52] Stephen's use of Nelson's monument as the site of a homely fictional epiphany of Dublin life suggests his attitude (*Ulysses* p. 119), while Joyce's view of monumental explanations and national political myths is most vividly figured in the 'Cyclops' episode where Bloom is the object of nationalist and antisemitic violence. The Citizen's one-eyed malevolence towards Bloom is treated with the broadest humour in the book, as if physical violence were too contemptible to have a place even in so encyclopaedic a work as *Ulysses*, yet when Bloom modestly offers his own alternative conception of history it is, necessarily, just as monumental:

Force, hatred, history, all that. That's not life for men and women, insult and hatred. And everybody knows it's the very opposite of that that is really life.
    What? says Alf.
    Love, says Bloom. I mean the opposite of hatred. (*Ulysses* p. 273)

Bloom's words are ultimately endorsed by the book as a whole, which is itself a monument, but it is a self-deconstructing one since the monumental conception is only justified within an understanding of its own status as an avatar of the mythopoeic. Consciousness of its nature as an enabling interpretation, of its kinship with fiction, gives the monumental spirit its true value, holds it within its proper boundaries, and protects it from fanaticism and false analogy. If the monumental spirit is a dangerous survival of the mythopoeic outlook in a post-mythic world, the answer is not to seek some Archimedean point of rational objectivity outside this condition, it is rather to understand the inescapability of the condition so that preferences in historical vision are recognised as being a matter of intrinsic assertion of values, perhaps embodied in transhistorical works of art, as much as an objective understanding of the world. Self-conscious mythopoeia acknowledges the condition whereas a spurious ideal of objectivity creates its own sphere of illusion.

If the monumental spirit, in its affinity with myth, is both an archaic and a permanent phenomenon, the antiquarian spirit is predominantly a feature of advanced cultures such as Nietzsche's or Joyce's. This spirit belongs to him who preserves and reveres – to him who looks back to whence he has come, to where he came into being, with love and loyalty; with this piety he, as it were, gives thanks for his existence. By tending with care that which has existed from of old, he wants to preserve for those who shall come into existence after him the conditions under which he himself came into existence – and thus he serves life.[53]

But this spirit, instead of serving life, can dwindle into empty nostalgia and be merely a symptom of incapacity to deal with the present. The modern British 'heritage industry' might be an example of this: 'everything old and past that enters one's field of vision at all is in the end blandly taken to be equally worthy of reverence'.[54] Joyce's attitude to his personal origins was at all times a vigorous counterblast to nostalgic reverence, and in *Ulysses* he soon touches on the specifically Irish and contemporary form of the antiquarian spirit by which he saw so many of 'the best spirits of his time' to have been seduced. The opening episode refers ironically to the Celtic revival which was so important in the literary Dublin of his formative years. When Mulligan quotes Yeats' 'Who goes with Fergus?' (*Ulysses* p. 8), it is not the line itself which is ironically distanced so much as the self-conscious recreation of an ancient Irish past. The Celtic revival, and attempts to spread the speaking of Gaelic, are understandable, but they risk turning the whole culture into a museum. Yet, curiously enough, the cultural template of Homer in *Ulysses* only throws into relief the localism of the modern setting and leads to what Nietzsche saw as the positive value within the antiquarian impulse, which was a love of place; a proper affection for one's locality of origin. In that regard, of course, *Ulysses* is a prodigious achievement. Joyce's ostentatious avoidance of the antiquarian spirit in *Ulysses* is a strategic device whereby he can secretly embody its positive meaning, much as Borges saw in Cervantes' treatment of the novels of chivalry not a satiric dismissal but a secret nostalgic farewell.[55] And the creation of Dublin is itself a function of the book's underlying metaphysic of world-creation; a local example of what all human beings do. The creation of a world is the archetypal and fundamental human act, although as active beings within our specific worlds we necessarily take this for granted most of the time. The world of *Ulysses* depends on the most fundamental kind of creative love: the disinterested sustaining of the object in existence. This, of course, is the achievement of Shakespeare who, in 'Scylla and Charybdis', exemplifies authorship as the sustaining spirit holding his characters in being on the model of the Christian, rather than Stephen's Flaubertian, God. Dublin is not overtly loved, which would run the risk of antiquarian sentiment, but is given something much more fundamental than that: it is brought disinterestedly into being. The book achieves *nostos* without nostalgia.

The ambivalence of both the monumental and the antiquarian spirits leads to the importance of Nietzsche's third category: the critical spirit. Whoever acts on this 'must from time to time employ the strength to break up and dissolve a part of the past . . . by bringing it before the tribunal, scrupulously examining it and finally condemning it . . . '.[56] The critical spirit does not seek the objectivity of the professional historian but serves, with some inevitable injustice, the immediate purposes of life. Such a critical spirit is hinted at in *Ulysses* by its cheerfully radical scepticism *vis à vis* so many discourses and beliefs. And Stephen's bitterness may represent a potential stirring of the critical spirit in him. But the overall effect of the book is more like that of Nietzsche's essay in meditating on the various possibilities. *Ulysses* offers a tangible realisation of Nietzsche' argument in that it proposes no solutions, but negotiates a course between the various illusions and pitfalls of historical consciousness through the adoption of a superhistorical viewpoint. This latter emphasis, however, remains a problem, and the diagnostic thrust of Nietzsche's essay focuses the ambivalence of *Ulysses* as both a critique, and an example, of the modernity it defines.

Ulysses: *a critique of modernity?*

Nietzsche's summary comment on modern culture as seen from the standpoint of ancient Greece is an uncanny anticipation of Joyce's method. *Ulysses* might have been written to answer Nietzsche's gibe at modernity:

That celebrated little nation of a not too distant past – I mean these same Greeks – during the period of their greatest strength kept a tenacious hold on their unhistorical sense: if a present-day man were magically transported to that world he would probably consider the Greeks very 'uncultured' – whereby the secret of modern culture, so scrupulously hidden, would be exposed to public ridicule: for we moderns have nothing of our own; only by replenishing and cramming ourselves with the ages, customs, arts, philosophies, religions, discoveries of others do we become anything worthy of notice, that is to say, walking encyclopaedias, which is what an ancient Greek transported into our own time would perhaps take us for. With encyclopaedias, however, all the value lies in what is contained within, in the content, not in what stands without, the binding or cover; so it is that the whole of modern culture is essentially subjective: on the outside the bookbinder has printed some such thing as 'Handbook of subjective culture for outward barbarians'.[57]

Bloom is a walking encyclopaedia in the Nietzschean sense: his mind is full of disconnected, half-understood items. The comparison of modern man with the ancient Greeks is a regular trope in German post-Enlightenment thought, and a variant of it has already been quoted from Matthew Arnold, but Nietzsche's thought-experiment of an imaginary meeting within one historical moment brings it close to the Homeric parallel. The book's overtly synthetic nature is a frontal recognition of Nietzsche's point that we can no longer be whole beings in the posited sense; but it is as if Joyce were seeking to absorb the point analytically while defusing its critical charge. The personality of Bloom answers Nietzsche in being a modestly humane exemplar of the modern condition. What is at stake is not the condition of modernity abstractly described, but the possible quality of life within it.

It is worth recalling here Hugh Kenner's treatment of the 'encyclopaedia' theme in *Ulysses*.[58] Kenner traced this theme from the original Enlightenment ideal of Diderot and his collaborators; through its debasement as parodied in Flaubert's *Bouvard and Pécuchet*; on through Bloom's ragbag consciousness of isolated facts and half-understood ideas; and to its terminal futility in Beckett. The original ideal of the encyclopaedia was to make the whole of knowledge universally available, but these writers show an increasingly radical corruption of understanding, and of language, by the very processes of mass education and the dissemination of 'knowledge' and 'ideas'. And this corruption has in turn left modern modes of knowledge only the more open to political and commercial exploitation. Intended as the vehicle of enlightenment and liberation, the encyclopaedia becomes the symbol of their degradation. Indeed the degradation runs so deep in the very language that these writers can only express themselves through a continual parody and subversion of conventional discourses; a strategy which Theodor Adorno described as 'negative dialectics'.[59] Although Kenner's account is highly illuminating, he rather passes over a radical problem in this strain of modern writing: to what extent it is itself enmeshed in the process it parodies. Of course, there is an obvious sense in which it is meant to be. As has been said, these writers express themselves through an ironic use of the available discourses. This is the creative paradox that Kenner and others have exhaustively explicated. But such a general formulation can cover a variety of implications. Within this creative strategy a writer can satirise without needing to imply any positive countervalue, so that we cannot always know to what extent the condition being satirised is to be seen as a deformation, or as a central representation, of human possibility. Is the satire aimed at a movable or an immovable object? Beckett's nihilism is clearly the latter. But the unease that James, Turgeniev, Lawrence and many others have felt about Flaubert is associated with a central equivocation in his work. Is Homais a comment on the ultimate value of human knowledge at large? Are the frail shoulders of Emma Bovary being asked to bear the weight of a tragic conception? Joyce on the other hand gave the theme a comedic and even celebratory inflection. The encyclopaedia theme may be absorbed into different universes of possibility, but in tracing its internal transformations Kenner stays largely within Flaubertian premises.

In that respect it is significant that Kenner does not include Nietzsche in his list of transformations, for Nietzsche gives it a radically critical meaning which would ultimately encompass Flaubert himself; and maybe even, to some degree, Joyce. However widespread it may be as a cultural condition, Nietzsche firmly rejects the 'walking encyclopaedia' condition as a human norm or necessity. His criticism of Flaubert's sedentary mode of composition is an emblematic comment on his aesthetic quietism, and some such critique of Flaubert is also implicit in Joyce's comedic transformation of the Flaubertian mode.[60] But if Joyce gives a more affirmative inflection to the Flaubertian technique one may still wonder what Nietzsche might have made of him. For Joyce veers away from both Flaubert and Nietzsche. Whereas Nietzsche presented the superhistorical standpoint as a way of ultimately affirming the importance of historical criticism and action, Joyce's superhistorical remove remains a dominant effect of *Ulysses*, and of his *œuvre*. The special aura of Joyce, and the widespread sense of reservation about him, are both attributable to this: his mythopoeia misses the embattled commitment of Nietzsche's essay. There is no point in objecting to some putative lack in Joyce's achievement, which is surely complete in its own terms, except perhaps to say that, where the appreciation of him is not balanced by a complementary sense of the significance of D. H. Lawrence, it is seriously deficient. But before considering Lawrence it is necessary to rehearse the problematic sense of identity and responsibility which is the inner dimension of modernist mythopoeia.

Bloom and the modernist self

The whole of *Ulysses* depends on the felt relationship between Bloom and the narrative discourses through which he exists. His personal qualities are adumbrated in a narrative medium which transcends, while ulti-

mately vindicating, him. Yet Bloom's relation to the parodically encyclopaedic narrative remains ironic and teasing. Given the equivocation
between organic and constructive conceptions throughout, can he be
understood as an intuitive whole? Is he the point of intuitive unity which
binds together the disparate discourses for the reader, or does the
narrative throw the intuitive unity of the self into question? If the
structure of the book is a synthetic myth held together through Bloom,
then he is himself part of a synthetic myth; the force of the term 'myth'
here being that the self has to function as an intuitive unity even if it
cannot be grounded as such. The functional horizon of myth has to
include the self.

I have argued that Joyce's focus on individual consciousness is the
means of an increasingly phenomenalised and dispersive presentation of
psychic life. Where the extremes meet, the terms 'subjective' and 'objective' start to reverse, or to dissolve. In this way, the narrative medium
constantly problematises, without dissolving, personal consciousness.
And, of course, the question of personal identity is repeatedly raised by
the characters themselves. Stephen ruminates obsessively on the continuity of the self as memory and possibility. The underlying historical
cultural reason for this is encapsulated, with the usual unwitting irony, in
Bloom's misunderstanding of Stephen's remark on the soul as 'a simple
substance and therefore incorruptible' (*Ulysses* p. 518). Stephen's theological definition points to the religious metaphysic which long sustained
the principle of personal identity, while Bloom's reply 'you do knock
across a simple soul once in a blue moon' points to the difficulty of
providing a post-religious account of identity, even if it were more
sophisticated than Bloom's. The word 'simple' has lost its theological
meaning, and within a secular metaphysic the notion of the self becomes
irredeemably problematic, although the ancient questions of free will,
responsibility, and so on, do not go away. There is an important motif
here, for modernism at large, which still seems frequently to be misunderstood.

Although the problem of personal identity is one of the pervasive
themes of *Ulysses*, the self continues to function as an intuitive whole in a
way that suggests this is the real point. Dr Johnson remarked of free will,
itself an aspect of the same question, that 'all theory is against it, all
experience is for it.'[61] Johnson supposed the truth to lie on one side or the
other and preferred to opt for 'experience'. There is a more complex
doubleness in much modernist writing in that it constantly deconstructs
the self analytically while simultaneously reconstituting it as a working

truth or necessary myth. The modernist self is the personal aspect of mythopoeic consciousness. For those who have seen the point, it too is a self-conscious myth. In this respect the modernist self already encapsulates the implicit posture underlying much twentieth-century cerebration devoted to exploding the self. Problems of agency and responsibility do not go away and have variously to be accommodated, whether inside or outside the given system of thought. Derrida has every so often to point this out to his more reductive readers.[62] By contrast, modernist mythopoeia encompassed this problematic holistically, within a form of life, rather than as a series of paradoxes within a system of thought. In this respect, modernism anticipated later thinking on this subject while avoiding reductively abstractive terms. In a recent study Anthony J. Cascardi has defined the postmodern self in pretty much this way as an arena in which different and often incommensurable discourses find a *modus vivendi*.[63] Cascardi exemplifies a common contemporary belatedness in not seeing that this is what modernism, with its radical critique of the 'old stable ego', was centrally about. Yet it is also a compliment to the great writers of the period that their implicit meanings have been imbibed unconsciously. For this reflects how the dissolution of the self was not usually the primary point of their works. At a moment of epochal transition, modernism gathered older and newer conceptions together while the urgent thematic concerns of these authors made their questioning of the self a necessary and integral part of their work rather than a self-regarding *trouvaille*.

Since the period of high modernism, however, the dissolution of the self has continued to dwindle into a truism whose very banality increases its ready adaptability for the purposes of would-be ideological critique. It would now be an obligatory entry in any contemporary *Dictionary of Received Ideas*: 'Individual: Does not exist; see also "Death of the subject" and "Social construction of the self" '. Fredric Jameson, for example, in a widely quoted essay 'Postmodernism and Consumer Society', invites us to share his self-congratulation on a purported sophistication at the expense of modernism.

The great modernisms . . . were predicated on the invention of a personal, private style, as unmistakable as your fingerprint, as incomparable as your own body. But this means that the modernist aesthetic is in some way organically linked to the conception of a unique self and private identity . . . Yet today, those of us who work in the area of culture and cultural and formal change, are all exploring the notion that that kind of individualism and personal identity is a thing of the past . . . There are in fact two positions on all this . . . The first one is content to say: yes, once upon a time, in the classic age of competitive capitalism, in the heyday of the nuclear family and the emergence of the bourgeoisie as the hegemonic social class, there was such a thing as individualism, as individual subjects . . . Then there is a second position . . . [which] adds: not only is the bourgeois individual subject a thing of the past, it is also a myth, it never really existed in the first place: There have never been autonomous subjects of that type. Rather this construct is merely a philosophical and cultural mystification which sought to persuade people that they 'had' individual subjects and possessed this unique identity. For our purposes, it is not particularly important to decide which of these positions is correct or rather, which is more interesting and productive.[64]

Jameson is undoubtedly true to the cultural facts. The sense of individual identity which was retained in modernism has since been largely lost or discredited. But half-truths lose their value when taken as whole ones and two aspects of his account particularly invite commentary. One is the slide between the modesty of the detailed claims and the corporate confidence of the whole. We are 'all' only 'exploring the notion' and it is 'not particularly important which of these positions is correct'. Maybe not. Perhaps it matters, however, whether either of them is. The second aspect is the supposed mystification of modernism. Undoubtedly, the affirmation of the self was a central feature of the period but within a radical questioning. In major works of modernism the self recognises over and again its own problematic status. It does not follow, therefore, that *any* conception of the self must be mystified, or that ideological awareness provides a more comprehensive understanding. In fact, a self-conscious commitment to a notion of moral selfhood is likely to enhance an awareness of its problematic and deceptive character while ideologically conceived critique, because it evades the nub of the problem, is increasingly susceptible to the confident reductiveness of orthodoxy which Jameson exemplifies.

I will return at the end of this study to the larger question of mythopoeia versus ideology. So far, I have emphasised the conscious world creation in *Ulysses*; its problematising of subjectivity; and its superhistorical or proto-ethical understandings. At the same time, although Joyce is not so quietistic, or indifferent to political questions, as was once commonly supposed, the aestheticism of *Ulysses* is primarily inflected towards the liberating impact of the superhistorical spirit against the historicist emphasis of the preceding century. Yet there is a different, complementary aspect of the mythopoeic conception whereby life is lived on the model of art: such a life becomes a continual act of radical choice; the momentary judgements of everyday existence are lived as primordial, as throwing into question a whole form of life. This radical alternative to Joyce's comedic superhistoricism, is to be found in D. H. Lawrence's puritan commitment to realising ultimate values in the momentary process of self-responsibilty in everyday life.

D. H. LAWRENCE: 'AM I OUT OF MY MIND?'

Language and myth

D. H. Lawrence had an inward understanding of mythopoeia inseparable from his whole view of life. That does not mean that he always got things right. In fact his capacity to get things wrong is literally vital. Like Nietzsche, he often thought in heuristic extremes which were the basis of uniquely penetrating insights. But as novelist, dramatist and poet he was disciplined by the experiential demands of his subject-matter. When engaged with a specific subject, Lawrence's creative capacity lay largely in a process of working through to get it right, to understand or to face the emotional issue, in a way that makes the capacity to be wrong an essential part of the process. Such a half-conscious, heuristic process can often be seen in the successive drafts of his works but, more importantly, it survives in the narrative medium of the final text. That is why the first difficulty in reading is to tune in to what he offers. If you read him as a body of doctrine you will have something not only useless, and possibly even damaging, but very un-Lawrencean. You have to attend to process and quality within the language itself; or, as he would say, you have to attend. He is a truly philosophical novelist because, in his case, this does not mean dramatic discussion of ideas, although it includes this, nor even the invention of a formal equivalent for a philosophical position, it is rather his awareness of the fundamental quality of being in all characters, in all states of feeling or consciousness.

Lawrence's rejection of the 'old stable ego' and the 'moral scheme' of nineteenth-century fiction in favour of 'what is physic – nonhuman, in humanity' showed his understanding of this.[65] Although expressed in terms of novelistic character, the dissolution of the ego carries with it an ontological, and a specifically anti-Cartesian, implication which Lawrence embodies most crucially within his narrative language. States of being are not detachable truths which can usefully be talked about in the abstract, they are qualities which have to be experienced, and that is the true force of his being a mythopoeic writer. For just as the philosophical dimension of Lawrence is not to be found at the level of 'ideas' or content, the same applies to his mythopoeic aspect. Of course, you can find myth, just as you can find ideas, at the level of something like content but that is not what makes him a mythopoeic novelist in any important sense. He is mythopoeic in his understanding of how we inhabit language as part of inhabiting the world.

Lawrence understood with a novelist's inwardness the psychological factor underlying differences in world view. The unconscious creation of worlds, or of different modes of being in the world, is Lawrence's primary subject in *The Rainbow* and *Women in Love* which were, to use his own term, the first mature expression of his 'metaphysic'. For an analytic purchase on this it is helpful to turn to Ernst Cassirer's 'philosophical anthropology' which drew on the same insights as Lawrence.[66] Ever since human beings consciously possessed civilisation they have imagined a 'primitive' other. But early twentieth-century anthropology, itself now largely outdated, gave a new twist to the notion of the primitive. Previously, archaic man had been seen as a simpler version of civilised man who happened to live in different circumstances, just as in Christian myth Adam and Eve were essentially like us except for not wearing clothes. Even *The Golden Bough* was still in that rationalistic tradition. But in the teens of the new century a generation of anthropologists created a picture of archaic man as having a radically different mode of being in the world; a different way of relating to nature, to the self and to time; all of which could be characterised as mythopoeic in a sense that stands in fundamental contrast to scientific reason. This was a view, notably expounded by Lucien Lévy-Bruhl, which saw early man as living in a felt continuity with the processes of nature so that sympathetic magic and natural piety rather than instrumental reason were his ways of influencing the external world.[67] Ernst Cassirer, as a Kantian, made sense of this new view of the 'primitive' as an alternative world view in which the Kantian categories of time, space, causality etc. were so conceived as to constitute a different, though equally coherent, world.

The new anthropological conception implied an inescapable relativity in the very instrument of discovery and observation, civilised thought and language, as modern instrumental reason itself became part of a world view. Cassirer formulated an inescapable relativity of world views standing in a tragic relation to each other since these two ways of knowing the world, the mythopoeic and the rational, were individually desirable and mutually incompatible.

Hence the unavoidable alternative which our knowledge faces: it can orient itself towards the real, but in this case it can never completely penetrate its object, but describes it instead only piecemeal and empirically, with respect to particular properties and characteristics; or it can achieve complete insight, an adequate idea which constitutes the nature and essence of the object, but then knowledge never leaves the sphere of its own concept formation. In the latter case, the object possesses only that structure which knowledge has ascribed to it by virtue of its arbitrary definition.[68]

The stark choice Cassirer offers here between sympathetic and scientific knowledge is questionable; and in his later years Cassirer worked towards an overall conception of aesthetic knowledge and symbolic form, itself highly relevant to the theme of this study, which would reconcile the two.[69] But this passage suggests the shock to the Kantian system when its fundamental categories are thrown into question; the shock of a world view suddenly made conscious of itself as a world view.

In the years immediately preceding the Great War, Lawrence absorbed the same recognition. Some of the thinking behind *The Rainbow* and *Women in Love* took place during his period by Lake Garda in 1912 which also gave rise to the volume of sketches entitled *Twilight in Italy*. The 'twilight' in question here is not a late nineteenth-century decline, as in *Twilight of the Gods* (*Götterdämmerung*), but the anthropological twilight (*Zwielicht*) between two kinds of world. The whole volume is a meditation on the meeting of different worlds. Most obviously, this refers to the worlds of northern and southern Europe which Lawrence had just traversed for the first time, but it also refers to other changes of world such as the Italians who emigrate to America, or the committed socialist to whom Lawrence talks with a respect founded partly on a recognition of his complete otherness of outlook. But the most fundamental is the encounter between the archaic world of the peasant and Lawrence's own world of educated modernity. He speaks of his encounter, which is hardly a meeting, with an old peasant woman spinning.

The spinner's indifference to Lawrence, even as he speaks to her, brings home to him the enormous gulf between his world and hers. Indeed, the very fact of language makes the gulf apparent. As he says, they 'divide', rather than share, the gift of speech.

> 'That is an old way of spinning,' I repeated.
> 'Yes – an old way,' she repeated, as if to say the words so that they should be natural to her. And I became to her merely a transient circumstance, a man, a part of the surroundings. We divided the gift of speech, that was all.
> She glanced at me again, with her wonderful, unchanging eyes, that were like

the visible heavens, unthinking, or like two flowers that are open in pure clear unconsciousness. To her I was a piece of the environment. That was all. Her world was clear and absolute, without consciousness of self. She was not self-conscious, because she was not aware that there was anything in the universe except *her* universe. In her universe I was a stranger, a foreign *signore*. That I had a world of my own, other than her own, was not conceived by her. She did not care.[70]

And he goes on at length to understand what it means to inhabit a radically different world. Whether he gets the woman's world right is not the point, even if it were possible to decide. What matters is the recognition of difference, and the way it emerges as a function of relationship. Only by attempting to understand her does he recognise her otherness. The themes and imagery of the passage were taken up in *The Rainbow* in which the mystery of personal otherness is linked to a similar sense of ontological mystery encountered in a foreigner. But in fiction his presentation of character as ontological quality must not be too self-conscious either for the character or for the reader which is why his subtle understanding of world creation is still missed despite its being the central concern of *The Rainbow* and *Women in Love*. In these books, Lawrence engaged the problem posed by Cassirer:

Have we been led into a fatal mistake by venturing on this course into the new world of symbols? Is it *possible* that by doing so man has torn himself loose from nature and estranged himself from the reality and immediacy of natural existence? Are the things he has exchanged for this really good? Or are they not the gravest threat to his life?[71]

The Rainbow and *Women in Love* are an elaborate, inward working out of the historical development of this dilemma; both books playing centrally on the terms 'reality' and 'knowledge'. I have indicated in detail elsewhere how the three generations of *The Rainbow* do not just cover a span of nineteenth-century and modern history.[72] Using the rival myths of origin associated with Eden and with Darwin, Lawrence gives through these three generations a synoptic account of the three phases of human cultural development postulated by Cassirer and, in various forms, by nineteenth-century thinkers. These are the mythic, the religious and the scientific. In the first, human life is part of a natural world charged with mana or divinity; in the second the divine becomes the supernatural and man separates from nature; while in the third there is no divinity and man stands in a merely instrumental relation to the natural world. But the subtlety of the book is that its central dynamic is never posed in these abstract categories; instead it enacts within the narrative language a gradually changing ontological relation to the world as the Edenic impulse, the desire to be rooted in a point of origin, struggles with the complementary, evolutionary need to escape the past. In *Women in Love*, when the Brangwens' story reaches the present day, historical narrative gives way to a spatialised one as Lawrence contrasts different world projections within a single modern generation. The geographical symbolism of Nordic and African becomes its principal axis as Gerald Crich's 'Nordic' being creates the icy and murderous world by which he is finally destroyed.

Lawrence was possessed by an ontological vision; a responsiveness to Being. He expressed this repeatedly in fiction, criticism, essays, plays, poems and travel writing. His successful works across these genres would make up a substantial *œuvre*. Of its nature such an ontological vision lay essentially in the proto-ethical sphere, and part of Lawrence's restlessness lay in his seeking always to relate it to the more ordinary processes of everyday life, both individually and socially. This is where many of his creative problems arose, as well as his achievements. He was increasingly at odds with his culture, and his rhetoric became at times empty or private while his novels, as I have shown elsewhere, are increasingly struggles with the realist novel form itself.[73] For the present, it suffices to give an example of his mythopoeic sensibility in the context of modernity. His story 'The Horsedealer's Daughter' is a rich example in which questions of language and being are given a narrative expression so seemingly natural that few readers see what is there. Indeed, the ability to see what is before your eyes is the question on which the story turns.

Language and vision in 'The Horse-Dealer's Daughter'

Lawrence's works frequently include discreet lessons in how to read him; and given his peculiarly holistic inhabiting of language, his works are often object-lessons in how to read at all. This aspect of Lawrence is especially important now as the linguistic 'turn' of the early twentieth century has gathered such an independent momentum as to become an empty parody of itself, a set of decadently self-fulfilling gestures. Saussure's cardinal recognitions, such as the arbitrariness of the linguistic sign and the relational nature of meaning, have not only dwindled into reductive orthodoxy, they have, more importantly, been assimilated to widespread attempts to understand language technically and scientifically or, as it were, from the outside. Accepting this scientific frame of reference, it took an apparent effort to arrive at Emile Benveniste's recognition that one can never be outside of language in that way.[74] But there was always a counter-tradition which considered language from the inside; which understood it as it is humanly inhabited. Philosophically, this emphasis is classically represented by Heidegger who insisted, for example, on the expressive value of sounds where Saussure had stressed the arbitrariness of sound as a linguistic sign:

It is just as much a property of language to sound and to ring and to vibrate, to hover and to tremble, as it is for the spoken words of language to carry a meaning. But our experience of this property is exceedingly clumsy, because the metaphysical-technical explanation constantly gets in the way, and keeps us from considering the matter properly.[75]

Lawrence is firmly within the 'Heideggerean' tradition and 'The Horse-Dealer's Daughter' is a concentrated embodiment of themes which Heidegger was to tease out in a more philosophical mode, particularly in his lecture courses entitled *The Fundamental Concepts of Metaphysics* and *Parmenides*.[76] Like Heidegger, Lawrence understood the philosophical tradition to have become enslaved to dualistic assumptions. Underlying the two modern traditions of thought about language, the 'scientific' and the 'poetic', lies the more fundamental conflict between dualistic and anti-dualistic metaphysics. Lawrence opens his essay on 'Why the Novel Matters' by defining the dualistic conception as a damaging illusion belied in the very act of writing.

We have curious ideas of ourselves. We think of ourselves as a body with a spirit in it, or a body with a soul in it, or body with a mind in it . . . It is a funny sort of superstition. Why should I look at my hand, as it so cleverly writes these words, and decide that it is a mere nothing compared to the mind that directs it? . . . My hand is alive, it flickers with a life of its own. It meets all the strange universe in touch, and learns a vast number of things, and knows a vast number of things. My hand as it writes these words, slips gaily along, jumps like a grasshopper to dot an i, feels the table rather cold, gets a little bored if I write too long, has its own rudiments of thought, and is just as much me as is my brain, my mind, or my soul. Why should I imagine that there is a *me* which is more *me* than my hand is? Since my hand is absolutely alive, me alive. Whereas, of course, as far as I am concerned, my pen isn't alive at all. My pen *isn't me* alive. Me alive ends at my finger-tips. Whatever is me alive is me. Every bit of my hands is alive, every little freckle and hair and fold of skin. And whatever is me alive is me. Only my finger-nails, those ten little weapons between me and an inanimate universe, they cross the mysterious Rubicon between me alive and things like my pen, which are not alive, in my own sense . . . And that's what you learn, when you're a novelist. And that is what you are very liable *not* to know, if you're a parson, or a philosopher, or a scientist, or a stupid person.[77]

The passage brings out the metaphysical ambiguity of a bodily organ considered in isolation. Both Heidegger's meditations on this theme and 'The Horse-Dealer's Daughter' focus on the eye as being either a detached instrument of the mind or a sentient organ. Indeed, as a way into the common territory of Lawrence and Heidegger, and keeping in focus the larger question of language and myth, it is helpful to ask to what extent the 'cleverness' Lawrence attributes to his hand is to be understood as a metaphor. Within Cartesian terms the expression is clearly metaphorical, but these are the very terms he is challenging. The understanding of common figures of speech may focus assumptions about how language is being understood generally.

An important metaphor for both Lawrence and Heidegger is the use of physical sight as an image of understanding. This usage is so ancient, and so culturally embedded, that it is hard to conceive of understanding without some implicit recourse to the metaphor of sight. In *The Fundamental Concepts of Metaphysics*, Heidegger noted the prevalence of this image in the Western tradition from Aristotle onwards, but instead of regarding physical sight as the relatively clear vehicle through which to understand the mind, he concentrates on physical vision as being itself the shifting and problematic quantity. For even at the 'physical' level, he argues, it is not the eye that sees, but the person. We do not see because we have eyes: we have eyes because we can see. We perceive the world because we have 'world' in which to do so. Lawrence likewise saw a metaphysical charge in the question of physical vision; he 'saw' sight as the most abstract and removed of the senses.[78] It is the traditional metaphor for intellectual understanding because it is the point at which sensory experience most closely approaches the intellectual. This conviction led him in part to privilege the other senses at the expense of sight, as is suggested in titles such as 'The Blind Man' or 'You Touched Me' (or 'Hadrian').[79] But more importantly the association of sight and understanding led him to discriminate *qualities* of sight. For sight may be employed in an abstractive way as a function of 'intellect', but it can also be the means by which what we call intellect can be rooted in the sensory. In other words, rather than being simply the most abstract of the senses, sight may represent the ambiguous centre of the human spectrum, and therefore provide a strategic point for questioning the nature and quality of the whole.

Heidegger and Lawrence focus this question by considering the organ itself, the eye, but, whereas Heidegger seeks analytically to unpick the metaphor of sight, Lawrence exploits its ambiguity. His essays on the unconscious, written between the first and final versions of the story, are concerned to understand psychic processes within a continuum of bodily process, and their language reflects this partial reversing of the Freudian turn whereby physical symptoms had been shown to be psychogenic. Accordingly, at one point Lawrence remarks that 'the breasts themselves are as two eyes'.[80] How metaphorical is this expression, we may ask, and are its terms reversible? Are the eyes the nipples of the head? They, after all, also respond to emotional stimuli by dilating and secreting. Have these capacities any relation to the function of sight? The relation between the eye as organ of sight and as centre of feeling and expression is most sharply focused in the act of looking into the eyes of another. Heidegger's meditation and Lawrence's story both turn on the enigma of the mutual gaze.

Heidegger makes the further emphasis that human sight is inseparable from language. It is language that gives us an intelligible world to see. Although Lawrence does not explicitly thematise this connection, his story is an object lesson in its truth. For he distinguishes qualities of attention in his characters' language as well as in their acts of vision. Meanwhile the language of the story, including that of its characters, is directed out towards the reader in such a way that reflection on the meaning of the narrative action leads us to appreciate the act of attention involved in reading it. In short, the interrelation of language and sight in the story turns its visual theme into an instructive commentary on the human relation to language. What actually *does* it mean to 'read' the story; or respond to language?

The story concerns the rescue by Dr Fergusson of Mabel Pervin as she attempts to drown herself in the nearby pond after the family business, along with the family home, has been broken up. A major narrative device is to withhold initially the information of Mabel's intention. When it becomes apparent, it does not act merely as the final twist of a conventional magazine story; it rather intensifies and focuses what is already half understood. The action is structured around an initial series of acts of vision between the characters and then a reversal of the same motifs after the rescue from the pond. As the close logic of this structure becomes clear, one can only marvel at the complete absence of literary or extrinsic elements in its organisation; that the artistic shaping is so completely inseparable from the emotional process. Of course, such a coincidence of subject and form is a critical truism. But the understanding of this truism is the beginning and end of discussing the story, for in this case it is not just an artistic principle: it is a general insight into what it means to inhabit language.

Before introducing the central characters, Mabel Pervin and Dr Fergusson, whose relationship in the story begins with looks, Lawrence describes two moments of looking between Mabel's brother Joe and his animals: the shire horses and the terrier bitch. Discussing the nature of the human look, Heidegger was also to draw an extended comparison with animals and, of course, the different otherness of animals and human beings is a pervasive theme of Lawrence's poetry. Heidegger's analyses bring out the implications of Lawrence's use of animals for, in both of them, the relation to animals highlights the hidden dimensions of the human look. Heidegger seeks to define the radical otherness of animals from human beings by insisting on the unknowability of the animal's world. Yet to do this he has to claim a certain knowledge. In particular he affirms that animals are, in his phrase, 'poor in world', or *weltarm*.[81] In other words, as compared to, say, a stone, an animal does indeed have 'world', but this is hardly comparable to the linguistically constituted world of human being. The lizard may seek out a warm rock, but it does not know this as a rock in the way a human being does. Heidegger uses this limited transposability of the human into the animal to explain what it means to have 'world' at all, but his argument does not depend on any positive knowledge of the animal's world. His use of the concept is heuristic: it is a square root of minus one in the total argument. Lawrence's characteristic use of animals has a similar doubleness which is worth pausing on as it has been known to confuse some of his more casual readers. The principal burden of the animal poems is to reveal the radical otherness of these non-human fellow-creatures with whom we none the less have a measure of transposability. The only way this can be brought into focus is through the use, and therefore the apparent imposition, of human terms just as Lawrence had to use his own terms in trying to understand the world of the spinner. Hence the characteristic device of these poems is what we might call a bracketed personification. Lawrence's objection to simple personification is expressed in an incident in *Women in Love* where Gudrun Brangwen briefly leads Ursula to see small song-birds as little 'Lloyd Georges'.[82] Ursula's subsequent reaction against this human appropriation is the import of many of the animal poems. Yet the initial imposition of human terms is not merely dispelled at the end of a poem like 'Snake'.[83] For the sense of relation, as with the spinner, is an essential condition of recognising something as radically other. Personification for Lawrence is therefore a necessary feint comparable to Heidegger's heuristic invoking of the animal. It remains, but under erasure. Once again, the underlying metaphysic is focused in a common figure of speech. The metaphor can only be used when it has been exploded; or, as one might now say, deconstructed.

And so Lawrence leads into his story of human relationship, and non-relationship, through relations with animals. Joe's attention is caught by the last group of shire horses leaving the yard. The horses embody a magnificence of life held in subjection but this implication comes over to the reader more than it does to Joe. And, in so far as he does obscurely intuit his own fate in the horses, it is by a mode of identification, a reversed personification, which rather collapses his humanity into their animal being. This sets the context for the following moment with a domestic animal, his terrier bitch. Having thrown the dog a scrap of bacon he waits for the 'creature' to 'look into his eyes'.[84] From the dog he has the comfort of power within a relationship of sorts. Of course, the dog does not offer a human relationship, but precisely because it lacks human consciousness it is free of certain human confusions. The dog includes the man in its world in the spirit of what Heidegger calls 'going along with'.[85] But, as Heidegger also points out, it is precisely the fact of human consciousness which frequently denies, or traduces, this fundamental relation. His comments on this topic bear upon the sense of isolation experienced by all the characters in the story. The reason they feel themselves to be isolated is a blindness to their own being

the illusion of such isolation arises from the circumstance that human beings factically move around in a peculiar form of being transposed into one another, one which is characterised by an indifferent going alongside one another. This illusion of a prior separation between one human being and another is reinforced by the philosophical dogma that man is initially to be understood as subject and as consciousness, that he is primarily and most indubitably given to himself as consciousness for a subject.[86]

For Heidegger, subjective consciousness cannot be the primordial condition because consciousness, particularly in so far as it is linguistic, implies a prior commonality and transposability with others. The moment with the dog helps to establish such a primordial level of creaturely 'going along with' against which the felt isolation of the human characters can be seen for what it is.

The whole opening movement with the animals sets the context for the relationship of Mabel and Fergusson. The first half of this is structured by three moments of looking in which physical sight grows more distant and obscure as emotional vision becomes more intimate. The first moment occurs shortly after the doctor has entered the room and had an exchange with the three brothers.

At this point Mabel rose from the table, and they all seemed to become aware of her existence. She began putting the dishes together. The young doctor looked at her, but did not address her. He had not greeted her. (*EME* p.140)

We have no omniscient insight into the meaning of the doctor's look. The narrative specification that he looks at her at all merely highlights his lack of attention to her. She has been part of the background, like the table and dishes, which become noticeable only when suddenly in motion. By a cunning indirection, Lawrence communicates the doctor's absence of attention while she has been sitting in full view only a few feet away from him. The next look that passes between them occurs when Fergusson, passing the cemetery, notices her tending her mother's grave. The two characters are now at some distance from each other but their mutual glance is deeply penetrating. Part of the reason for the intensity to which he responds in her look is that, unbeknown to him, she intends this to be her last act before drowning herself. Although the situation is extreme and unusual, it brings out a mixture of transposability and enigma which Heidegger sees as characteristic of the human glance as such. In other words, although the world of the animal is unknowable, the creature does not conceal it. The animal, Heidegger says, 'is excluded from the essential realm of conflict between concealment and unconcealment. The sign of this essential exclusion is that no animal or plant "has the word"'.[87] By contrast, the human capacity for self-disclosure, which may occur in the look, rests upon concealment just as memory implies forgetting. Hence although human beings disclose themselves in the look, Heidegger says, they only do so 'so as to let concealing and the abyss of their essence be present in what is thus unconcealed'.[88] Disclosure and concealment are inseparable in the exchange with the human other. The third moment of vision completes the pattern. In the darkness of the late afternoon in autumn, and at a considerable distance across the fields, Fergusson sees a figure making for the pond. He cannot recognise her, but intuits that it 'would be Mabel Pervin' (*EME* p.145). To continue to see her at all in these conditions requires him to be 'like a clairvoyant, seeing rather with the mind's eye than with ordinary sight' (*EME* p. 145). Yet there is nothing mystical about it: 'he could see her positively enough, whilst he kept his eye attentive' (*EME* p. 145). The emphasis of the opening encounter is now reversed, so that emotional transposability is at its maximum as physical sight fades.

These three moments lead up to the story's turning-point in the pond when both characters go under its surface and lose their vision entirely. After the rescue, the motifs of this earlier pattern are very precisely reversed. This is centrally figured in Mabel's awkward clutching at the doctor's knees. Her gesture echoes his groping for her in the pond which was just as desperate, convulsive and unpremeditated. The significance of the echo lies in the question of who is rescuing whom. For clutching may mean rescuing, possessing or drowning. Such is the gesture with which Diana Crich drowns the young doctor who attempts to rescue her from the lake.[89] In the present story the doctor rescues Mabel from drowning, but she is the one who more significantly rescues him and shows the greater courage in doing so; she does it by appearing to be the one in need. So too, whereas the first part of the story treated the eye as merely the instrument of sight, attention now turns to the eye as an organ of sentience in its own right. The pond remains an important point of mediation between the earlier focus on sight and the subsequent focus on the eye itself. For when Fergusson looks into Mabel's eyes they become his pond. They are the fascinating yet fearful medium in which he is also to risk losing himself with the possibility of emerging with a different self. The reversal of the pond motif is quite specific, although so natural as hardly to emerge as a pattern of imagery. Where the water of the pond was deathly cold, her tears are repeatedly described as 'hot' (*EME* p. 149). In contrast to the clayey bottom of the pond, her eyes are 'unfathomable'. Again the word is repeated (*EME* pp. 149–50). And where the pond water was stagnant, her eyes are constantly 'filled', as from an inner source, 'like some slow fountain coming up' (*EME* p. 149). As they now look into each others' eyes, the pond motif has reversed the apparent transparency of physical sight into the enigma of the gaze. What, after all, do we see when we look not at, but into, someone's eyes? Do we look at a person, through the 'windows of the soul', or at a physical organ which might, in certain moods, be merely 'vile jelly'. In the light of both Heidegger's comments and Lawrence's story we may retain the traditional image of windows if it is inflected away from the usual implication of transparency. Windows are for looking out rather than for exposing the interior. As Fergusson and Mabel now look at each other in the light of a greater knowledge their gaze still encounters a frightening concealment and strangeness which remains until, and beyond, the end of the story. Although they agree to marry, the story makes no promises about the outcome of the relationship.

The look into the eyes as pond has a further implication which Heidegger makes explicit. Human beings, he says, see each other as mortal. Mabel has faced her own mortality with desperate directness in the pond. He also has nearly drowned. Now they each look into the eyes of the other with a mixture of fear, need and courage arising from this glimpse of their own mortality and reinforced by the still unresolved note on which the story ends. The emphasis on fear and courage throughout is also pointed up by the doctor theme from which Lawrence draws a number of meanings. The immediate irony is that of 'physician heal thyself'. At the beginning of the story Fergusson has a cold, but through their joint immersion in the pond Mabel not only saves her rescuer but cures her doctor. More significantly, he has always used his professional distance as an alibi for human distance although he has also sought, from this safe remove, the vicarious energy of the Pervin brothers. His reversed idealism in seeing the suggestively named Pervins as vigorous and sensual (*EME* p. 144) is not, of course, Lawrence's own view but is a class projection arising from Fergusson's own lack of life and his fundamental bad faith. He identifies with them only on the condition of class distance but Mabel breaks down his bad faith by a leap of emotional logic. When she comes to herself before the fire she asks who has undressed her. His reply that he did so to 'bring (her) round' is followed by a long gaze after which she says 'Do you love me then?' (*EME* p. 148). In her culture no man would see her naked, even her brothers, except for a husband. And a husband is someone who would love and care for her. The final 'then' quietly enforces the backward leap of her emotional intuition. He must love her. He, of course, has undressed her without erotic feeling just as he should have done in the same circumstances even were he not a doctor. But, because his professional distance is habitually used as a means of self-protective bad faith, it crumbles before the directness of her question and the deeper nakedness, the challenging self-exposure, of her gaze. Her question gives words to her gaze. And it is appropriately a question if, as Heidegger claims, the gaze is always partly a negotiation of concealment. Yet it is a question whose very posing is also an affirmation, a disclosure, on her part. The relation between gaze and speech at this point is typical of the story at large. The characters' speech throughout embodies the varying quality of their 'going along with each other' that has been seen in the acts of vision, and the real interest of the vision theme for present purposes lies in its bearing on the story's language at a number of levels.

As with Mabel's question, the characters' speech constantly reveals their whole way of being. The story opens with Joe's question to Mabel 'what are you going to do with yourself?' (*EME* p. 137). When we discover that she may already be resolving to do away with herself the question takes on a chilling dramatic irony, but this is only a way of focusing the nature of the utterance itself. In asking such a question in a tone of 'flippancy' and without 'listening for an answer' he reverses its semantic meaning. It becomes a refusal of concern; an instance of Heidegger's 'indifferent going along with'. Meanwhile, an opposite pregnancy of meaning can be seen in another of Mabel's questions to Fergusson:

> 'Did you dive into the pond for me?' she asked.
> 'No,' he answered. 'I walked in. But I went in overhead as well.'
>
> (*EME* p. 147)

The exchange is a classic example of the difference between 'male' and 'female' speech as defined by Deborah Tannen.[90] She distinguishes the predominantly functional and practical purposes of what she calls male speech from the emotional and relational purposes of female speech. So here, Mabel's question, beginning and ending with personal pronouns, is purely relational: 'Did *you*... *me*?' His reply, by contrast, focuses on the functional question of how he actually entered the water. His avoidance of the emotional issue here is equivalent to his flinching from her gaze.

The different meanings that can be seen in Joe's and Mabel's questions do not depend upon semantic ambiguities. They arise from different qualities of tone and commitment. In this respect, Lawrence is doing something similar to George Eliot in *Middlemarch* when she distinguishes the different tonalities with which several characters ask 'What can I do?' But the Lawrencean metaphysic is closer to Heidegger's than to George Eliot's, and specifically so regarding questions of ego and egotism. This emerges in Mabel's crucial and repeated question to Fergusson when she first comes to consciousness after her near drowning.

'Was I out of my mind?' she asked.

and then again with reference to her present position:

'Am I out of my mind now?' (*EME* p. 147)

Mabel's phrase has a resonance beyond its immediate context; a resonance which is more metaphysical than ethical. For beyond the simple meaning of 'madness', which Mabel clearly intends, the experience in the pond was indeed an involuntary escape from what Lawrence would call 'mental consciousness'. It was an escape from the dualistic assumptions of the word 'mind'. Being out of her mind, in this sense, is exactly what both of them need to achieve. The fact that this resonance of the phrase is not conscious on her part does not undermine its significance for her. On the contrary, were it to be self-conscious it might be merely a function of her consciousness, an abstract idea, and not really 'out of her mind' at all. That there is a truth for her in the experience signalled by the phrase lies rather in the way Mabel's language is porous to such meanings. And, of course, gazing into her eyes will have a similar value for Fergusson because that too is a non-verbal experience. Precisely because he is usually so well-defended in words, he must be fruitfully exposed to a dimension outside of his mind. His own plunge into the fearful medium she represents for him is caught in the concluding sentence:

'No, I want you, I want you', was all he answered, blindly. (*EME* p. 152)

'Answered blindly' is another of those oxymoronic Lawrencean loc-utions which hardly give pause while reading, but which prove on inspection to be subliminally linking quite different realms. Here, at the very end of the story, visuality and language are being merged and, in using language 'blindly', Fergusson too is getting 'out of his mind'.

If Mabel's language is porous to meanings beyond her conscious intention, it is differently so from the unwittingly thematic remarks quoted from Bloom and Stephen in *Ulysses*. In Joyce's case, the meanings were created by the text as part of our knowledge rather than the characters'. In Mabel's case it *is* her knowledge although, of course, she does not 'know' it in any sense that she could articulate. To some extent the level of narrative and the level of character correspond to the levels of consciousness and unconsciousness which Lawrence is constantly dis-solving. Furthermore, what has been said of the characters here applies to the reader too and indeed the final example has already gone beyond the characters' speech to the language of the narrative itself. In other words, a proper understanding of the narrative subject has a compelling, if implicit, bearing on how we respond to the story. The so-called 'characters', after all, are themselves strictly rhetorical figments and their 'visual' experience is itself 'only' a play of words. Quite apart from the characters' speech, therefore, everything that is 'visual' for them is purely verbal for us. Hence all that has been said about the qualitative discrimi-nations in the visual realm has a doubly linguistic equivalent for the reader and, in that sense, the act of sight in the story is a running metaphor for the language in which we are reading of it. For the crucial

issue here is not sight but attention. Properly attending is as hard in
language as in physical vision, as Lawrence's own literary criticism
exemplifies. His seminal studies of the classic American writers, for
example, are subtly attuned to the authors' struggles to retain conscious
control of their material while he shows how their power is often a matter
of their nonetheless being able to be 'out of their minds'.

The story enforces a general truth about language which Heidegger
expresses in his close readings of poetry while, as a novelist, Lawrence
saw a proper responsiveness to Being as the compelling question in all
uses of language, even the most humble and everyday. Whereas Plato,
and even the 'beastly' Kant, saw reality as lying beyond the world of
phenomenal appearances, Heidegger and Lawrence saw the difficulty as
one of adequate attention to the Being of what is openly there to view.
The openness of Being, like that of the eye, is mystery enough. As
Heidegger puts it: 'The task of properly seeing what we have had in front
of us all along may appear to be very simple, yet this kind of seeing and
grasping is actually very difficult'.[91] The point is truistic when stated in
the abstract but it is especially significant in the reading of fiction where a
damaging version of the traditional dualism is constantly encouraged by
the academy. In trying to account for the power of particular works of
fiction readers will often appeal to meanings or patterns lying beyond the
realist appearance of the text. This may lead to misreading not at the
level of semantics or interpretation, but at the level of attention; misread-
ings which are the equivalent of Fergusson's avoidance of Mabel's gaze
and questions. In the present story, for example, the pond is evidently a
grave. It is square, clayey and deathly cold. Equally evidently it is a
womb. The doctor who pulls Mabel from its waters is giving her a new
birth. But the problem lies in the imaginative value of this tomb/womb,
death and rebirth, motif. Students are often encouraged to think that
such a mythic pattern gives a further 'depth' to the realistic story. But this
pattern, when isolated as such, is not experienced as myth so much as
reduced to a general concept. The search for deeper meanings usually
results in shallower ones and resorting to the myth kitty is the surest
symptom of the death of mythopoeic sensibility. That is why for Heidegger the true function of myth is to avoid conceptual fixture and to catch
the transitory relation to Being. The *mythos*, he says, 'is the sole appropriate kind of relation to being in its appearing'.[92] The true depth of the
story is to be experienced at the bottom of the specific muddy pond, as
realised in the narrative language, rather than through a general symbol
of rebirth. As Janice Harris has rightly observed, the scene by the fireside

repeats the earlier action in the pond in order to bring its meaning into consciousness.[93] But bringing it into consciousness is not the same as reducing it to an object of consciousness. In that regard, it is appropriate that Mabel repeats her question in the past and then the present tense: 'Was I out of my mind?' and 'Am I out of my mind now?' The crucial quality of the experience has not been lost.

Of course, the desire to explain the power of the story in terms of its mythic motif will often come from a reader who has genuinely responded to it, but the trouble is that a reader who has not so responded can still perform the same critical exercise. What is wrong with such accounts is that they do not distinguish the qualities of response. Even if the story has not been responded to as banal, it is reduced to banality in the critical account. Meanwhile there are readers who come to Lawrence expecting banality, and for whom the conventionally mythic reading confirms the expectations. For Lawrence truly challenges the banal, not with 'deeper' meanings which are themselves banal, but with a deliberate courting of the banal, as it were, on its own territory. That is why would-be sophisticated academics constantly fall into the trap of assuming Lawrence's own banality. In the present instance, Lawrence has written a highly accessible magazine story; indeed a love-story involving a young doctor, which is a classic theme of modern popular romance. His reversal of romance expectations is particularly focused in the ending which recognises the deep-lying problems any relationship between Fergusson and Mabel will have to negotiate. But the reversal is going on throughout. Everything he does with the material, including his treatment of the conventional value of the doctor as a socially desirable male, is such as to invest the everyday material with a different depth. In this respect again, the visual theme provides the central focus. Heidegger speaks of the human look as the entry of the 'divine' into the everyday, and some of the more intense glances in the story would bear out that insight.[94] That again is easily said and may mean little. Lawrence's creative difficulty was to find the proper relation between the 'divine' and the everyday. His title for the original 1916 version of the story was 'The Miracle' while the title of the 1922 published version has moved to the other end of the tonal spectrum. Apart from the deliberately mundane flatness of the reference to Mabel, and her being identified entirely through her relation to her father, the later title perhaps echoes a standard verbal formula of British schoolboy humour: 'She was only an x's daughter, but she...' In the present case it would be something like: 'She was only the horse-dealer's daughter, but she knew how to give you the ride.' Whether or not such an echo was in Lawrence's mind, it catches precisely the world of crude male sexuality in which she has lived and catches it at a specifically verbal level. A significant challenge to the banal within the realm of the banal has to be through the detailed quality of language and attention. Lawrence's special power, as Jessie Chambers affirmed in her memoir, was constantly to discover the numinous (the magical or the divine) in the everyday.[95] What is at stake is a quality of attention, and symbols of death and rebirth are not the cause of this: they are only made meaningful by it.

The story is typical of Lawrence in that its full force eludes a purely naturalistic explanation at the level of social, ethical and personal psychology although, moment by moment, the action seems to be conducted in these terms. Some sort of transformation of the habitual and the everyday, a transformation for which miracle is a good popular term, is of the essence. Or, in other words, the proto-ethical, Heideggerean dimension of responsiveness to Being underwrites whatever occurs at the level of personal relationship. But Lawrence, rather better than Heidegger, shows the necessary relationship between response and responsibility, and indeed exercises a demonstrative tact, and clarity of relevant focus, in leaving open the pressing questions, at the everyday personal level, about the possible future of the relationship. He presents these as part of the whole situation but with an exact sense of their proportional weight in relation to the experience that the characters have just passed through. Lawrence's mythopoeic consciousness is most crucially to be found not in his overt allusions to myth, but in this way of relating the personal and the impersonal, the conscious and the unconscious, in a holistic, flexible exploration of human being-in-the-world. Above all, his way of inhabiting language is crucial and distinguishes him most significantly from other modernist writers. Whether or not the late twentieth century is more prone to sex in the head than Lawrence's generation, it is undoubtedly more prone to have language in the head. Even in so far as Lawrence is recognised to be a challenging writer, the nature of the challenge is often misunderstood. The significant locus lies at the level of language rather than of doctrine, and readers of Lawrence must let his story do for them what Mabel does for the doctor. Yet much published commentary reifies the action of his fiction, and even the question of language, in a way that is precisely a self-confident equivalent of Fergusson's emotional evasion. It is a fundamental error, existential rather than intellectual, to read Lawrence against the grain of his own holistic inhabiting of language. A crucial capacity in anyone offering to comment on him is to know what it means to be 'out of your mind'.

Language in the head

For a writer, an attitude to Being is an attitude to language. Lawrence's use of language is, I believe, unique in that its very informality, whether we take this to be real or apparent, reveals aspects of the creative process which are doubtless representative, but which, in other writers, are not normally part of the eventual product. Most evidently, his way of inhabiting language is at the opposite extreme from the imposition of authorial will which is the ideal of much post-Flaubertian modernism. It is not in conflict with the related ideal of artistic impersonality, except that Lawrence's impersonality is of a different kind, as he makes clear in his discussion of Giovanni Verga whose truly artistic disinterestedness, Lawrence says, makes his borrowed Flaubertian principles seem like absurd Parisian readymades: 'And when he starts putting his theories into practice, and effacing himself, one is far more aware of his interference than when he just goes ahead. Naturally! Because self-effacement is, of course, self-conscious and any form of emotional self-consciousness hinders a first rate artist: though it may help the second rate.'[96] Lawrence does not allow here for the possibility of the mature Joyce whose aesthetic impersonality became a metaphysical statement. Lawrence is thinking within a realist mode in which language serves the narrative and, more importantly, impersonality of feeling was for him a human quality before it was an artistic one. It was in *The Rainbow* he first developed a coherent account of impersonality as a quality of feeling within the characters. When Tom Brangwen, for example, looks at his wife after childbirth with an 'impersonal' look, we understand this as quite different from detachment or indifference.[97] Less explicitly, the relationship in 'The Horse-Dealer's Daughter', in taking the characters out of their Cartesian minds, is a new opening to something impersonal in themselves. But, of course, the concern for impersonality of feeling, which was so central to Lawrence at the level of subject-matter, and which ultimately underwrites his mythopoeia, has implications for his own writing. He has to write in something of the same spirit. His remark, therefore, that 'any form of self-consciousness hinders a first rate artist' may not be universalisable, but it is, perhaps for that very reason, a telling illumination of his own relation to language.

Lawrence goes on to speak of Verga's deliberate redundancy, or circling repetition, as embodying the process of emotional recognition.[98] Doubtless he recognised his own method here, and in his case it was a risky procedure leading to some of his notoriously empty and private rhetoric, but it was also essential to his unique capacity to get beneath conscious mental controls. Many other modern writers shared Lawrence's interest in subconscious process, and its relation to creativity, but Lawrence was unusual in the way he made this a truly creative principle. Of course, there is a large unconscious factor in all creativity but in Lawrence it becomes a subliminal dynamic of the narrative language in which the reader is required to participate. In this respect, the author to whom Lawrence stands in starkest and most significant opposition, even more than Joyce, is Thomas Mann, because he openly thematises the same questions, and for an abstractly similar purpose, and thereby shows the radical difference in conception. Lawrence and Mann, of course, had no time for each other. Reviewing *Death In Venice* Lawrence remarked 'Thomas Mann is so old – and we are young.'[99] And, when Karl Kerenyi drew Mann's attention to *The Rainbow* as a significant precursor of the project which was to become *Joseph and his Brothers*, Mann impatiently dismissed Lawrence's 'hectic sensuality'.[100] Yet the two authors are mirror-images of each other and comparison brings out Lawrence's relation to language, and through that his relation to modernism generally: apparently at its periphery, substantively at its centre.

Women in Love and *The Magic Mountain* are pivotal works in each writer's *œuvre*. Each novel was conceived before the Great War and was modified by incorporating the wartime experience. Both novels analyse the condition of contemporary European culture through a small group of unusual but representative figures whose inner state is symbolised by their seclusion in the snowy mountains at the centre of the European continent. The significance of this location is that the action of each novel is played out against the background of a psychic map of Europe: Mann's extending horizontally from Russian to American, and Lawrence's vertically from Nordic to Italian. Europe represents the range of a complete human psyche within which the common theme of the two books is an unconscious struggle between eros and thanatos, as apparent forms of life and health are shown to be the symptoms of a deeper sickness unto death. Love is one of the most important of these ambiguous forms, and in each novel the word 'love' itself is anatomised for its possible falseness. Both novels seek finally to honour life despite the ambivalences that enfold it, and the apparent triumph of the death principle in recent history. It follows that the significant action of each novel takes place at a partly unconscious level and constantly eludes direct verbal definition. Indeed, the nature of language and speech is an important theme of each work as the psychic map provides a backdrop against which the characters' attempts to articulate their own understanding are constantly illuminated as by an ironic X-ray vision. When speech itself is seen in this way as the rationalising activity of consciousness against the background of the unconscious process or condition then it becomes in itself a primary dramatic element. It is not just what is said, but the very fact and quality of speech, that comes into question. At this point, however, the differences begin to come into play. That Lawrence's psychic map should be based on a North/South polarity rather than an East/West contrast, a vertical rather than a horizontal axis, is appropriate, since Lawrence's novel works in terms of psychic depth where Mann orchestrates broad cultural historical themes.

Mann's critical view of speech and language focuses on these elements, not in their individual use, so much as in their general nature. Using the wordless form of music to which Hans Castorp increasingly turns, he exposes the underlying emptiness of the great dialogues in which Naptha and Settembrini adumbrate fundamental attitudes to life in European culture from the Middle Ages through the Enlightenment. Mann does not ironise the importance of the questions they raise. He rather recognises that the meaning of these rival world views lies not in their claims to objective or historical truth, but in their expression of psychological dispositions. The novel is a textbook instance of the consciousness of world views, and was published in the same year as *A Passage to India* which shares the same concern. Although they are argued passionately by their proponents as vital beliefs, these world conceptions are recognised by the narrative as something more like aesthetic creations. They are internally coherent, emotionally compelling, and an inescapable way of illuminating the external, historical world. But we cannot judge one over the other simply on truth grounds, although we recognise that vital preferences are involved. Hence, Mann has a certain narrative identification with Settembrini's humanistic impulse, but does not privilege him philosophically, or discriminate his quality of speech. Meanwhile, it is the unintellectual Castorp who, at an intuitive, unarticulated level, learns properly to love life. The 'characters' themselves are really only lay figures through whom Mann meditates, brilliantly, on these themes. The danger in this, which explains the common resistance of English readers, is that Mann himself seems to suffer from having world views 'in the head'. But, of course, this is, at least partly, unfair.

The point is that by his own logic Mann cannot give a grounded view of his own. There is no where else to go.

The speech theme in Lawrence is the opposite of that. In *The Rainbow*, where the characters were less individuated, their thought and speech were typically merged with the mythopoeic narrative voice, and thereby gathered into an ontological reality which remained unselfconscious for them. The characters themselves could not articulate their deepest experience without traducing it. But in *Women in Love* the characters are highly articulate so that speech and consciousness become, as in *The Magic Mountain*, problematic themes in their own right. Lawrence is concerned to define his characters' fundamental relations to Being, which is itself wordless, and that is the light in which the quality of the characters' speech is to be understood. Speech itself is always, as Birkin says, a 'gesture' or a 'dumbshow' that must be interpreted rather than taken at its semantic face value.[101] Emotional quality is communicated in the saying rather than in what is said. As the naturally most articulate character, Birkin also recognises that articulacy is a possible snare and is 'irritated and weary of having a telling way of putting things'.[102] He frequently becomes inarticulate, and is the figure who signals the wordless significance of some of the book's memorable episodes such as 'Moony' and 'Water Party', in which the conscious relations of the characters, including their speech, are set against a symbolic insight into their inner, unconscious states of being. Since the novel is concerned with the characters' responsiveness to Being, such as has already been seen in the much simpler case of 'The Horsedealer's Daughter', there is no generalised value accorded to 'speech', so much as a constant process of discriminating individual qualities of utterance and response. The classic treatment of the speech theme in *Women in Love* is by Michael Ragussis who links it to a romantic tradition of thought on language.[103] Ragussis traces in detail how the 'struggle into conscious being' thematized by characters such as Birkin is enacted in the narrative language itself.[104] Lawrence's apparent dogmatism is only one half of a dialectic whereby his fundamental commitments, which are indeed absolute, seek to find expression in the relative realm of individual and social relationships. This contrasts with the spirit of much modernist writing in which a highly conscious artistic will is imposed, even when the importance of the unconscious is being stressed. From Lawrence's point of view, a writer like Mann traduces his material, or forecloses its meaning, by his very language. Thomas Mann saw Freud as a co-worker in the same field:

Freud's ambition to bring into consciousness what was formerly unconscious, and thereby to control it, was sympathetic to Mann's own
outlook; and, of course, it involved a corresponding view of art and
language.[105] By contrast, in his essays on Freud, Lawrence objected to
Freud's colonising of the unconscious, and saw the conscious ego, with
its assertion of its own will, as the mischievous element, while the
unconscious realm was a principal source of health.[106] This was no
simplistic reversal, of course: consciousness was not all bad, nor the
unconscious all good. Lawrence's works are a continual negotiation
between conscious and unconscious, where discrimination is always
specific and relational. The experience of Mavis and Fergusson in the
pond is rehearsed in the moment by the fire, and the combined experience is carried into an uncertain future.

If *Women in Love* and *The Magic Mountain* are the two works in which
these authors come closest, once allowance has been made for the
fundamental differences in conception, there is a sharper contrast between their respective reworkings of Genesis in *The Rainbow* and the
Joseph novels. Both works are concerned, in Mann's words, with 'the
birth of the ego out of the mythical collective'.[107] Each incorporates the
nineteenth-century scientific understanding which had dislodged biblical authority and more recent anthropological thought which was giving
a newly fundamental value to myth. These works reaffirm Genesis as a
central myth of origins, while simultaneously demonstrating that the
mythic is the ultimate category of human understanding. They are
concerned with the past as a resource by which the characters can
successfully accommodate the new experience of the present. For the
'mythic' is most essentially present, not as the overarching structure of
the historical narrative, but as an inner resource of the characters. But, in
their understanding of how this resource is present in the characters, the
two works differ sharply. Mann makes it a matter of self-consciousness
for the characters themselves. The central figures in each generation are
aware at moments of crisis that their ancestors have encountered comparable experiences. The legendary inheritance is their conscious guide.
It is no more than a guide, of course, because the ancestral models have
constantly to be adapted, not merely followed, but they face life with the
confidence of inheritors. They see themselves as characters within a
much larger story whose outcome is unknown, at least to them, but
which they are helping to shape, and which will in turn give significance
to their individual lives.

Lawrence presents the Brangwens as inheritors with a comparable blend of confidence and humility. They too belong to something beyond themselves. But Lawrence's subtlety was to communicate this as a resource which remains unconscious for the Brangwens themselves and largely subliminal for the reader. The 'mythic' is present for them not as an idea, or even as a story, but at a pre-reflective level in their way of being. The characters' experience is typically merged into a narrative prose which represents, imitatively and enactively, their inner condition. When the opening paragraphs describe the life of the early Brangwens in language such as this: 'the pulse of the blood of the teats of the cows beat into the pulse of the hands of the men', some readers wince from what they see as Lawrence's heavy-handedness.[108] But these readers are actually responding to part of his meaning. The opening prose poem is not merely affirmatory: it also expresses the intolerable claustrophobia of this life from which some of the characters wish to escape, or evolve. The ambivalence is expressed in the gestural rhythms of the prose running counter to its overtly celebratory semantics. Lawrence's double myth of origins combines the ascending Darwinian evolution from the Marsh with a fall from Eden. The struggle between these two principles, and the struggle to prevent them falling apart, is the living myth of *The Rainbow*. Once again, as with the pond in 'The Horsedealer's Daughter', the overtly mythic references are not the significant locus of mythic meaning. This lies in the shifting quality of being-in-the-world, and the corresponding clash of world views, communicated within the language and usually below the self-conscious awareness of readers, let alone of the characters. Where Mann is consciously mythopoeic, Lawrence has mythopoeic consciousness.[109]

But there remains something more specific to say about Lawrence's relation to language in explaining his remark that 'any form of emotional self-consciousness only hinders a first-rate artist'. For what has been said so far has only defined an attitude and indicated its thematising in his fiction. When Lawrence's remark is thought about more closely, or is taken very literally, it is an extraordinary claim. It is sometimes said that Lawrence's attempt to express unconscious life was a contradiction in terms. It is helpful to state the problem in this bald way, but it is the beginning rather than the end of the question, for Lawrence's claim corresponds to something unique in his writing. In effect, Lawrence takes as literally as one could conceive Heidegger's direction to listen to language.[110] In some of his more unbuttoned works, like *Mr. Noon*, Lawrence shows pleasure in word-play, often extending the same motif over several pages as he does in that novel with the word 'spoon'.[111] Once one is aware of this proclivity in Lawrence, one becomes attuned to its more subliminal working throughout his fiction; his prose is full of potential word associations floating just beneath the surface of consciousness. Whereas most of us labour to clarify meaning, and struggle against unwanted associations and importunings of language, Lawrence seems deliberately to submit himself to this as part of a process of creative discovery shared subliminally with the reader. When he writes most effectively, it is often by seeming to write in a clumsy, unfinished way.

The recent systematic editing of Lawrence has revealed more clearly his processes of composition. It was commonly believed, based partly on odd remarks of Lawrence himself, but more from the final effect of his writing, that he was not a reviser so much as a fluent rewriter of new drafts. It has now become clear that he was indeed a careful reviser, but in a manner that actually reinforced the apparent effect of fluent informality. In revision he seems typically to confirm, or even to add, the repetitions and infelicities that another writer would seek to remove. A minor example occurs in the opening of a sentence already quoted from 'The Horse-Dealer's Daughter': 'At this point Mabel rose from the table.' Flaubert would not have passed this opening clause. Bellowing it aloud in his room at Croisset, he would soon have detected the ugly internal jingle of 'Mabel' and 'table' (*EME* p. 140). But actually the rhyme is appropriate since Mabel is no more than a piece of furniture to the men in the room, and the wooden tone it imparts to her name, a name so pointedly omitted from the story's title, is also appropriate. Without getting embroiled in the inanities of the 'intentionality' argument, a close reader of Lawrence will find such effects to be characteristic, and vital to the overall narrative effect, and yet it is extremely difficult to believe that they are all consciously sought. It is as if he had an intuitive way of riding the language in which much of the process, like the 'cleverness' of his hand in writing, was not a matter of mental consciousness. Similarly, in the second sentence of his story 'The Primrose Path', which concerns the aggressively insecure virility of the main character who is working as a cabman, we find the group of cabmen 'jerked themselves erect' (*EME* p. 123). When it is quoted in isolation, the masturbatory suggestiveness of this is immediately apparent, but in the narrative context any such effect is at best subliminal.

His story 'England, my England' opens:

He was working on the edge of the common, beyond the small brook that ran in the dip at the bottom of the garden, carrying the garden path in continuation from the plank bridge on to the common. (*EME* p. 5)

The sentence is not comfortable to read. The long parenthetical clause creates a momentary ambiguity as to whether 'he' or the 'brook' is now the subject of 'carrying', while the concluding repetition of the word 'common' falls flat. Indeed, the interpolated clause accentuates the repetition of this word. As the story proceeds, however, it becomes apparent that Egbert, the central character introduced here, is neither a worker nor common, and the word 'common' becomes an important motif of the story. There is a deep historical ambivalence about the word 'common' which has become a term of social disapproval while retaining its meaning of social solidarity, as in the seventeenth-century use of the word 'Commonwealth'. Egbert's being on the edge of the common, and even a certain syntactic labouring of the sentence itself, turn out to be appropriate in both senses. Work is a strain for him because he does not really afford it a proper place in his life, or in a communal life, although he may have some unconscious nostalgia for it. In Lawrence's England, it transpires, the values of commonality and wealth are typically usurped by class and money, and Egbert is an unconscious victim of this. As in the opening of *The Rainbow*, the crucial 'action' is enacted in the language below the level of semantics. For at the conscious level, this effect, if it is one, only works retrospectively. The sentence has no Joycean or Jamesian wit to point up these implications. It is as if Lawrence, if he was aware of the pregnancy of the word, wanted the process of recognition to occur slowly and subliminally within the reading, rather than be signalled immediately as a stylistic effect. And it was probably not so self-conscious anyway, but rather an obsessive recurrence of a key term as Lawrence developed this complex of themes. His language typically presents a body of fluid material to be worked over in the course of the story.

Lawrence's habit of verbal repetition is the most overt aspect of this general proclivity as in his play with the words 'reality' and 'knowledge' in *The Rainbow*.[112] These words prove to have fluid meanings constantly modified, and even reversed, in shifting contexts. But this more consciously heuristic play, of which the reader has also to be at least half-conscious, rests on a broader relation to language in which a multitude of such shifts or suggestions remains subliminal in the reading and, one surmises, in much of the process of writing too. Whatever the process of composition, Lawrence's language enacts the desideratum of the Verga essay. Its meanings constantly lurk just beneath the surface of consciousness, which is why Mann and Lawrence, as true parallels, could never meet. Lawrence's modernity included a fundamental critique of artistic modernism, and no account of it should leave him out. His critique of modernity and modernism was based on a lived mythopoeia, a flexible responsiveness to Being in language, which quickly detected the ersatz versions of those who have myth, or language, 'in the head'.

CHAPTER 3

Countercases: T. S. Eliot and Ezra Pound

The three writers considered so far offer a spectrum of mythopoeic possibilities, although others, such as Pablo Neruda, Rainer Maria Rilke or Wallace Stevens are equally relevant. To claim that mythopoeia, as defined in the preceding chapters, is central to modernism, is not to impose a monolithic account. There are authors for whom an emphasis on consciously inhabited world views is not primary; while in Kafka and Beckett the mythopoeic conception applies rather in a reverse or imploded mode. *Finnegans Wake*, although a monumental example of mid-century mythopoeia, is so completely focused at the level of language, is so intra-mythic, as to have moved away from the specific theme of personal conviction within a world view. None the less, mythopoeic consciousness, in the sense I have outlined, is a significant criterion by which to read other writers, as is evident from two borderline cases.

Pound and Eliot are among the first instances that spring to mind when thinking of myth in relation to Anglo-American modernism, yet both stand outside the definition formulated so far. For what is in question is not the use of myth, but its significance. To *use* myth is not necessarily to be mytho*poeic*, and may even pre-empt that possibility. What distinguishes both these poets, despite their mutual differences, from the three writers already considered may be approached through their attitudes to the linguistic turn. They had a common concern to 'purify the language of the tribe': through poetry and criticism, they wished to keep language rich, subtle and accurate as the public medium of expression and understanding.[1] This ambition influenced the methods, and sense of purpose, of university English studies up to the mid-century. In retrospect, however, it assumed a very direct relation between linguistic form and cultural condition. The one is taken as an immediate index, or cause, of the other. That there *is* a relation may be readily agreed, but how immediate a relation is the question; and that leads to a peculiarly modern development in the consciousness of language which has its roots in the modernist period.

When Nietzsche insisted on the radical metaphoricity of language, 'truth is a mobile army of metaphors', his claim was so all-encompassing as to leave everything unchanged, since, having absorbed the metaphorical nature of all language, we have to carry on as before, making the same practical, internal distinctions. For everyday purposes some uses of language are more metaphorical than others. Yet it also makes all the difference. His recognition is an aspect of the mythopoeic awareness, that sense of the human creation of meaning, seen in the preceding authors, and it has the same effect of putting brackets around the whole of experience without necessarily changing its internal relations. In that sense it changes everything; it modifies consciousness and the relation to one's own convictions. But Eliot and Pound resisted Nietzsche's implication of radical metaphoricity, and in that respect they reflected a different line of twentieth-century interpretation. This saw the same world-forming power of language as making language the total index of a world and therefore revealing it. Wittgenstein's aphorism, 'the limits of my language mean the limits of my world', implied a certain scepticism; it meant that you would need, in order fully to understand any use of language, to bring the whole 'form of life' into consciousness.[2] And that is impossible because a form of life is not only too vast and complex, it is largely implicit; and even if you *could* bring it fully into consciousness, you still could not know for sure that you *had* done so. So too, individual usage, however indicative, is always part of a larger implicit background which we cannot be sure to have encompassed in exercising verbal critique on others. My one-time French landlady's apparently anti-semitic remarks took on a different meaning when I learned she had risked her life to save her Jewish neighbours in the Second World War. But, over the latter half of the century, there has developed an excessive confidence in the critical scrutiny of language as exposing the reality of its user. This intra-linguistic, or backdoor, literalism has had extensive consequences in later twentieth-century thought in the form of ideological critique, and it stands in opposition to the creative or responsible scepticism of the mythopoeic consciousness.

Eliot and Pound were on the watershed, or as it has turned out, the faultline, between these two possibilities. Their mutually deprecating view of Nietzsche is an index of this; and particularly in so far as the reading of Nietzsche requires an intuitive appreciation of the way he himself uses language. He had no yearning for transcendent or objective truth, but Eliot and Pound *did* want something like this, and could not, therefore, adopt the mythopoeic posture as defined so far. Each wanted a certain literalism for his own world view. Of course, this needs to be carefully formulated. Literalism cannot now be taken too literally, and no poet rejects metaphor. Pound's desire to get beyond metaphor is the motive of his metaphorical power. In seeking unmediated contact with the earth, the GEA TERRA, he says 'Wisdom lies next to thee / Simply, past metaphor' and in doing so, of course, he uses metaphor, consummately.[3] What is really at stake, therefore, is not so much the relation of language to world as the internal relation of the speaker to language. Geoffrey Hartman's study of Wordsworth and other poets, entitled *Unmediated Vision*, might as accurately have been called *Mediated Vision*, but his title points to the inner dynamic and motivation of these poets' language, and that is the focus for considering Eliot and Pound. They each had a keen insight into modernist mythopoeia, but Eliot directly resisted it, while, for Pound, it was the locus of a catastrophic internal conflict.

T. S. ELIOT: RELIGION VERSUS MYTH

Eliot's remarks on myth in his review of *Ulysses* clearly had an eye to his own method in *The Waste Land*.

> In using the myth, in manipulating a continuous parallel between contemporaneity and antiquity, Mr. Joyce is pursuing a method which others must pursue after him . . . It is simply a way of controlling, of ordering, of giving a shape and a significance to the immense panorama of futility and anarchy that is contemporary history . . . It is, I seriously believe, a step towards making the modern world possible for art.[4]

These comments echo Pound's 'scaffolding' image by seeing the mythic structure in an essentially external way. But, whereas Pound dismissed the mythic parallel to focus on the text, Eliot privileges the mythic means itself, and that is the connection with his own creative concerns. Despite the disarming 'simply', Eliot's formulation contains a significant ambiguity. Is myth merely a technical method enabling the artist to *express* the futility and anarchy, or is it a principle of meaning that actually *opposes* it? Although the sentence slides from 'controlling' to 'giving . . . significance', the general context, and the emphasis on technique, imply the former meaning, and that is how the remark is usually understood. Yet the ghost of the second meaning lurks in the pathos of the historical generalisation and in the fact that myth is patently not an arbitrary or neutral framework. In *Ulysses* itself these different possibilities are self-consciously present. The numinous holism of myth is set in counterpoint to an ostentatious constructivism, and to that extent Eliot's formulation, precisely in its doubleness, is to the point. But, in so far as his formula turns Joyce's luminous complexity into an apparently unwitting ambiguity, it points to the confusion lying at the heart of *The Waste Land*. For *The Waste Land* is a great poem of religious quest in which the essentially inner or spiritual theme is ambivalently projected both on to an external social plane and on to a mythic backdrop.

The poem is about fertility, or the lack of it, and sexuality is thematically central. The general strategy of the poem in this respect is well known. Images of sterile sexuality are interspersed with occasional glimpses of other possibilities, but what strongly communicates is a disturbed distaste for sexuality *per se*. Of course, the poem always provides reasons for the sexual distaste in the inner emptiness or the selfishness of the participants, but we can now see that these reasons are partly alibis. Eliot was vulnerable to the English class mystique in a way that his fellow Americans, Pound and Henry James, were not, and we now know much more about his unhappy personal situation and first marriage. For many years the premisses of the poem were acceptable to readers who broadly shared Eliot's social attitudes; as in 'One of the low on whom assurance sits / Like a silk hat on a Bradford millionaire', or the typist's 'drying combinations'.[5] But a typist's need to launder her underclothes has no implication for her personal or ethical nature, and the irrelevance of the detail highlights the real emotion, the sexual repulsion and social snobbery, of the line. The emotions of the poem, while patently genuine, partly mistake their object.

This aspect of the poem, however partial with respect to the whole, clarifies the role of the fertility myth in the poem's emotional dynamics as opposed to its official symbolism. The Grail myth is a more subtle alibi than the social and ethical ones already noted, and Eliot spoke more truly than he realised in speaking of the mythic method as one that could be put to 'use': in representing the value of fertility, and therefore sexuality, in a remote and impersonal form, it at once fills, and disguises, the emotional gap. Eliot did not inhabit the fertility myth emotionally, even under the negative sign of an emotional lack, and his use of the myth was at the opposite extreme from the mythopoeic sensibility of Lawrence or Pound. His underlying condition, indeed, was expressed very frankly when he spoke of:

the void that I find in the middle of all human happiness and all human relations, and which there is only one thing to fill. I am one whom this sense of void tends to drive towards scepticism or sensuality, and only Christianity helps to reconcile me to life, which is otherwise disgusting.[6]

Here is a textbook case for Nietzsche's analysis of Christianity as a negative life symptom, and it is no wonder that Eliot's allusions to Nietzsche were pre-emptively contemptuous. In effect, Eliot found in the mythic allusions of *The Waste Land* an impersonal and culturally prestigious vehicle through which to project unexamined or unresolved emotions. But, by the same token, once those emotions were projected into the myth, it did indeed become their poetic formula. The power of the poem is the power of these emotions expressed in perhaps the only way he could have expressed them at that time. His essay on *Hamlet* is relevant here: in describing Hamlet as having feelings in excess of their apparent cause, feelings in search of an 'objective correlative', Eliot might again have been speaking from his own case.[7] But, in offering as *his* objective correlative a vast cultural myth, his unconscious subterfuge was less likely to be detected; even by himself. The outcome is that the fertility legend of *The Waste Land* became a genuine modern myth, but not in such a way as to achieve a critical self-consciousness about its own status. It could not recognise its own highly personal and tendentious nature.

It later became clear that Eliot's true importance was as a religious poet, and he increasingly confined the expression of his social views to prose. This provides a sharper focus on his use of myth, since religious faith, for him, was essentially incompatible with mythopoeic relativity. He would not, in principle, accept his own belief as myth. In fact, of course, his most ambitious religious poems, the *Four Quartets*, were mythopoeic. They were genuinely of their time in that, while speaking of religious faith, they do not assume it in the reader. When reading much religious poetry of earlier periods, such as Herbert's or Milton's, the modern agnostic makes an historical adjustment which includes a 'suspension of disbelief', but in the *Four Quartets* this attitude of aesthetic sympathy would actually be inappropriate since the poetry seeks to engage precisely this question. Eliot himself stressed the distinction between 'devotional' poetry, which depends on a faith shared by the reader, and 'great religious poetry', which includes not just Dante, but Corneille, Racine, Baudelaire and Villon.[8] Religious poetry is a broader term and may express a religious view of life unconsciously or negatively. So too, he speaks of Tennyson's 'In Memoriam' as being religious not 'in the quality of its faith, but because of the quality of its doubt'.[9] *The Four Quartets*, even more than *Ash Wednesday*, are in Eliot's sense religious rather than devotional, and the spiritual struggle of which they speak does not depend upon specifically religious terms. F. R. Leavis, despite his radical critique of Eliot, saw the heuristic process in these poems as exemplifying a whole conception of language akin to what has just been seen in Heidegger and Lawrence. Although he would not have called it so, Leavis offers a mythopoeic reading which it is not necessary to repeat here.[10] But his critique of Eliot, even in these poems, relates to Eliot's tendency to swerve, self-defensively, against his own creative process. Unlike the speaker of 'Among School Children', he could not, at the crucial moment, allow himself to be carried by it.

The discursive equivalent of this can be seen in the velleities and archness of Eliot's essays, and, in relation to the present theme, his way of recognising, without accepting, the relativity of world views. He continually touches on the problem of belief while wisely avoiding a definitive treatment of it, and he comes closest to articulating modernist mythopoeia by his resistance to it. Two topics are particularly relevant here, humanism and religious belief, which lie on each side of the mythopoeic possibility. In his essays on 'The Humanism of Irving Babbit' and 'Second Thoughts about Humanism' Eliot recognised that the true enemy of religion in the context of modernity was not militant atheism so much as humanism.[11] He wishes therefore to expose it philosophically and takes the traditional religious high-ground that humanistic values are an afterglow of religion and have no ultimate grounding without it. The trouble with this is that humanism is not a philosophy; it is, in Nietzsche's sense, a myth. That it to say, it is the working horizon of value of many modern individuals and communities. It knows it has no grounding beyond itself; and it believes religion does not either. Indeed, to require humanistic values to be given theological or philosophical support might actually be damaging to them; particularly if such support is not forthcoming. If our values require philosophical justification then what is their value in the first place? In practice, of course, the desire for such justification often arises from the need to have one's values accepted by, or imposed on, others, and in that respect Eliot's position is essentially the common British vulgarism of supposing that the church is a kind of ministry of public morals. But the weakness of Eliot's social understanding, particularly in the British context, is really the sign that his true interest lay elsewhere, in the suffering and surrender of the spiritual life. It was not on the question of humanism, therefore, but of belief that his thought ran deepest.

In a lengthy note to his 1929 essay on Dante, Eliot meditated yet again on the question of poetic belief, taking as his point of departure I. A. Richards' notion of poetic utterances as 'pseudostatements'.[12] He seeks to clarify the relation of poetry and belief by avoiding two simplistic extremes: the poet's beliefs cannot be ignored, yet response is not in any simple way conditional upon sharing them. He wants, in other words, to distinguish artistic sympathy from sharing the belief, while avoiding generalised answers to the problem; particularly such as would separate poetic belief too sharply from real belief. He therefore sees the emptiness of I. A. Richards' notion of the 'pseudostatement'. As he says: 'The theory of Mr. Richards is . . . incomplete until he defines the species of religious, philosophical, scientific, and other beliefs, as well as that of "everyday" belief.' Eliot sees the abstract ungraspability of the question. Literature does not give a special category of belief different from scientific, religious, ethical or 'everyday' belief, yet it somehow implies a special, partly dramatic, relation to all belief, including one's own. From this point of view, 'poetic belief' or 'pseudostatement' are deceptive categories resting on their distinction from real belief while distracting attention from its equally problematic character. These terms do not just shift the burden of the problem, they keep it permanently circling, like an intellectual pass-the-parcel, while Eliot's own passing of the parcel, his refusal to adopt a position, is the negative counterpart of what I have characterised as modernist mythopoeia. For in modernist mythopoeia, instead of poetic belief being the problematic term to be explained by contrast with real belief, it is rather the mystery of belief at large which is problematically focused by poetic belief. Poetic belief stands for any belief raised to a level of self-conscious bracketing. But for Eliot this philosophical aporia was unlivable.

Yet in his late lecture on 'Goethe as the Sage', Eliot introduces a new term which gets closer to the spirit of mythopoeia in his own way.[13] While he is still unpersuaded by Goethe's 'thought', he is now persuaded of his wisdom. He sees in Goethe a maturity expressed in the poetry itself not at the level of aphoristic content, but as an experiential quality embodied in language. A similar recognition occurs in his late lecture on Yeats. Eliot's comments on impersonality in 'Tradition and the Individual Talent' had acquired an inexpungable notoriety despite his attempts to distance himself from them. He now recognises, with eloquent clarity, the mature Yeats' capacity to speak in the first person in a truly impersonal spirit, and his comments could as well apply to his own use of the first person in the *Four Quartets*.

There are two forms of impersonality: that which is natural to the mere skilful craftsman, and that which is more and more achieved by the maturing artist. The first is that of what I have called the 'anthology piece'. . . The second impersonality is that of the poet who, out of intense and personal experience, is able to express a general truth; retaining all the particularity of his experience, to make of it a general symbol.[14]

Eliot sees an irreducible quality in the poetry, something which cannot be expressed in other terms. Although he hesitates to attribute wisdom even to the mature Yeats, he sees in him a Blakean honesty which answers to this more profound order of impersonality; the same quality that Leavis missed in Eliot himself. With this clue, Eliot might have reread Lawrence with a new appreciation. This impersonality is closely connected to the mythopoeic impulse and has to be understood as an inner and qualitative, rather than an outer and technical, affair. By the time of the Yeats lecture, that is to say, Eliot was in a position to rewrite the latter part of 'Tradition and the Individual Talent', seeing imperso-nality not as an 'escape' from personality, but as a different modality of it. But that is the weak part of the essay, while Eliot's opening account of tradition is his nearest discursive approach to acknowledging the mythopoeic spirit. Where 'orthodoxy' is the spirit of obedience to an inherited order, tradition is a more subtle matter. Tradition, for Eliot, manifests itself in a less conscious way and not least when the individual writer consciously reacts against it. An active relation to tradition is both conscious and unconscious, never completely one or the other; a point that seems to be missed by Michael North in his excellent treatment of this theme.[15] It also follows that tradition will live in creative activity rather than in discursive thought. Tradition is Eliot's nearest equivalent for modernist mythopoeia.

If tradition was Eliot's working myth, the 'dissociation of sensibility' over the seventeenth and eighteenth centuries is to be understood in its light. The controversial impact of this idea, and its continuing power even after it had been repeatedly exploded as an historical claim even by Eliot himself, indicates its mythic nature. It really expresses the pervasive damage of the Cartesian split as perceived by the modernist generation, and its particular historical location was bound to be flexible. Eliot later came to see John Donne's poetry not as a late embodiment of unified sensibility, but as a stage in its dissociation. The truly unified sensibility he now located much earlier, in Dante. Yeats likewise placed Dante, along with himself, at phase seventeen of his visionary system; the phase denoting the highest 'unity of being'. In placing the historical Dante at the centre of his system, Yeats gave him a frankly mythic status. And Yeats, as a mythopoeic writer, was concerned with the quality rather than the content of Dante's faith, just as his own desired unity and faith sought no support from theological doctrine. But when Eliot pushed the moment of unified being back to Dante, he linked it to medieval religious belief. He still resisted seeing it mythopoeically.

In sum, Eliot's religious outlook and philosophical training gave him a keen insight into the problematic relations of poetry and belief, while leading him to reject the model of modernist mythopoeia whereby poetic belief became the model of all belief. On this model, of course, belief remains just as enigmatic, but the locus of the problem changes. It is 'everyday' belief which now becomes self-consciously mysterious, while art and criticism provide clues as to how best to live it. Although Eliot saw quite clearly that no world view has a transcendental grounding, his religious faith kept him from accepting his own beliefs as myths. That helps explain his peculiar potency as a maker of modern myths.

ODYSSEUS UNBOUND: THE CANTOS OF EZRA POUND

Pound is a troubling figure on whom readers are divided not just between, but within, themselves. As with Heidegger, we are faced with a major, formative intelligence who colluded, on principle, with a fascist regime. Without offering yet more retrospective moralising on flawed genius, the relationship between the public life, on the one hand, and the body of thought or poetic vision on the other, remains a vital question. Someone may be morally small, as seems the case with Heidegger, or deluded, as was the case with Pound, without this invalidating all their insights in their specific field. Indeed, some narrowing concentration is often the condition of such achievements and this may apply even to a philosopher of 'concern' or to a poet whose great theme is a just and truthful vision of human society. But there is a more positive point to be made here. Ideological critique, because of its very generality, may not be really to the point when it subsumes, but cannot take account of, individual ethical quality. As Pound said: 'An idea has little value apart from the modality of the mind which receives it.'[16] It is common practice to identify an ideology and assume that it leads to certain kinds of actions or consequences. But what frequently matters is not so much the ideology as the individual's relation to it, the way of living it. The dogmatic literalism of Pound's beliefs is at least part of the problem. His poetic power lay largely in his mythopoeic sensibility while his catastrophic flaw lay in a lack of that inbuilt relativity and scepticism I have characterised as modernist mythopoeia.

Pound's understanding of myth was within a conception of language, and a poetics, which lent itself to what I have called intra-linguistic or secondary literalism. Kathryne Lindberg has argued that Pound had a Nietzschean conception of language, but, as I have suggested above, the linguistic turn to which Nietzsche gave classic expression was inflected in a different direction by Pound.[17] When Pound speaks metaphorically of a 'Wisdom . . . past metaphor', this hints at the contradictory burden in the language of the *Cantos*. For this contains both a mythopoeic experience transcending language and an ideological conviction that language reveals the reality of others. These combined pressures gave a literalistic inflection to his poetic voice and allowed his authentic mythopoeia to be governed by a spurious ideology.

Some of his most explicit thinking about myth was in his early study of Provençal poetry, *The Spirit of Romance*. His remarks have a characteristically modernist elusiveness. 'Speaking aesthetically,' Pound says, 'the myths are explications of mood' and hence, even for moderns, if they have the relevant emotional experience, 'these things are real'.[18] At the same time he remarks of Ovid that he 'walks with the people of myth'.[19] This suggests that Ovid himself was no longer one of them so that for modern man too, perhaps, the experience can be emotionally 'real' only under something like aesthetic conditions. His essay on Arnold Dolmetsch catches the spirit of the transition at first personally and then historically:

I have seen the God Pan, and it was in this manner: I heard a bewildering and pervasive music moving from precision to precision within itself. Then I heard a different music, hollow and laughing. Then I looked up and saw two eyes like the eyes of a wood creature peering at me over a brown tube of wood . . . The first myths arose when a man walked sheer into 'nonsense', that is to say when some very vivid and undeniable adventure befell him, and he told someone else who called him a liar. Thereupon, after bitter experience, perceiving that no one could understand what he meant when he said that he 'turned into a tree' he made a myth – a work of art that is – an impersonal and objective story woven out of his own emotion.[20]

Ovid's poetry offered Pound a literary twilight zone comparable to the anthropological twilight Lawrence found in Italy. Pound had one of the most mythopoeic sensibilities of all modern writers and this underwrites, or largely constitutes, his own poetic. His difficulty lay in interfusing the mythopoeic and the modern; his very authenticity exacerbated the problem which deepened as his poetic career became increasingly invested in the *Cantos* and was caught up in the changing circumstances of twentieth-century history.

The cardinal issue for the *Cantos* is the relation between the order of economics and the order of nature, for the *Cantos* rest on Pound's reassertion, in non-theological terms, of the medieval Christian view that lending for profit is usury and a sin against the natural order. Money should not breed money. From the standpoint of modern instrumental reason, the medieval religious outlook was closer to myth in maintaining a sense of the divine in nature. Hence Pound recovered with other aspects of medieval culture, particularly from Provence, its residually mythopoeic sensibility. This cultural geology works powerfully in the Usury *Cantos* partly because the modern voice, the medieval thought, and the mythopoeic response are combined but not confused (*Cantos* pp. 229–30). Usura is not a mythic figure, she is a literary personification, yet she provides a synoptic middle term exposing modern economic practice to the critical weight of a mythopoeic natural piety sharpened to a philosophical edge by its medieval form. Pound's moral passion carries an impersonal and traditionary weight enabling him to speak with a Blakean simplicity and authority such that his critique of the modern economic order is still eloquent and pertinent. But the case is not always so straightforward. The relationship between the mythopoeic vision, the artistic method and the historical analysis remains problematic.

The encyclopaedia theme in Joyce and Nietzsche focused the incommensurable accounts of the world available to modern culture. It is not just that there is too much information but that the different disciplines cannot be brought to common terms. Pound, like other modern writers, refused to acquiesce in this cultural fragmentation but his refusal took a different form. Yeats, Joyce and Lawrence, all sought to dissolve this multiplicity of discourses into an encompassing human viewpoint which depended on a common metaphoricity, on their all being forms of human projection and response. Most clearly, Joyce's successive techniques in *Ulysses* are strictly metaphorical evocations of the various disciplines. Lawrence's essays on the unconscious, written partly in opposition to Freud's scientism, showed a similar awareness which is equally present in his narrative prose. But Pound wanted to resist relativistic fragmentation while maintaining the literal integrity of the disciplinary fields. Kathryne Lindberg has traced the dispute between Eliot and Pound on this matter.[21] Eliot wanted to keep the discourses of economics and religion separate with religion as the authority. Pound wanted to mix them but for him, science, economics, politics, philosophy and history were not to be dissolved into metaphors. He studied these disciplines so as to incorporate them literally into his poetry; or, as a critic, into his sense of the meaning of poetry.[22] Any unity was to be found in affinities between the disciplines themselves. The biologist Louis Agassiz and the anthropologist Leo Frobenius were models whose methods and insights were to be applied directly to his own poetic concerns.

It was therefore harder for Pound to bring such different materials into a coherent single understanding, and more so when they involved the political realm. Pound's mythopoeia in the *Cantos* seeks to find the proper human viewpoint overall; the Archimedian point from which the whole culture can be judged and improved. He typically interweaves different discourses, therefore, often including direct quotations from historical, philosophical or economic texts, and, at its best, the effect is a counterpoint with each element in separate concert with the others. At the same time, all these historical situations and discourses are seen from the standpoint of a mythopoeic relation to the natural world. Mythopoeia is the fundamental point of reference for all these other discourses, but it does not absorb them, does not convert them into metaphor. There is a peculiar integrity about this, but also an insoluble difficulty. And, since Pound sought not just a Blakean diagnostic critique but political and economic solutions, the equivocal relation of the economic and the mythical begins to matter. Ironically enough, it was precisely because he wanted his different disciplines to maintain their own integrity that they were vulnerable to a fatal ambiguity.

Although he would not have welcomed the suggestion, the contemporary with whom Pound had the most significant affinity was D. H. Lawrence, and the comparison brings out what is at stake in Pound's mythopoeia. These two writers were diametrically opposed in many of their literary techniques and allegiances, and, after a period of initial friendship in pre-war London, they grew apart personally. None the less, they were both prophetic iconoclasts who looked back to a pre-Socratic mythopoeic world as the criterion from which to criticise their present culture. Each experienced the mythopoeic as a psychological fact in his own life and refused to accept that it was barred in principle to modern man if he would open himself to it. Behind their more obvious differences, therefore, the artistic and mythopoeic visions of Lawrence and Pound had a common missionary purpose creating similar strengths and difficulties. In particular, their difficulty lay in enforcing their mythopoeic vision on an incomprehending or hostile world so that, after an early period of hopeful discovery, they each suffered an estrangement which was personally and artistically damaging. In this respect, the Cantos contrast with Lawrence's *The Plumed Serpent* (1926). *The Plumed Serpent* is a largely disastrous, if fitfully brilliant, speculation on modern social renewal from ancient mythic sources. When he subsequently rejected its 'leadership' ideal, Lawrence was partly rejecting such extra-artistic forms of prophecy on his own part; or rather he could continue to be a prophet and a moraliser, but his 'art speech' was not to be confused with everyday speech or with political programmes. More significantly, his rejection of 'leadership' was anticipated within the work itself. Apart from the heroine, Kate Leslie's, misgivings about the revival movement and its leaders, the realist novel form itself can be seen crumbling, almost consciously, under the pressure of prophecy and the author's awareness of his own moral isolation. As I have indicated elsewhere, the demands of the novel form helped to bring the unreality of the project to a point of conscious crisis.[23] As a novelist, as a creator of fictional worlds, Lawrence was especially obliged, despite himself, to engage the ethical and social domains which, as J. P. Stern has pointed out, were largely missing from Nietzsche's thought.[24] Lawrence subsequently turned to fable, as in *The Escaped Cock* (originally published as *The Man who Died* in 1929); or in *Etruscan Places* (1930) he contrasted the quality of ancient Etruscan life to Roman with an eye to the political revivalism of Mussolini. Fundamentally, Lawrence did not confuse the aesthetic and the prophetic because he understood their meeting in the mythopoeic. Although he was constantly tempted by utopian schemes, these were for himself and his friends, and he never fully lost the recognition he affirmed late in life that he had no solutions to offer in the realm of practical politics: 'As a novelist, I feel it is the change inside the individual which is my real concern. The great social change interests me and troubles me, but it is not my field . . . what steps to take I don't know. Other men know better.'[25]

Pound always knew better than the practical men, and was willing to tell them so, and he lived on to a more difficult wartime era in which myth had acquired a sinister meaning. In the latter half of the century, largely in response to fascism, there has been a general turn against 'myth'. A classic moment in that turn was the account by Adorno and

Horkheimer of the bound Odysseus listening to the Siren song of pre-civilised mythic powers.[26] In their view, myth represents for the modern only a sentimental atavism, and it is quite understandable that, in the face of fascist triumphalism, these authors should see myth as a seductive power to be resisted, although their political emphasis, and generalised purview, blur the aesthetic and metaphysical aspects which I have been tracing in the previous writers. They, therefore, used Odysseus as the image of a man caught between incompatible cultures at the very time that Pound was using the identical figure to make his historical understanding of modernity 'cohere'. What is importantly at stake in both these accounts of modernity is the function of the aesthetic standpoint which, for Adorno and Horkheimer, is focused in the image of the bound Odysseus, while the *Cantos* also present an Odyssean voyager whose meaning ultimately hinges on the problematic nature of his aesthetic bounds.

On analogy with Wittgenstein's remark that 'if a lion could talk we would not understand him', we may say that if the pre-conscious collectivity of myth *could* be apprehended by a self-conscious individual it would be incomprehensible.[27] There is no return to the former condition. Hence, as Jakob Taubes has argued against Adorno and Horkheimer, in being bound *by his own choice* Odysseus converts the mythopoeic encounter with the Sirens into a different meaning for the mythic experience *within* Enlightenment.[28] Once his being bound is understood not just as an external condition for encountering an earlier state, but as part of the intrinsic structure of the different experience he now has, then it becomes an image of the creative paradox of modern mythopoeia. The bound Odysseus takes on his proper metaphysical value when we see the bonds as essentially aesthetic. For Adorno and Horkheimer, the bourgeois master Odysseus enjoys, under conditions of self-repression, an aesthetic experience denied to the labouring crew but they do not see the binding as an image of the aesthetic condition as such. They assume a binary literalism whereby Odysseus either regresses to the mythic or must be externally restrained. Yet for artistic modernism, as opposed to political modernity, the mythic is time and again not just conditional *on*, but is internally conditioned *by*, the aesthetic. Myth is only to be experienced under an aesthetic sign, and to understand the internal dynamic of modernist mythopoeia it is more useful to see the binding as an image of the aesthetic condition *per se*. Joyce's *Ulysses* used Homer as a necessary term to define a consciously constructed modern equivalent. *Pace* Adorno, the meaning of 'Bloom as Ulysses' lies not in an atavistic nostalgia, but in the aesthetic double consciousness implied in a *self*-bound Odysseus. It is Mann's 'late and mature' form which is in question here, rather than the 'early and primitive' one which is none the less necessary to define it. Hence, where Adorno's hero is torn between conflicting worlds, Joyce keeps both worlds in distinct but inseparable focus as mutually necessary terms. This is the context in which Pound's view of the Homeric parallel as 'scaffolding', necessary to the writing but not to the completed work, becomes revealing, for what Pound misses here is the function of the running parallel in defining Joyce's aesthetically constructed mythopoeia. He dismisses this whole dimension. He sees the satiric objectivity of *Ulysses*, but not the metaphysical construction of objectivity itself; Joyce's acceptance of inescapable mediation.

Joyce, Yeats, Mann and Proust all had a strong sense of aesthetic boundaries as defining the limits of their fictive worlds, while simultaneously understanding such fictive projection as the model of all human worlds. That is why their world projections may be understood as mythopoeic rather than as simply fictive or historical. But in Pound and Lawrence there is the frequent threat of a more literalistic elision of aesthetic boundaries. Rather than an overt aestheticism functioning as an image of world creation at large, the aesthetic understanding seems merely to be overridden, didactically, within the work. In major works of Lawrence and Pound, the prophetic or didactic motif repeatedly threatens to override aesthetic limits. Pound's image of the *periplum*, a map which follows the forward course of a journey, catches the ambivalence here. It is an admirably open-ended voyage of discovery, but one in which this voyager makes unbounded, literalistic claims to historical exemplarity and political application. Pound's catastrophic error lay in the Quixotic literalism of his claims as much as in their specific content, and it is not enough, therefore, just to winnow the poetic wheat from the fascistic chaff, for it is the spirit of the whole, the turning of a vision into a programme, which is in question. I am less concerned, therefore, with the internal complexity of the Poundian vision, admirably expounded by other critics, than with its overall imaginative status. This was the order of question Yeats had in mind when he defined *A Vision* as 'an aesthetic arrangement of experience . . . holding in a single thought reality and justice'. Pound's master narrative was not to be viewed in that way, but he needed to ask some equivalent question about the meaning and consequences of believing in it. The method of the *Cantos*, however, did not encourage this; indeed, it actually exacerbated his literalism.

The condensed allusions of the *Cantos* are a way of making the poetry active and educative. The method involves the reader in a process of exploration, of seeing new connections. As if in direct refutation of Nietzsche's 'walking encyclopaedia' trope, Pound picks up the most isolated items from cultural history and illuminates them within his master narrative of economic corruption and artistic decadence. There partly lies behind this his reading of the anthropologist Leo Frobenius who developed the term *Paideuma* to mean a cultural form by virtue of which any individual item, such as a jug or a form of speech, could be recognised as expressing that particular culture.[29] The paideuma was not myth, or ideology, nor a structuralist system, yet it was a way of seeing a whole culture in the light of a detail; what Pound called a 'luminous detail'.[30] For Pound, too, found nothing random in his diagnostic reading of cultural history. But paideuma was a term developed by Frobenius for the anthropological study of historical cultures, and it is not clear that it can be applied in reverse as a creative artistic principle. Leon Surette has pointed out that Pound adapted Frobenius' descriptive term as an evaluative one, and invested it with personal rather than public meaning; although it is worth noting that Frobenius saw the paideuma as a creative resource analogous to Eliot's tradition.[31] In effect, the fundamental technique of the *Cantos*, what Pound called the ideogrammic method, attempts to convert the paideuma into a way of actually creating and judging cultural meaning.

It is also worth recalling that Pound's ideogrammic method arose from his interest in the Chinese written characters. Following Ernest Fenellosa, Pound saw the Chinese written character as expressing ideas with an immediate wholeness, and visual directness, unknown in Western writing.[32] The real value of this to Pound was in providing a corroborative parallel for his thinking about poetic language in his imagist phase. It is sometimes objected that the value Pound saw in the Chinese character might not apply to native users for whom the signs would be merely conventional. Only under the Western eyes, perhaps, of Fenellosa and Pound did the Chinese character have such a quasi-literalistic power. But the origin of Pound's ideogrammic method involved either a tendency to read cultural signs in a literalistic way or attraction to a form that allowed this. His interest in the ideogram is interestingly contemporaneous with the early, one-for-one, picture theory of language in the *Tractatus* which Wittgenstein later abandoned. The *Cantos*, however, went on to develop the ideogrammic principle into an extended structural device concerned to express not just 'a complex of emotion in an instant of time' as in the imagist poem, but wide-ranging complexities of historical process.[33] Hence, historical figures, allusions and anecdotes, most notably from Renaissance Italy, post-independence America and Confucian China, are juxtaposed to exemplify the radical and pervasive damage done by private capitalism and the banking system, which separate profit from labour and make money breed. The overall vision and the local successes of the *Cantos* are such that few readers can follow them without acquiring a further education in doing so; and the ideogrammic compression is intrinsic to this. We have the sense of a mind grappling to create a map, or to establish the landmarks of an essential history behind the obfuscations of official or inherited versions. At the same time, the modernist spatialising suggested by the image of the voyager is problematic as a way of reading the processes of history. The individual vignettes of the *Cantos* have time and again an imagist concentration and power, but, as critics have repeatedly pointed out, they always depend on the master narrative. The poem has not so much an imagistic immediacy by-passing argument as a suppressed argument. We are given the outcome without the process of interpretation. You can, of course, go and do homework on it which will frequently prove instructive and persuasive, but the ideogram can only make sense in Pound's terms. The method of the *Cantos*, therefore, encouraged the dogmatic tendency in their author. In effect, it imposes a mythic overview upon history without acknowledging its own essentially mythopoeic status. So too, while Pound admires the great individuals of his historical narrative, their *virtu* is ideologically defined. Ideological critique tends to be outwardly directed rather than introspective since, even when the self is questioned, it is in the light of this objectified perception. And so Pound's ideological, rather than mythopoeic, conception is reflected in the poetic self of the speaker.

The Poundian self

The question of the self evidently underlay the growing mutual aversion of Pound and Lawrence. Lawrence came to see Pound as too given to external posturing, too conscious of his effect.[34] Pound, by contrast, seemed to be reacting to Lawrence's personal intensity, his confident possession of what T. S. Eliot, with withering intent, called the 'inner voice.'[35] Without taking Lawrence as an unproblematic yardstick, Pound's aversion is symptomatic. His early poetics of objectivity, like his social personality, seem partly a natural innocence of self-inspection. Daniel Pearlman has analysed Pound's antisemitism as the classic projection of a man who did not look into himself.[36] Yet this occlusion of self has a truly tragic structure, as well as stature, in that it is equally the basis of the impersonal spirit of his finest poetry; including such highly personal works as the Pisan *Cantos*. It also underlies the unique selflessness which made him an indefatigable midwife to the talents of others. In so far as his own true Penelope was the impersonal aesthetic of Flaubert, he echoed that great romantic *malgré lui* in becoming the true tragic hero of his own '*œuvre*.

Whereas Yeats, Joyce, Proust and Mann variously placed their autobiographical material under sometimes devious but always firm aesthetic control, in Lawrence and Pound the prophetic exigency constantly blurred the boundary. This is not in any simple way 'inartistic'. Their prophecy was not separable from their art and each took artistic risks such that even their failures are an important part of the whole. When Lawrence 'shed his sicknesses' in his work this was part of a self-righting introspection by which he could turn his own errors and confusions to account. But for much of his career Pound's strength lay in the opposite direction, and his rather slighting attitude to romanticism, as aired by Daniel Bornstein, is an index of this.[37] What Pound missed by his aversion from romanticism was its sustained and sophisticated introspection. He was oblivious to the complex, post-romantic metaphysic which Lawrence and Yeats variously absorbed. In *The Spirit of Romance* Pound refers dismissively to 'nature worship' with an evident intention of encompassing the whole subsequent tradition passing through Wordsworth.[38] He has an important point in seeing the idealised reification of 'Nature' as a symptom of modern alienation, and one applauds his revival of Provençal romance behind modern romanticism. None the less, his dismissive view of a later romanticism left him largely indifferent to, or unaware of, the post-romantic examination of the self and particularly as it constitutes the metaphysical condition of all experience; the chapter of European thought which has been absorbed into modernist mythopoeia. This contrasts with Thomas Mann, for example, whose deep implication in post-romantic German thought was the condition of the painful revision he achieved in *Doctor Faustus*. Mann's technique of historical montage is a close cousin of Pound's ideogrammic structure as he used the constructivism of modernist mythopoeia to deconstruct the evil myths spawned by, or at least laid at the door of, the same post-romantic tradition. Mann constructs his historical montage according to a theory of music and of the significance of music in German culture.[39] The sources from which he derived this theory intended it literally but the novel does not require this of the reader. The theory itself may be taken as an encompassing metaphor, and Mann was taken aback when Arnold Schoenberg was offended by his attributing the use of twelve-tone technique to the Faustian hero.[40] That does not apply to historical theory in the *Cantos*. Likewise, *Doctor Faustus* is autobiographical to the point of being confessional, but this aspect remains under firm and appropriate dramatic control with Mann's own potentialities split between the diabolically inspired hero, Leverkühn, and the humanist narrator, Zeitblom. Of course, Pound's personal voice was also highly controlled, but not always in a way that would lend itself to dramatic introspection or self criticism.

Pound's impact on the modernist generation was partly a confident loathing of the second-rate. But his clarity of critical vision was connected to a literalistic impatience and a dismissal of metaphysical self-consciousness. Other modernist writers saw the problem in Emerson's question 'Why should not we also enjoy an original relation to the universe?'[41] This central dilemma of modern thought was to be in itself a source of artistic inspiration and technique. Aesthetic mythopoeia was one way of negotiating it. Lawrence made the dilemma itself his central theme. Both strategies offer a prophylactic against the spirit of dogmatism. But Pound's peculiar strength was inseparable from his implicit denial of the problem; until it caught up with him, that is, and the confident declaration 'Le paradis n'est pas artificiel' (*Cantos* p. 438) acquired the after-thought 'l'enfer non plus' (*Cantos* p. 460). And hence, whereas some of his contemporaries transformed an earlier generation's aestheticism or romanticism into a subtly mythopoeic view of life, Pound kept a residual nineties aestheticism along with a political literalism. And, because the elements did not merge, they were subject to merely collapsing literalistically together. In that respect, Adorno's dualistic interpretation of the bound Odysseus is appropriate to Pound's case except that Pound is aesthetically unbound. Vital affirmations, such as the Usury cantos, jostle with highly specific historical claims. At such moments the poetry is dependent on a doctrine external to itself and its vision of human culture is then neither history nor poetry. As the poem wanders its historical *periplum* in search of its true home, it becomes evident that this might have been found in a stronger recognition of its own status as a modern myth. Such a solution was not acceptable to Pound, and yet, in the Pisan Cantos, like Eliot in the *Four Quartets*, he came remarkably, and unexpectedly, close to it.

'*Dove sta memoria?*'

If Pound's ideogrammic method is a version of modernist montage, the technique varies significantly from author to author. Mann's underlying model in *Doctor Faustus* is the scholarly lecture form juxtaposing spokesman characters giving synoptic, but reasoned, accounts of German cultural history. Joyce's typical spirit is parody, incorporating the past without being bound by it. Eliot's allusions, at least up to *The Waste Land*, are most commonly nostalgic traces often implying an absence of present power and vision. Pound's characteristic form is literary 'imitation', whereby the past is made usably contemporary. In Mann and Joyce the meaning of allusion tends to be more systematically worked out within the text, while in Eliot and Pound the allusion is usually more glancing, although the underlying vision may be just as systematic. They characteristically invoke isolated cultural touchstones carrying a self-evidently representative charge. I wish to dwell on the emotional dynamics of allusion in these two poets, since this level is often ignored when they are considered in terms of their public 'meaning' although much of the effect is of a more private emotional kind.

Two kinds of 'luminous detail' may be mistaken for each other. The detail may be revelatory of the paideuma or be an intrinsically trivial feature which happens to be invested with personal emotional memory in the way that Proust has classically defined. As far as their overt meaning is concerned, allusions to Dante, Homer and Cavalcanti, for example, in Pound and Eliot have the force of paideuma in that they provide public landmarks for an understanding of cultural history. But they also represent moments of private emotional recollection which gives them a potential ambiguity. Important processes of learning and recognition occur, for all of us, in purely private ways. Chance occasions, of no special significance in themselves, become triggers or foci for general understanding as we pick up, largely unconsciously, broader cultural structures. This is particularly the case in acquiring language which is not done simply by following grammatical rules so much as by imitating and adapting expressions heard in use, and especially so with the mother tongue acquired at an early and unreflecting stage of life. This is even more evident when assimilating a new language and culture at a mature age. A chance phrase may then linger in memory with a representative charge without having any intrinsic value; like the inane, but carefully constructed, phrases in a language primer. For the individual concerned this trivial expression can quite legitimately have the value of the paideuma. It may not be easy therefore to distinguish moments of genuinely public cultural perception from the more ordinary, purely personal, process of cultural acquisition. Meanwhile the personal, emotional associations of the individual may give a further, quite arbitrary, value to any detail which is what Proust explored in relation to words and names as well as to sensory experiences. Hence there may occur that slide from the neutral anthropological meaning of the paideuma to the evaluative which Surette points out in Pound. Eliot and Pound, as well-read cultural diagnosticians, coming to Europe with the cultured American's 'complex fate' of being at once an outsider and an inheritor, lived at an unusually high level of recognition in this regard. Their alertness to its paideuma allowed them to focus the inner being and historical formations of European culture. Indeed, the process was so self-aware as to become a poetic principle. But the very self-awareness carries its own dangers. The apparently objective meaning of the luminous detail as paideuma may rest on its Proustian value of a personal emotional memory.

Eliot's poetry always had an intuitive awareness of this Proustian dimension even when seeking to be most public. His allusions are typically felt as fading echoes, cultural traces disappearing as we strain to catch them, whereas Pound tends to transliterate the past into the present, to give it a renewed life. So too, the allusions in Eliot's early poetry are held together as personal associations objectified within the poem. This did not need to be a deliberate strategy on Eliot's part. Indeed, in *The Waste Land*, the reverse seems more likely to have been the case: that it was partly an intuitive subterfuge arising from Eliot's deep reserve about his private experience. The reader of *The Waste Land* feels its private associations the more vividly because of their very inexplicitness, because of the lurking sense that the whole poem is an unconfessed confession. The outcome is that the real force of Eliot's master narrative of emotional and cultural sterility is generated by the personal emotions of the poem rather than the other way round. When Eliot himself disowned the cultural significance that readers had insisted on attributing to his 'rhythmic grumblings', he was acknowledging, without quite revealing, the truth beneath the standard reading.[42] And perhaps he was right, as a poet, to preserve the mystery. For *The Waste Land* is a compelling poem in which much traditional commentary has re-enacted the emotional subterfuge of the poem itself; and thereby perhaps protected it; somewhat as years of grime unwittingly preserved many London buildings whose cleansing exposure threatened with decomposition. Pound's allusive technique in *Hugh Selwyn Mauberley* is almost diametrically opposed in its inner, emotional dynamic. While Eliot's title announces a public theme, its poetic life is highly personal: Pound's title focuses on an individual with autobiographical traits, but the poem does not have the evident emotional hinterland of Eliot's.[43] Although the relationship between Mauberley and Pound is highly elusive and ironic, the elusiveness is not just a matter of irony and self-critique. It is rather that personality as such is not really in question for Pound at all. In contrast to Eliot's confessed need to 'escape from personality', Pound seems to have seen himself as a public event in a way that made him able to use a partly autobiographical *persona* in a highly instrumental, dramatic spirit. For him, there is no straining after impersonality. Where Eliot's personality is revealed in his effort to disguise it, Pound's impersonality is revealed even in his self-reference. It simply serves the paideuma by being part of it. In *Mauberley* this is highly appropriate. In the *Cantos*, however, the personal voice is more problematic, and the preceding comments on affective memory have some bearing on why this is so.

Minds of the calibre of Eliot and Pound, exercising at all times a highly original and penetrating cultural perception, are especially liable to slippage between the two significances of paideuma and personal emotional memory, and this repeatedly happens in the *Cantos*. Pound's use of the Iñez da Castro story, in canto xxx, is a case in point. This concerns the waiting woman who had secretly married the crown prince Pedro of Portugal and was stabbed as she went with him to beg pardon from the king. When the prince succeeded to the throne he exhumed her body and made the courtiers kiss her hand. One could find in this anecdote an extreme morbidity, or a gesture of romantic defiance, or both. Pound seems to have the former aspect principally in mind, but this is not necessarily evident without our knowing it independently. Pound commented on Camoens' use of this episode in the *Lusiads*.[44] He saw a difficulty for Camoens in making artistic use of an event which 'life' had already made so completely articulate. Although he has an artistic point here, his remark suggests a certain literalism as if the event could somehow speak, uninterpreted, for itself. The *extremity* of the event may be hard to contain aesthetically, but its *meaning* is open. Yet in his own use of this episode in the *Cantos*, it is the meaning that Pound seems to take for granted.

Yet precisely this aspect of the poem was to become the condition for an unexpected development of the *Cantos*. When Pound defined epic as 'a poem including history', his phrasing implied a generic dualism.[45]

Rather than the merging of history and art argued in Nietzsche, and enacted in Yeats and Joyce, Pound sees them as distinct categories within the text. The poem is not identical with history as in the mythopoeic conception. But history, which was meant to be contained within the poem, was itself to enfold the *Cantos* in an unforeseen sense which enforced on them a mythopoeic dissolution of categories. Pound in the 1940s, like Pablo Neruda in the sixties, was driven in upon himself to review the whole political commitment on which his most ambitious poetic project was based. Neruda's response has been recognised as having a Proustian aspect, and the same essentially applies to Pound too.[46] The sixty-year-old Pound, in as opposite a situation as could well be imagined from the 'sixty-year-old, smiling public man', of Yeats' 'Among School Children', none the less experienced a comparable reversal which, like Yeats', took its meaning from his former artistic quest. We could not truly understand it without the rest of the '*œuvre*. Imprisoned in the cage at Pisa after the war, Pound had not only to review his past, but was heavily dependent on memory to do so. A man whose achievements had largely depended on his not being by nature introspective was forced to undergo a radical and sustained self-examination, using as his materials the former self which had been projected for so long within, if not as, his own artistic creation.

The Pisan *Cantos* are widely recognised to be among Pound's most important poetic achievements and a general case for them is not argued here. I wish only to consider their relation to Pound's remembered past as invoked by themes from the earlier cantos. In effect, the luminous details are the focus for an ambiguous conflict between the outwardness of the paideuma and the inwardness of Proustian memory. Proust's *A la Recherche* is the story of an emotional and artistic quest in which the narrator finally discovers his paradisal state only when the consciously willed search has proved abortive. He discovers that the desired experience lay always to hand but was actively obscured by the very deliberateness with which it had been pursued. Yet the long and misapplied search was not really lost time, either for him or for the reader, for when he finally encounters the paradisal state it is with a peculiar dependence on earlier moments; while the self-conscious nature of his earlier quest means that the reader too, by knowing the earlier volumes, is able to share the experience.

Pound's entry into memory is very different. Where Proust emphasised the triviality and arbitrariness of the emotional trigger, Pound suffered a catastrophic and highly relevant external shock. He is more like Lear on the heath suddenly exposed to 'feel what wretches feel' and aware that he had 'ta'en to little care of this'. And so Pound tries to put his world together with his old objectivity, yet, when he sees the telephone wires, with birds like notes on a stave of music, this catches a new note in his relation to the external world (*Cantos* pp. 485–7). His meaning is now aware of being highly personal and internal to the point of fragility. The outer world reflects the inner and is indeed the only way of achieving an inner order and security. Where Pound once praised Joyce for his treatment of 'subjective matters' in an objective spirit, he now subjectivises the external as a way of handling his own inner life. In the deeper European ancestry of Proust there lies what, in the English context, we may think of as the Wordsworthian paradigm. Far from being 'nature worship', it is a profound form of self-awareness, particularly for a disturbed psyche. It does not just use the external world as an internal symbolism, it relieves the burden of the enclosed or disintegrating self by experiencing it as part of that external life. Pound has rediscovered the Wordsworth of 'that uncertain heaven / Received into the bosom of the steady lake.'[47] Or nearly so, for it is still very much in his own terms, just as the birds sit on the linear clarity of man-made wires, and are translated into the cultural, indeed the graphic, image of the musical stave.

Since the Pisan Cantos are concerned with memory, and dramatically speaking are created through memory, it is fitting that one of Pound's remembered resources should be Cavalcanti's poem 'Donna mi prega' with its theme of memory in the phrase 'dove sta memoria' or 'where memory liveth'. This phrase was a leitmotiv in earlier cantos where it retained the impact of an external cultural allusion, the value of the paideuma. The relation between Pound's canto xxxvi, which is a near translation of Cavalacanti, and the original has been luminously discussed by Peter Makin.[48] In making it so much his own, Pound preserved a tension between the original and its new inflection. It still importantly belonged, that is to say, to Cavalcanti even while being co-opted by Pound. But when the single phrase comes back in the Pisan Cantos, it has suffered a sea-change. The phrase 'dove sta memoria', which had been repeated with the value of a mantra, needs only a shift in intonation to become an interrogative. Where indeed does memory live? Proust had meditated on precisely this question and decided that it truly lives not in the analytic and voluntary consciousness, which is Pound's habitual and continuing resource, but in the involuntary welling up of affective memory which Yeats tapped in 'Among School-Children'. This is the poignant new potentiality with which the phrase now returns,

recalling not so much Cavalcanti himself as Pound's earlier, self-confident use of him. If Pound had used the Cavalcanti allusion for the first
time in the Pisan situation, its impact would be significantly different.
The two-stage process of recalling his own earlier usage allows the
phrase, like Vinteuil's musical phrase in Proust, to become a formula for
Pound's present experience without being fully explicable in terms of
either present or past alone.

Yet Pound does not ask the Proustian question; he stays in the mode of
affirmation. Whereas Yeats' 'Among School Children' is a dramatically
controlled enactment of another sixty-year-old's experience of an over-
whelming recognition occurring through his submission, after initial
resistance, to a Proustian emotional memory, this is the possibility that
Pound seems both to need and, just as rightly perhaps in his case, to
resist. The inner drama of the Pisan Cantos is their fragile negotiation
between two possibilities, since the speaker needs to recognise past error
and yet cannot afford, for several reasons, to let himself go on a tide of
feeling. There is no coming to terms with the past except through his self
and yet this self, as has been seen, is not an introspective one. In fact it
may be thought of as an essentially pre-modern one, of a kind antedating
the development of modern individuality as described, say, in Charles
Taylor's *Sources of the Self*.[49] Peter Nicholls has remarked how little Pound
actually concedes politically in relation to his years of fascist support, and
this perhaps reflects an underlying psychological truth of Poundian
identity itself.[50] Pound needed most of all to survive as a self, but he had
always conceived of his self, in keeping with his earlier poetic sense of his
own personality, in the pre-modern style of, say, Villon, whom he had
quoted in 'Mauberley', or of the Provençal poets. Villon typically speaks
of himself as if he were simply a given fact of life among others, with an
impersonality quite in keeping with his being able to write a poem made
up entirely of proverbs. Or, when he was imprisoned, like Pound,
expecting a death penalty, he imagined his body, quite unsentimentally,
as an object for others on the gibbet. Pound, indeed, had set Villon's
Testament to music.[51] Villon is an accumulation of experience rather than
an arena of personal consciousness, and his character is no more up for
ethical discussion than a rock might be. Just as 'Mauberley' was concerned with 'l'élection de son sépulchre' and with one who 'passed from
men's memory in *l'an trentuniesme / De son eage*', so in the Pisan Cantos
Pound, now twice that age, is still concerned with the public memory he
will leave. If this is not self-serving it is partly because of the pre-modern
mode of self which he maintains.

Pound maintains this self while needing to assimilate a modern, post-Rousseau introspection which would threaten it. His encounter with the goddess in canto LXXXI negotiates these two necessities at the moment of greatest introspection. Being a felt presence rather than a clearly embodied appearance, she is ambiguously separate from him and yet a manifestation of his emotional condition:

> There came a new subtlety of eyes into my tent,
> Whether of spirit or hypostasis,   (*Cantos* p. 528)

Her eyes are not those of a separate self such as Dr Fergusson plunges into in Lawrence's story; nor such as Yeats saw staring at him 'in momentary wonder'. The 'goddess' first addresses him with the supportive emotional knowledge he needs, 'What thou lovest well shall not be reft from thee' (*Cantos* p. 521), after which her voice goes on increasingly to merge with his own as he faces his past: 'Pull down thy vanity / How mean thy hates / Fostered in vanity' (*Cantos* p. 521). The female figure here, instead of the confidently outward-directed allegory of Usura, is an inner voice which has to be externalised to be heard at all. The emotional impulsion, not quite acknowledged as an aspect of the self, is refracted through a figure who yet clearly arises from within as an effect of his extreme condition, and whose voice then merges with his. As he goes on to accuse himself, it is still half under this protective device. And much of the struggle is sub-textual, enacted more in the imagery and dramatisation than in what is directly said, although the latter is part of it too, like a melody against a bass. Indeed, throughout the canto, and the ones into which it leads, there is a ground bass, or chthonic base, in the continual interplay between the elements of firmness, imaged largely as stone, and of fluidity. This metaphoric complex runs through Pound's work, but here it acquires a special poignancy, as if its meaning, as a deep-lying formation, were at last being revealed. Earlier, in canto LXXX, tears were referred to in French:

> Les larmes que j'ai creées m'inondent.
> Tard, trés tard, je t'ai connue, la Tristesse,
> I have been hard as youth these sixty years.   (*Cantos* p. 513)

Now tears, still distanced in the Greek form DAKRUON, are the inner principle of fluidity to which he must yield, while stone, often in sculpted form, provides the hardness to contain or resist it. And so the various lines 'Gemisto stemmed all from Neptune / hence the Rimini bas reliefs' (p. 528), 'why not Dei Miracoli / mermaids that carving' (p. 529), 'the sage / delighteth in water / the humane man has amity with hills' (p.

529), 'panta rei' (p. 529), 'he was standing below the altars / of the spirits of rain' (p. 529), 'green pool, under green of the jungle / caged' (p. 530) are all followed by the memory of Yeats giving himself to the flow of creation like the contained yet natural noise of 'the wind in the chimney' (p. 533) to produce 'aere perennius' (p. 534) in 'Stone Cottage' (p. 534). The imagery recalls Wordsworth's 'steady lake', except that here the conflict between the elements remains both unresolved and sub-textual.

At the end of canto LXXXII the speaker gives himself to the earth as bride, mother and grave:

> Fluid ΧΘΟΝΙΟΣ o'erflowed me
>   lay in the fluid ΧΘΟΝΙΟΣ;
>   that lie
> under the air's solidity
>   drunk with the ΙΧΩΡ of ΧΘΟΝΙΟΣ
>   fluid ΧΘΟΝΙΟΣ, strong as the undertow
>   of the wave receding.
> but that a man should live in that further terror, and live
>   the loneliness of death came upon me
>   (at 3 P. M., for an instant)   (*Cantos* p. 526)

'Undertow' suggests the danger for him of this chthonic dissolution which is yet the condition of new birth, and the reference to 3 P. M. sculpts that fleeting moment of emotional time into an objective chronological order, like a reverse gravestone 'that', in an earlier phrase, 'has carved the trace in the mind / dove sta memoria' (*Cantos* p. 457). Even now, to echo another phrase from earlier in the sequence, it is as if he would say 'remember that I have remembered' (*Cantos* p. 506). Once again, he seeks no Proustian nostalgia so much as present survival and an example for the future. In the next canto the female chthonic principle returns in the form of the wasp. It is initially 'Brother Wasp', almost as from the folk world of Uncle Remus and echoing the brotherhood of other prisoners, some of whom are black. Yet the initial maleness only sets off the transposition into the female 'La vespa, *la* vespa, mud, swallow system' (*Cantos* p. 532). She creates a womblike container of earth mixed with water which becomes hardened and systematic. It is like a swallow's nest, but the word 'swallow' also continues the liquid emotional associations, just as the name of 'Mr Walls' a few lines later picks up the image of stone and containment.

The power of the Pisan Cantos lies in their restraint; in what they do not say. But they also enact dramatically and subliminally the inner need for this restraint, so that what is not said is the more felt. Maybe that is why more penitence has sometimes been read into them. The unexpected change of circumstances caused Pound to enter the hell and purgatory of the Pisan captivity after the earlier literary evocations of these states. He now saw paradise as 'spezzato', or 'in fragments', as 'the smell of mint', and, despite his resistance to affective memory, he experienced ethical relations with a transcendent simplicity reminiscent of Lear or of Proust's Marcel (*Cantos* p. 438). Simple acts of kindness, hardly noticed by the persons concerned, became not the luminous details of a cultural paideuma so much as the luminous centre of a human world. Exposed to inner as well as outer dissolution, he had to sustain his identity while relinquishing ego. His transcendence of ego in this sequence was a way of sustaining a self within a world, and it brought him close to the spirit of modernist mythopoeia as defined by some of his great contemporaries.

CHAPTER 4

The politics of modernist mythopoeia

JOSEPH CONRAD AND THE 'AFRICA' WITHIN

By the latter half of the twentieth century the very idea of myth had become irremediably tainted through its co-option by fascism. Despite the hopeful efforts of Thomas Mann and Karl Kerenyi to keep myth as a humanistic resource, the political conservatism of several modern writers, including Pound's commitment to Mussolini, gave a strong colour of conviction to the view that this association was an intrinsic one.[1] The sentimental literary acquiescence in the mythic by much Anglo-American academic criticism, or the covertly religious system building of Northrop Frye, only reinforced this interpretation, while Adorno and Horkheimer's *Dialectic of Enlightenment* provided a classic left analysis supporting such a view; although the inner structure of their argument actually leaves itself open to other evaluations, in so far as they present myth not just as a primitive power to be escaped but as an inner and inescapable correlative of Enlightenment itself. From this stand-point it might be more productive to recognise myth as a power to be lived with; and to be understood critically from within. That is one of the strong implications of the modernist writers discussed so far, and it is a more than theoretical possibility, for although the *idea* of myth, particularly in leftish critique, has now acquired almost invariably a reductively negative slant, a great deal of the *literature* of the latter part of the century has been conducting a nuanced and critical participation in the mythic. The positive significance of myth as embodied in modernism does live on, but is largely unrecognised both in its meaning and in its ancestry. Since the significant shift in the latter part of the century, which is to be discussed in the next section of this study, has been from the *metaphysical* to the *political* aspect of myth, it is worth reconsidering the moment from which this later literature descends, and to see how the specifically political implications of the earlier period have been retrospectively distorted.

The work of Edward Said has been the most influential example of this misappreciation. Said has articulated a post-colonial recognition of the Eurocentrism of the colonial period at all levels of culture. His broad project is a political and cultural necessity of the late twentieth century, but his reading of Conrad, and of modernism, is seriously blinkered. The term 'Eurocentric', when used polemically, is problematic in itself since it combines the meaning of a damaging myopia with that of a legitimate and inevitable point of view. What else could Europeans be? The point is not merely 'semantic': it touches the heart of Said's project from *Orientalism* onwards. In *Culture and Imperialism*, after an extended critique of Conrad's *Heart of Darkness*, he has a brief, slightly grudging, note on modernism as the period when writers were partly forced to acknowledge non-European cultures.[2] But in following Conrad up the Congo, Said partly muddies the waters. A more inward understanding of modernism would make it possible to appreciate the significance of *Heart of Darkness*. Rather than modernism being reluctantly disturbed by an incipient late-colonial conscience, although that is part of it, modernism was itself the means for a diagnostic understanding of the colonial mentality. With respect to this period, T. S. Eliot's principle applies: that we know better than our forebears because they are part of what we know.[3] We see better by standing on their shoulders, and we may understand our own position better if we do not suppress its history. Accordingly, the present purpose is to place *Heart of Darkness* in its relevant modern context rather than offer yet another reading of the work.

In the early decades of the twentieth century, some of the most significant European writers, stimulated partly by the fact of colonialism, and partly by the internal crisis of their own civilisation, conducted an important self-examination for which the techniques of modernism were a crucial means. The widespread interest in 'primitive' cultures and artefacts was an important aspect of this, but the significance lies in the reception; in how these elements were internalised in the European psyche. As has been said earlier, there was a rebound by which the otherness of primitive cultures was reflected back, or internalised, as a self-recognition. It is, therefore, necessary to appreciate how the motif of the 'foreign' was absorbed into the psychic and projective configurations of modernist mythopoeia so that a critical, rather than a delusive, internalising could occur. Nietzsche's image of the mobile horizon was not emptily relativistic, because it enforced a critical recognition of what it means to inhabit a constructed world. It entails responsibility not just

at the level of moral agency, but in sustaining the whole world of values
in which the ethical is lived. Of course, there remains an evident and
irremovable danger of self-enclosure, and particularly so when encountering anything radically other, but the consciously mythopoeic recognition provides the inward and homeopathic insight needed to appreciate
this truth. It is only paradoxical till you start to think about it that a true
recognition of the other should, in the first instance, be a recognition of
the 'other' within. The *meaning* of the other as 'other' is necessarily
internal. Much post-colonial critique, although it may be a cultural
necessity of our time, is the unwitting inheritor, rather than the dis-
coverer, of this process.

The force of this point for the modernist relation to colonialism can
be seen by briefly comparing the typical use of the foreign or foreigner
in Victorian writers such as Charlotte Bronte in *Villette* (1843), Dickens
in *Little Dorritt* (1857) and George Eliot in *Middlemarch* (1872). Each
used the foreign to highlight English provincialism, but with the ultimate effect of affirming the normative nature of the home culture. The
foreign viewpoint was for them satellitic. It provided a temporary
standpoint outside the normal world of author and reader but not as an
independent, equal planet. In the modernist generation, by contrast,
the foreigner typically came to be more radically internalised as part of
a new relation to the other and to the self. Since, as was remarked
earlier, D. H. Lawrence and Thomas Mann are diametrically opposed
in their outlook and techniques, their common exemplification of the
point is especially illuminating. Their differences highlight the common ground.

When Lawrence's initially projected novel, first entitled *The Sisters*,
and then *The Wedding Ring*, became the two novels *The Rainbow* and
Women in Love, he differentiated sharply between them adopting, for the
pre-modern part of his story, a nineteenth-century historical form and,
for the second, a spatialised modernist structure. The treatment of the
foreign element in each case changes in keeping with this difference in
the form of life. The Brangwen family of *The Rainbow* are yeoman
farmers from the English midlands, but in the first generation of the story
Tom Brangwen marries a 'Polish lady'.[4] Although Lydia Lensky's
foreignness occasions a mixture of attraction and fear in Tom, which is
crucial to the dynamic of the relationship, it is not ultimately significant
in itself. It is rather Lawrence's naturalistic means of highlighting what
for him is the vital truth of all human relationships: that another person
never can, or should, be fully known. As opposed to the romantic ideal of

twin or merged souls, Lawrence saw the the body as a locus of irreducible otherness. The 'arch' symbolism of the book likewise focuses his sense of how the strength of a relationship depends on the separateness of the two points at which it rests upon the ground. Another person must not be possessed emotionally, and therefore cannot be possessed mentally either. Hence it is finally said of Tom with regard to Lydia that 'He did not know her any better, any more precisely, now that he knew her altogether'.[5] But the felt need for mental and emotional possession is often in compensation for an inner emptiness, and in the novel's dialectic of rootedness and change, as modern individuality struggles to transcend inherited emotional forms, it is once again a half-Polish character, Ursula's soldier lover Anton Skrebensky, who embodies the fall into empty individualism. His foreignness, as opposed to Lydia's, now echoes the cosmopolitan vacuity of Ursula's Uncle Tom, the colliery manager, and points forward to the possessive willpower of Gerald Crich, the militaristic, German-educated, mine owner of *Women in Love*. Foreignness in *The Rainbow*, in other words, is a shifting value, yet it has always an internal, psychological meaning within a local English world. At the same time, while the foreign is now highly internalised as a psychological value when compared with its typical Victorian usage, its meaning still depends on its indeed being foreign.

In *Women in Love* the foreign theme is more radically internalised again; just as it is in *The Magic Mountain* to be published four years later. I have already indicated that both books create a psychic map of Europe: Mann's guests in the Davos sanatorium extend from Russians to Americans with the Germans in the middle, while Lawrence projects a range of psychic possibility extending from the Nordic abstraction associated with Gerald Crich down to the African statuette in which Rupert Birkin sees a culture of pure sensuality. In each case this symbolic map defines a possible equilibrium and wholeness within the individual psyche. Lawrence's version, of course, is the more radically internalised of the two. In the 'Snow' chapter of *The Magic Mountain*, for example, Hans Castorp has a vision of barbaric horror lying at the heart of a Mediterranean paradise. Mann's implication is that this is a permanent truth of the psyche which must be acknowledged. Lawrence, by contrast, was not only more sympathetic to the instinctual and unconscious realms, he saw their meaning as highly relational; they take their value from the way they are perceived. For him, the supposed 'instinct' to violence and power, or the lapse into barbarism, comes not from some generalised realm of unmediated instinct, but from the specific habits of repression.

So Gerald Crich, for example, sees the instinctual life as aggressive and dangerous because his own life is held so completely within the grip of his personal will. His fear of himself is what makes him dangerous. Hence the novel consists of a number of episodes in which the subconscious states of the characters unwittingly project their quite different 'realities'. In Gerald's case it is a murderous, and ultimately self-destructive, one. He projects, or creates, the world by which he is destroyed. Rather than changing through experience, he assimilates everything to his own *a priori* projection. He cannot experience the other as other at all. Hence the importance of spatial form and a symbolic geography in *Women in Love* as opposed to the historical and developmental process highlighted in *The Rainbow*. But it is noteworthy that, as the whole map of Europe becomes the model for a single psyche, so the purview of the geographical symbolism reaches out to encompass Africa, and thereby raises the question of the 'primitive' within this model of psychic wholeness. It is a complex story which has to be understood in its inward, or psychic, dimension.

The internal, and therefore relational, value of the unconscious and instinctual realms for Lawrence is made particularly evident in the early chapter 'Fetish', set in an artist's flat in London, where there is an African statuette of a woman in labour. The characters react differently to the carving. Gerald finds it repulsive, while the artistic circle find it exotic. Being himself the most substantive example of modern primitivism, Lawrence detected the primitivist fashion, in much early twentieth-century art and thought, as a decadent symptom. Loerke, as the proto-typical modern artist, appreciates South Pacific and Mexican masks in a spirit of formalist exoticism. Birkin, on the other hand, sees in the artistic concentration of the African statuette an extremity of experience which is alien to him, but which suggests inner possibilities crucial to his self-understanding. What he understands as the pure sensuality of the statuette completes the meaning of the Nordic mental reduction by being its opposite extreme. It is both an aesthetic counterpart to Loerke's art of willed abstraction and the psychological opposite to Gerald's will power exerted in the social and personal realms.

Far from seeing the African merely as a superseded form, Lawrence is in effect comparing the decline of the great, still only recently discovered, African culture of Benin with the possibly impending, inner dissolution of contemporary Europe. Africa figures the European future and an earlier title of *Women in Love* had been *Dies Irae*. How literally this apocalypticism is to be taken is not really to the point. The novel is visionary as well as historical. What matters for him in this is that the Nordic and the African are opposite poles of cultural and psychological reduction which, in their extremity, prove to be similar; mirror images of each other. The statuette is, therefore, a term in a deeply internal process. Modernist universalism treats the African past as a potentiality of the European present, and the essential concern throughout is with the meaning of the statuette within a white consciousness rather than within its own culture; although, of course, its Africanness remains a vital term in its European meaning.

In *Women in Love,* as throughout his works, Lawrence explores the possible meanings of 'primitive' cultures for his own. But to see how his internalising of the primitive provides a fruitful model for understanding Conrad's use of the colonial 'other' the best example is the episode in *The Rainbow* where Anton Skrebensky speaks of Africa on his return from colonial service. Although Ursula has long come to recognise his personal hollowness, she is momentarily aroused by him here. Apart from a touch of vicarious perversity and exoticism in herself, the attraction lies in a momentary intimacy which he offers only because he is unaware that Africa has aroused a repressed aspect of himself. Its unconscious significance for him is evident in his mixture of fascination and horror.

Then in a low vibrating voice he told her about Africa, the strange darkness, the strange, blood fear. 'I am not afraid of the darkness in England', he said. 'It is soft, and natural to me, it is my medium, especially when you are here. But in Africa it seems massive and fluid with terror – not fear of anything – just fear. One breathes it, like a smell of blood. The blacks know it. They worship it, really, the darkness. One almost likes it – the fear – something sensual.'

She thrilled again to him. He was to her a voice out of the darkness. He talked to her all the while, in low soft tones, about Africa, conveying something strange and sensual to her; the negro, with his soft loose passion that could envelope one like a bath.[6]

Skrebensky is fascinated because this 'Africa' is his own repressed self: equally, he is horrified because it is the self he must deny. Only as it is projected onto Africa can this unconscious and self-fulfilling structure come into expression at all, albeit still under the sign of denial. This is a remarkable diagnostic dramatisation of the inner structure of a colonial exoticism as the return of the repressed, yet I have never seen it referred to in the now vast body of commentary on the post-colonial theme. Is there another repression going on? Of course, Skrebensky himself gains no insight into its meaning and after his break-up with Ursula he goes off to colonial service in India. This 'Africa' is entirely the white man's internalised Africa, and the scene is appropriately set, to use George Eliot's phrase, in the heart of England.

A closely related point has to be made about *Heart of Darkness*, although Conrad, who was writing before the turn of the century, did not have Lawrence's insight into this psychic structure. If Skrebensky, when reduced to 'a voice out of the darkness', is reminiscent of Kurtz, this only highlights the essential differences, including the fact that Kurtz never faces *his* fiancée; and nor do Marlow or Conrad do so on his behalf. Conrad was still inside the colonial order as Lawrence was not, which is why his partial recognition of its evil and emptiness is so tortured and mystified. There is no Lawrencean exposure in Conrad, only a first peering into the horror. But Conrad had crucially recognised that the horror is in the heart of Europe, in Brussels not Africa. His displacement of the evil contradictions on to Belgium is part of the indirection. No doubt loyalty to his adopted country led him to see Britain as still representing the civilising 'idea' which alone could justify the colonial venture.[7] But this was also the condition under which his critical insight could be expressed at all. Conrad took the crucial step of internalising the question which is why his book has been able to tell a truer story than he perhaps bargained for, and which only a post-colonial world can fully appreciate.

Conrad's Africa is still, of course, exotically conceived, and his understanding governed by contemporary stereotypes. Although the darkness is European, Africa is presented within the understandings of Conrad's day including the brooding jungle, the magnificent black woman and cannibalism. His admiration for the African crew's restraint, as opposed to the European lack of it, is predicated on a 'Freudian' assumption of necessary control, just as Freud's interest in primitive cultures provided him with a model for relating to the instinctual realm. It may be that if Conrad had been able to write a novel about the real Africa, as well as the 'Africa' within, it might have been a greater work, but properly to appreciate Conrad's achievement is to see both the unlikelihood of such a recognition in his day and Conrad's contribution to making this recognition possible, indeed banal, for us. The point can be put more strongly: a novel about the real Africa might well not have had the intense concentration on its inner theme which Conrad achieved. The light had first to be directed inwards. The process by which a European culture comes to a self-understanding in relation to colonialism is necessarily an internal and tortuous one, although once one awakes from such dreams their elements of emptiness, absurdity and cruelty are, in a double sense, blindingly obvious. *Heart of Darkness* is not essentially a novel about Africa, any more than *A Passage to India* is about India. These countries are necessary terms, but they are not really the point.

The critical difficulty is that these books necessarily face in two directions. Although their essential meaning is intra-European, their construction of their colonial backdrops will almost inevitably arouse the distaste of present-day readers; and especially those from the cultures in question who have not asked for their countries to be used as moral gymnasia for Europeans. Chinua Achebe's attack on *Heart of Darkness* is, therefore, an honourable and entirely pertinent human document, while remaining for all that an inadequate response to the novel.[8] Of course, these books are racist because they are stirrings of critical consciousness within a racist culture. If they were not documents of that culture they would not need to have been written in the first place. So too, Achebe is himself an inheritor of the critique Conrad helped to initiate, and speaks from the broader standpoint of progressive Enlightenment developed within the European tradition; if his standpoint were merely Africanist it would undercut itself. But my present concern is with the nature of this critical consciousness in the modernist decades. The slowly-dawning recognition that the colonial or primitive 'other' is a function of the European psyche is enabled by the awareness that, for the European, so is everything else. After the partial perception of this in *Heart of Darkness*, it is in the teens of the century that the recognition becomes clear, and quite evidently as part of the broader modernist awareness of world projection. This is abundantly, almost programmatically, clear in the case of Skrebensky where the colonial and primitivist themes are subordinate to the larger mythopoeic process of world projection in Lawrence's analysis of modernity. In *The Rainbow*, conceived as it were backwards from *Women in Love*, Lawrence is only *adopting* the form of the nineteenth-century historical novel. Internally to the narrative he understands the relativity of its competing world views. The novel's combination of biblical and Darwinian myths of origin puts the whole narrative under the sign of mythopoeic relativity. His understanding of the inner process behind Skrebensky's 'Africa' is inseparable from this broader conception. Indeed, Lawrence's diagnosis of colonial exoticism is a by-product of his quite specific analysis of modernity as the imposing of a world view.

Once again, *Ulysses* provides the classic instance for this theme. Composed largely during and in the wake of the Great War, Joyce's novel has a manifest distaste for tribalistic nationalism. The 'Cyclops' episode is the most direct thematising of this, and even here the violence is largely deflected by mock heroic humour. In the run-up to an anti-semitic attack Bloom is asked 'What is your nation?' to which he replies, simply and complexly, 'Ireland. I was born here', while the preceding conversation has mocked the possibility of definition.[9] Despite the abundance and quality of published discussion on the question of nationalism, particularly in the last twenty years, it is not evident that the matter has been significantly advanced beyond Bloom's naive yet pithy formulation.[10] 'Nation' is one more of those terms whose mixture of potency and unreality Joyce exposes, and, once again, mythopoeic consciousness provides the underlying condition for this perception. Bloom's parallels with Shakespeare and Odysseus, the frequent use of his outsider's perceptions as the effective narrative standpoint, and above all the conscious play of discourses throughout the book, all underlie this destabilising of nationality as an intuitive or essentialist mode of identity. National identity is still powerfully there, of course, but is placed firmly under the sign of myth. Once again, as with Lawrence, the specifically political theme is governed by the prior, and more general, question of constructing any human world.

Although *The Rainbow* and *Ulysses*, both conceived in the early teens of the century, raise critical questions about empire, both are set within the British Isles; and a full account of their views on nationhood would have to include the dimension of social class. But Conrad, as well as his more patrician background, gave hostages to fortune in setting *Heart of Darkness* in Africa; and the subsequent, largely delayed controversy over the book expresses the new world awareness that was to grow up. *A Passage to India* (1924), although it is set in India, has escaped such bitter criticism for a variety of reasons, including the fact that it is an explicitly metaphysical work placing in open-ended relativistic conjunction the Christian, Muslim and Hindu world views. It belongs more fully and overtly, though also more two-dimensionally, to the mythopoeic recognition, the clash of world views, at the centre of modernism. Yet the use of a real India creates some of the unease aroused by the Africa of *Heart of Darkness*, and this may be partly because a new awareness was already pressing upon it. The internal drama of European self critique could only last so long before becoming evidently Eurocentric in the damaging sense. Increasingly, it would become necessary to write about the real India or Africa, as well as the symbolic country within, and the change of consciousness can be seen, in retrospect, to have occurred at a brisk pace.

Lawrence's *The Plumed Serpent* (1926), coming a little later again, reveals this change more urgently than does *A Passage to India*. One reason for the imaginative disaster of the book is that, in attempting more seriously and radically to escape the white Western world, it only imposes its symbolic project the more violently upon the contemporary historical reality of post-revolutionary Mexico. Instead of the coherently syncretic symbolism of a fable like 'The Woman Who Rode Away', Lawrence wanted, and in a sense needed, to root his utopian project within a contemporary reality. Hence there remains a fundamental formal uncertainty as to how far the novel is realistic or is to be taken as a utopian thought experiment, and this uncertainty is located in the meaning of Lawrence's 'Mexico'. The man who had so brilliantly understood Skrebensky is himself drawn, for opposite reasons, into a structurally similar projection onto the other. For Lawrence is now assuming the radical inferiority or decadence of the Western world, and furthermore is seeing that much of the psychic disorder and violence of Mexico is precisely the result of its colonial past which has left it with a double cultural disinheritance. It has lost its old culture without gaining a new one. But the fact that Lawrence's 'Mexico' is so clearly imposed on the real Mexico is not just a matter of Lawrence's internal evolution, it is also the sign of a generally changing consciousness. By 1930, the period of high modernism, to which a universalist mythopoeia was central, was giving way to more political, and relativistic, emphases.

The Plumed Serpent was a dead-end for Lawrence, as he himself soon recognised. Much of the time it was an unwitting parody of his truly mythopoeic perception. He repudiated its 'leadership' ideal, particularly when he saw the rise of the fascists in Italy.[11] And he always recognised that 'we cannot return to the primitive, to live in tepees and hunt with bows and arrows'.[12] Yet the book represents a growing point, if not for Lawrence himself, then for subsequent fiction. It expresses the point at which modernist universalism is no longer able to hold together a European psychic action and the reality of non-European culture in a mythopoeic synthesis. And, of course, once this recognition is there it acts retrospectively; you then realise that you never really could do so. When George Gissing expressed his irritated admiration at Dickens for having written great summative and ethical fiction of a kind that was not possible by Gissing's own time, his irritation included the recognition that Dickens could not have got away with it either if he had known what Gissing, in his generation, now knew.[13] That is how the late twentieth century stands in relation to Conrad who, like most of those who exercise critical consciousness at any time, was wise within his generation. But

Lawrence, who pushed so consciously and radically against the forms of his own historical culture, reveals the dilemma which was to have important consequences for a newly relativistic understanding of culture and for the development of appropriate fictional forms. Carlos Fuentes' 'Quetzalcoatl' novel *Change of Skin* (1967), for example, is different in literary kind as well as in cultural outlook from *The Plumed Serpent*. It is not accidental that Latin American fiction should, by the latter part of the century, have provided some of the most fruitful forms of post-modern mythopoeia, and is also the area of the world which, by virtue of its mixed heritage, largely eludes the analyses of Said, which are more appropriate to classic situations of colonial domination whereby the cultures in question have remained distinct. As a way of considering the gradual break up of the modernist synthesis by the end of the 1920s and its relation to post-colonial cultural relativity, we may usefully join Thomas Mann on his first journey to America, as he reread the Hispanic classic *Don Quixote*, and meditated on his own mythopoeic novel sequence set in Africa: *Joseph and his Brothers*.

PART III

CHAPTER 5

The break-up of modernist mythopoeia

NOVEL, STORY AND THE FOREIGN: THOMAS MANN,
CERVANTES AND PRIMO LEVI

Thomas Mann's 'mythic phase' was a self-conscious development start-
ing in the late nineteen twenties, with the Joseph novels, and covering the
rest of his career encompassing *Doctor Faustus*. If the Owl of Minerva flies
at dusk, Mann's self-consciousness about the mythic makes him an
excellent lens through which to consider both modernism and the period
of its break-up. The historical, formal and thematic aspects involved can
be approached in the sidelong fashion adopted by Mann himself in an
apparently casual essay on the reading of Cervantes. In May 1934
Thomas Mann, already living in exile in Austria, made his first journey
to America where he was to spend the war-time years. In the previous
year Hitler had come to power and Mann had published *The Tales of
Jacob*, the first volume of the tetralogy *Joseph and his Brothers* which was not
to be completed until the latter part of the war.[1] His essay 'Voyage with
Don Quixote' records his rereading of this foundational European novel
on the journey.[2] The essay is commonly read as a piece of casual
journalism, but its apparent casualness is part of a highly crafted insight
into Mann's consciousness of his own historical world and the contemporary significance of his mythic phase.

Mann intersperses the narrative of his voyage with passages of commentary on *Don Quixote*. His apparently random procedure frees him
from the need to argue a case, or even to see Cervantes's text from any
consistent viewpoint. But the essay interweaves several themes with the
complexity and open-endedness of a work of fiction. In fact, as in *Don
Quixote*, the apparent randomness is the basis for a more subtly thematic
structure by which the world of Cervantes' book and the world of the
voyage are significantly connected. For, as Erwin Koppen has noted,
Thomas Mann's reading of *Don Quixote* actually occurred some months

before the voyage.[3] Writing to Karl Kerenyi in March, he had already
advanced some of the observations about the archetypal meanings of
asses, and Cervantes' relation to novels of Greek antiquity, which are put
forward casually and tentatively, as if for the first time, in the essay.[4] In
other words, the voyage and the reading are both historical events of
1934, but the voyage to America reading *Don Quixote* is strictly a fiction.
As a fiction, it is close to the mode of philosophical metafiction being
contemporaneously developed by Borges. In several of Borges' pieces
Cervantes provides a starting-point for another level of reflection, and
Mann's apparently casual and literal framing narrative of the voyage has
also to be seen in this light.[5] The events and characters of the voyage
retain an historical reference, but they acquire a fictional significance
which no one, even Koppen, seems to have appreciated. This explains,
for example, Mann's inconsistency in commenting on an episode from
Part II when by any literal logic he has only just started Part I. And there
are suspicious congruities too. What *was* the weather on the Atlantic that
week? Was it really so iron grey at the beginning while Mann reflected on
the inhospitable element on which he was setting forth and the ominous
future of the continent he was leaving behind? Was it so sunnily distant
from Europe in mid ocean? Was there a convenient mist around New
York to turn the Statue of Liberty into a 'goddess' and Manhattan into a
Quixotic 'land of giants'? These questions are inconsequential in themselves, but they alert us to the recognition that everything in the 'essay'
serves a thematic purpose, and the author of *The Magic Mountain* knew
how physical setting can create the sense of time and distance. In short,
as in *Don Quixote* itself, we appear at first to have a fictive world set against
an actual world only to discover, with a slowly dawning consciousness,
that we have two planes of fiction.

The double-layered fiction is Mann's deep compliment to Cervantes
underlying the often critical note of his overt commentary. And this in
turn suggests the nature of Mann's own creative assimilation of Cervantes. For literary 'influence' can be most significant when least readily
detectable; when it has been absorbed completely into a different
organism. The ultimate interest of the essay is to reveal a Cervantean
dimension in Mann which is so integral as to be barely visible. This is
indicative of Cervantes' impact on subsequent twentieth-century fiction
too, in that it is not really concerned with the thematics of romantic
projection so much as with Cervantes' exploration of his own narrative
means. One of Mann's first comments is on the dizzying meta-fictional
awareness created in Part II of *Don Quixote* when Quixote and Sancho

meet their own readers ('Voyage' p. 441). But this is only the most striking moment in a pervasive Cervantean interest in the interrelations of imagined and lived experience. Cervantes, for example, constantly interweaves parallel stories not just to develop the themes of the main narrative, but to explore the effects of narrative itself. The refraction of experience through narrative is one of his abiding concerns. So, for example, the cautionary tale of the 'Impertinent Curiosity' is read out of curiosity by characters who are themselves part of another interpolated episode.[6] In Mann's essay, the world of the book and the world of the ship remain formally distinct in the mind of the voyaging narrator. There is no Cervantean dissolution of the fictional frame; no stepping forward of the hero to meet his reader. Yet, as Mann's final dream of actually meeting Don Quixote suggests, there is an equivalent in the way Mann's own narrative of the voyage increasingly enfolds and expands the original text. For, just as Alonso Quijano is ultimately no less fictional than Don Quixote, so is the 'Thomas Mann' we meet within the tale of the voyage. This Mann, another nearly 'sixty-year-old, smiling public man', is travelling first-class and develops a lively antipathy to a younger man, who appears also perhaps to be a writer, but who remains mysterious because of his habit of leaving the first-class to go and play shuffleboard with the Jewish exiles in steerage. Mann finally complains to us of this figure who

travels first-class and takes his meals with us in a dinner jacket; but offensively abjures our intellectual diversions and betakes himself to a foreign, a hostile sphere. People ought to know where they belong. People ought to keep together. ('Voyage' p.452)

Read on the purely biographical plane, this querulous mixture of snobbery and xenophobia is simply authorial, but within the fictional development it acquires a different significance. We recognise a narrating character who resents being faced with a disturbingly courageous *alter ego*. The other man is another Mann.

For Mann's culminating comments on Don Quixote dwell on precisely these same themes of exile and xenophobia as seen in the episode of Ricote the Moor ('Voyage' pp. 456–60). When Mann recounts how Sancho meets his erstwhile neighbour, Ricote the Moor, travelling disguised as a Christian pilgrim, as he can no longer endure his homesickness after the Edict of 1609 banishing the Moors from Spain, the earlier, casual references to Jewish *émigrés* on the boat come suddenly into focus, and Mann points up the historical irony of Ricote's praising

Germany as the most tolerant country he has found in his exiled wanderings. A significant moment in the modern reception of Cervantes was Americo Castro's reversal when he came to see such moments of apparently unselfcritical xenophobia in Cervantes not as something shared with his age, but as the crucial point of a profound critique.[7] Unlike Sancho, who has the self-confidence of being an 'old Christian', both Alonso Quijano and the author, Castro argues, were new Christians, or converted Jews. It would certainly make sense for the greatest identity crisis in world literature to have come from a Spanish *converso*. Although Castro's case has not been universally accepted among Hispanists, it is significant that it should have been made at all, and in the same decade of triumphant fascism as Mann's essentially similar reading.

Like Castro, Mann sees the critical force of the Ricote episode as deriving in significant measure from Cervantes' apparent acceptance of the Edict. Even Ricote is anxious to declare his loyalty on this point. The practical impossibility for Cervantes of directly criticising the Edict, in other words, is incorporated as a narrative strategy. The inhumanity of the Edict, and Ricote's attachment to Spain as his native country, acquire a telling self-evidence precisely from their not being questioned by the narrator. And this is Mann's own method in the essay as 'he' responds to the unknown figure who fraternises with Jews. In adopting the conventional posture which the whole narrative is designed to expose, Mann once again celebrates the example of Cervantes by incorporating his method. In short, Mann, who thought Joseph Conrad was the greatest modern novelist, uses the Conradian circumstances of the ocean voyage for a multi-layered, dramatic meditation on home and exile and on the ambivalence of nationhood and community.[8] The sense of community is a precarious necessity which must be consciously upheld, yet it can hardly be separated from a spirit of exclusion. It tends to define itself by its perceived outsiders. Mann's personal situation gives the question a concrete urgency. It also leads him to see in Cervantes and himself a cousinship across a gulf. And this gulf is not simply personal, it is historical and generic. For, having argued that the power of the Ricote episode lies in Cervantes' narrative strategy, he goes on in his next passage of commentary to undercut this with a deeper and less personal analysis bearing on the historical and artistic distance between Cervantes' time and his own.

Mann notes the difference between an earlier conception of the artist as craftsman and the post-romantic conception of individual genius.

Cervantes, Mann insists, was not just pretending to go along with the Edict. He was a man of his time and accepted its assumptions ('Voyage' pp. 458–9). Precisely because he did not see himself as an artistic prophet opposing contemporary wisdom, his critique arises impersonally from the nature of the case. But as Mann draws this large scale contrast, and raises the problematic character of the post-romantic or modern artist, we may expand his reflections in the light of his own artistic practice. In a sense, Mann implies, Cervantes had it easier because his craft conception, his being essentially *of* his cultural community, spared him a responsibility that the modern artist cannot avoid. Yet if Cervantes did not have the modern artist's problems, he may well hold vital clues to their solution, as becomes evident in Mann's assimilation of Cervantes in *Joseph and his Brothers*. To appreciate the significance of this, it is necessary to recognise the precise moment of the Cervantes essay in Mann's novelistic 'œuvre.

The Joseph tetralogy and modernist mythopoeia

In effect, Mann's essay represents the awareness that he and Cervantes are as two book-ends enclosing the historical period of realist fiction. While producing some of the masterworks of the realist tradition, Cervantes still had one foot in the world of romance. Mann has a similar duality in reverse. Having produced one of the masterworks of European realism in *Buddenbrooks* at the opening of his career, he had participated in the modernist transposition of realism, most notably in *The Magic Mountain*, and now, as he remarks in the Cervantes essay, he was developing the mythic method which was the central modernist means of assimilating, and yet transcending, realist form. Historically, Mann can look at Cervantes as a comparable eminence across a large valley. In their very distance they have something in common. Both have a larger outlook than the practice of realism. Earlier realist form had come to be seen as narrow in two relevant ways: philosophically, in its relation to science, and politically, as the expression of specific national cultures. A brief overview of each aspect explains what was at stake in Mann's modernist transcendence of realism by myth.

The period of the realist novel was roughly contemporaneous with the prestige of Newtonian science. The physical sciences provided what seemed for a long time the paradigmatic form of truth statement, whereas modernist mythopoeia is an attempt to combine the lived, intuitive, spontaneous nature of belief with the recognition of philosophical relativity. But, where Thomas Mann, and others of his generation, found a restriction in the older conception of scientific truth, Cervantes lived before science had acquired its modern prestige. When Anselmo, the foolish young husband in the 'Tale of the Impertinent Curiosity', first asks his friend Lotario to test the virtue of his wife, Camila, Lotario gives a resonant reply. He says Anselmo is like the Moors who would wish to have the existence of God proved mathematically. Anselmo meanwhile insists on an empirical test like the assaying of gold.[9] To submit a matter of faith to such criteria is a profound intellectual and moral error. Behind Anselmo's desire to test his wife, there lies the model of a blasphemous impropriety; a point which is ironically highlighted, perhaps, by his bearing the name of the theologian responsible for the ontological proof of the existence of God.

Without taking Lotario as an authorial spokesman, we can recognise the force of his appeal to a religious criterion over the head of the rationalist or scientific. In a sense, the same psychological testing of ethical quality, or search for a chimerical ethical essence, is conducted by Richardson's Lovelace on Clarissa and by Laclos' Valmont on la Présidente de Tourvel. But in these later instances the religious criterion becomes progressively more vulnerable within the increasingly secular premisses of the novel. Indeed, there is a large theme here. Hans Blumenberg and Peter Sloterdijk have both written on the theme of 'curiosity' and its 'epochal ambivalence', in Blumenberg's phrase, during the transition from a theological to a scientific culture. For the older culture it represents a moral danger while in the scientific world view it is a primary virtue. Cervantes' title, 'La novela del curioso impertinente', stresses, not just the excess, but the misplaced, nature of Anselmo's curiosity. Without returning to Cervantes' world of religious faith, Mann is similarly seeking to escape the criterion of a narrowly instrumental or scientific reason, and of its associated form of realism. Already in *The Magic Mountain*, as in Joyce's *Ulysses*, physical science had become simply one of the systems by which the human world is constructed. In short, modernist mythopoeia has more in common with the openness of Cervantes than with the scientific hegemony associated with an earlier realism.

The realist novel has been seen as representing another kind of narrowness in reflecting the worlds of its particular national cultures; a question that is central to the Joseph novels. This is a problematic claim, but it bears on the modernist reaction to realism. The view that the realist novel had an intrinsic relation to nationalism has been most notably argued by Benedict Anderson and seems to have won a measure of acceptance. The realist novel, he suggests, tended to invoke national consciousness because it dealt with 'imagined communities', largely defined, as it happens, by bourgeois interests and functions.[10] Since the totality of such functions cannot be known directly, it can only be invoked imaginatively through the concept of the nation. On this view, rather than the novel being a fictive reflection of social reality, its fictive status is itself a reproduction of the imaginary nature of the national identity or socio-economic whole. I suspect that realist form is more like a chameleon taking on the colour of its context. Yet the novel has undoubtedly embodied national formations, both consciously and unconsciously. Dickens and George Eliot, for example, have a highly self-conscious Englishness, while René Girard, in *Deceit, Desire and the Novel*, is quite unaware how culturally specific is the myth of feeling which he analyses as a universal one.[11] For present purposes, what matters is that national consciousness was an important critical theme for Thomas Mann and other modernist writers, and that the mythopoeic basis of their fiction has a strategic value in this regard. It makes Anderson's point. Lawrence's use of Genesis in *The Rainbow*, or Joyce's use of Homer, are ways of undercutting conventional evaluations of their characters' worlds. The universality of modernist mythopoeia, even if it has itself come to seem increasingly questionable and Eurocentric, was most importantly a progressive motive, a dislodging of national or metropolitan perspectives, so that an Irish Jew or a provincial farmer could see the world from an equally, if not more, human viewpoint. Not surprisingly, therefore, Cervantes 'universality' is the first aspect on which Mann's essay focuses. 'Universality', that most hapless of literary critical clichés, represents a real and vital problem. By drawing this term into the thematic field of 'home', 'exile' and communal beliefs, Mann revivifies the complex questions underlying the cliché.

The self-conscious relativism of modernist mythopoeia, its awareness of itself as a human construction, was a prophylactic against naive universalism or cultural essentialism. It encompasses the fact of human cultural variety; of the jostling differences within the recognisably human. Hence, as Mann reaches 'the stage of myth' so the relativity of culture is the primary theme he seeks to explore ('Voyage' pp. 455–456). In Mann's contemporary world, the primary significance of the Joseph tetralogy lay in the sheer fact of a German writer working, throughout the Nazi period, on a celebration of the Jewish story as the universal story of humanity. And two of his most important intellectual sources were

Sigmund Freud and Karl Kerenyi, both Jews. But, more importantly, within the story of Joseph, Mann explores the theme of cultural relativity and embodies it in the very mode of the narrative. An important clue to this lies in his running references to Nietzsche in the essay. He comments as follows, for example, on Cervantes' capacity to subject Spanish national grandeur to ironic scrutiny.

That is winning, and ridiculous. But what would a Don Quixote at the other extreme be like? Anti-idealistic, sinister, a pessimistic believer in force – and yet a Don Quixote? A brutalised Don Quixote? Even Cervantes, with all his melancholic humour, had not gone as far as to conceive that. (Voyage, p. 438)

It is not clear whether this is a reference to Hitler, to Nietzsche or to Nietzschean thought as traduced by national socialist ideologues. But, if the problematic nature of post-renaissance modern identity was introduced by the emblematic figures of Don Quixote and Hamlet, then its latest phase in Mann's own century had been ushered in by a figure similarly inseparable from the image of madness. At the end of his essay Mann recounts his dream of talking to a Don Quixote with Nietzsche's features, and finds him 'tactful and courteous' and understandably 'beloved', in Cervantes' words, 'by all that knew him' ('Voyage' p. 464). The combination of Nietzsche and Don Quixote is highly ambivalent, but it leaves till *Doctor Faustus* a full analysis of Nietzsche as representing the dark side of German culture. Here it suggests the more positive side of Nietzsche; the Nietzsche who underwrites philosophically the self-conscious mythopoeia of the modernist generation.

Nietzsche and Cervantes

The sea voyage invokes very naturally the image of an horizon shifting with its moving centre; the image by which Nietzsche expressed the necessity for spontaneous, believing action within a relativistic awareness. Mann attributes the same insight to Joseph in his discussion with one of the merchant's sons with whom he is to go to Egypt (*Joseph* p. 447; *Joseph in Ägypten* p. 7). When the son, Kedema, is affronted at Joseph's suggesting the merchants are to 'take' him there, Joseph explains that, although he and Kedema are only feet apart, they inhabit different universes. In the universe of which Kedema is the centre, says Joseph, his observation is perfectly just. But in the universe of which Joseph is the centre it is as if the merchants are indeed there to perform this function. Joseph's reply is eminently 'tactful and courteous', he appeals to imagination rather than argument, and he eventually charms the merchants as he does almost everyone who matters in his life. But, for all the distance from Nietzsche's iconoclastic tone, the essential thought is Nietzschean and typifies Mann's humanistic assimilation of the central Nietzschean recognitions.

Alasdair MacIntyre, and others, have argued that narrative fiction is the proper model for the spontaneous and holistic nature of ethical life and community. Nietzsche preferred the image of theatre. There is a different emphasis as Nietzsche, seeking to deconstruct as well as affirm, makes the self-consciousness of acting his model of ethical identity, while MacIntyre, seeking to overcome the reductive abstraction of conventional moral philosophy, invokes the holism of narrative fiction. Mann, like Cervantes, combines both emphases. He recounts his narrative of Joseph in such a way as to imbue it, and his characters, with Nietzschean, performative self-consciousness while preserving the intuitive wholeness of personality and world. The way narrative tends to naturalise its own grounding is a feature that both Mann and Cervantes regard with suspicion, but wish, not so much to expose, as to negotiate. Mann's project is to retell the biblical tales of Jacob and Joseph with a modern psychological and anthropological consciousness. Hence the inordinate length to which he swells the Genesis version. But the effect is to recover and reaffirm the originals for his own day. Whereas Borges' Pierre Menard gave Cervantes' text a different meaning by preserving its exact verbal form, Mann rewrites his original to preserve its meaning.[12] His difficulty lies largely in the psychology of his antique characters whose personal motivation includes a recognition of their own mythic importance. He encompasses this by a means which is as Cervantean in method as it is Nietzschean in meaning.

All the major figures, and some of the minor ones, recognise themselves as enacting roles within a story. The characters thus create their story without feeling it to be merely their own. The whole story, as summarised in the final sentence, is ambiguously a 'god-invention'. We do not know whether it has been invented *by* God or is the story of the invention *of* God. But, either way, the characters have many earlier models on which to form their present. Jacob and Joseph negotiate the crises of their lives by reflecting on similar episodes told of their ancestors. No previous occasion provides an exact model, but the consciousness of the need to act in keeping with the model is a crucial and enabling aspect of their psychology. To be sure, the very notion of personal identity changes over the course of the story, since the whole tetralogy recounts, in Mann's words, 'the birth of the ego out of the mythical collective'.[13] This may be why the story becomes more Cervantean as it goes on. To base the whole psychology on the conscious re-enactment of archetypal models known through story, and to try constantly to adjust these models to an unpredictable historical present, is squarely Quixotic. Hence, while it is possible that Mann's reading of Cervantes in 1934 influenced the later volumes, the increasing development of conscious personal identity in Joseph by comparison with his father and ancestors, makes the Cervantean, or Nietzschean, consciousness of acting within the demands of a story something that must inevitably grow more pronounced. Whereas Jacob tends to govern his behaviour by ancestral models, Joseph is more innovative and thinks forward, like Don Quixote, to the posterity for which he will himself be a model.

Joseph's sensibility is as much artistic as religious; he increasingly stage-manages events. His punishment of his brothers, and subsequent reconciliation with them, is like Prospero's. And, although one hesitates to attribute his dual consciousness merely to Cervantes' example, there are moments where Mann seems consciously to echo Cervantes just as his characters echo, with similarly creative difference, their forebears. And so, when Joseph is suddenly promoted after interpreting the Pharaoh's dream, he calls for his former jailer, Mai-Sachme, a mere provincial official, to be his steward. As he does so, he encourages the jailer to pursue his ambitions as a story-teller for

Great is the writer's art! But truly I find it greater yet to live in a story; this that we are in is certainly a capital one, of that I am more and more convinced the longer I live. And now you are in it with me because I brought you; and when in the future people hear or read of my steward who was with me and at my side in exciting moments, they will know that this steward was you, Mai-Sachme, the man of poise. (*Joseph* p. 998; *Joseph der Ernährer* pp. 240–1)

He chooses his Sancho. When reading the episode with no thought of Cervantes, the parallel hardly springs to mind. All the elements of Mann's story are necessary and of a piece. Yet, in the light of the Cervantes essay, the Quixotic echo is like a broad wink. Furthermore, Mann's own historical situation, in chronicling these events, is exactly that of Cervantes' fictitious Arab historian, Cide Hamete Benengeli, who wrote up Don Quixote's adventures in a language foreign to the characters themselves. In both cases, a profoundly national tale is told through the language of its enemies, while giving the characters a value they themselves had not conceived. Indeed, the significance of both works comes to lie as much in the narrative mediation as in the action. The epic whole of Don Quixote's own, unwritten romance, the version he imagines will be written, parallels that of the Bible which the characters from Genesis equally cannot yet know. Both narrative wholes are therefore invoked, but are only experienced as separate episodes and tales. This dissolution into tales is given a thematic import within both texts, and in Mann's case it provides an intimate commentary on contemporary transformations of fiction at large.

Story and belief

Joseph's consciousness of living within a story takes its force from the importance of story-telling in the culture, psychology and action of the book. Joseph can always fascinate with words. Even a utilitarian arithmetical sum he turns into an engaging narrative (*Joseph* p. 453; *Joseph in Ägypten* pp. 15–16) He is a story-teller in every sense. He tells tales on his brothers (*Joseph* p. 51; *Geschichte Jaakobs* p. 81). He tells fibs such as that he can make pancakes (*Joseph* p. 450; *Joseph in Ägypten* p. 12). And, of course, he retails his ancestral tales. These different senses of fiction, history and lie are interrelated. As Joseph matures, he comes to recognise, like Jacob before him, that the literal truth may, for creative and honourable purposes, give way to the archetypal. Like Don Quixote after the episode of the fulling mills, he sees that for the dignity and meaning of the subsequent legend certain details need not be told; just as they would not have been in Don Quixote's version of his own story as romance (*Don Quixote*, trans. Jarvis p. 168; *Don Quixote*, ed. Riquer p. 39). Or the characters on occasion connive at a self-deception reminiscent of Don Quixote's refusal to test his homemade visor (*Don Quixote*, trans. Jarvis p. 26; *Don Quixote*, ed. Riquer p. 39). When Isaac 'mistakenly' blesses Jacob instead of Esau, it is with a half-conscious awareness of what is going on (*Joseph* p. 131; *Geschichten Jaakobs* pp. 198–9). And Jacob does the same in turn with Joseph's sons (*Joseph* p. 1182; *Joseph der Ernährer* pp. 514–15). Furthermore, the bystanders in these episodes, as so often in *Don Quixote*, connive at the willed delusion. These characters are not just in a story, they are fed on story and feed themselves stories.

In the Joseph novels a culture of story-telling gives pyschological force and metaphysical point to these figures living self-consciously within a story, but Mann also absorbs it into the structure and texture of his own narrative. He does this by the fluidity of his narrative horizons. The whole work is a *roman fleuve* based on a brief part of the first book of the

Bible. Hence a larger horizon is repeatedly hinted at which, since it is unknown to the characters, is not encompassed within Mann's narration other than as a complex of separate stories. The first volume is called *The Tales of Jacob*, in the plural, and Mann recounts these tales in their order of present relevance rather than their original chronology. They therefore constitute a body of model experiences all individually equidistant from the present in which they are creatively invoked. Indeed, the stories are not only retold, they are likely at any moment to be re-enacted, as if timelessly, in the present. In this way, Mann dissolves his ultimate narrative horizon and privileges the constantly shifting horizons of particular stories. Only through their mutual echoes do we intuit the larger shaping.

This narrative structure is Cervantean in reverse. Where Cervantes stuffed his main narrative with stories, Mann deliberately dissolves his biblical whole into a multiplicity of stories; consistently privileging story at the expense of any overarching frame. The story-teller, he says, is a wanderer.

> The story-teller's star – is it not the moon, lord of the road, the wanderer, who moves in his stations, one after another, freeing himself from each? For the story-teller makes many a station, roving and relating, but pauses only tentwise, awaiting further directions, and soon feels his heart beating high, partly with desire, partly too from fear and anguish of the flesh, but in any case as a sign that he must take the road, towards fresh adventures which are to be painstakingly lived through, down to their remotest details, according to the restless spirit's will. (*Joseph* p. 32; *Geschichte Jaakobs* pp. 50–1)

The ancestral inheritance is a constant process of development, and the mobile horizon of the stories in which it is embodied is honoured by Mann's narrative. Walter Benjamin had a similar thought in his essay on 'The Storyteller'. Only a few years before, towards the end of the period of high modernism, both E. M. Forster and Boris Eichenbaum had independently spoken of 'story' as the primitive and relatively uninteresting substratum of the novel.[14] Benjamin, writing at the time of the Joseph tetralogy, reverses this evaluation. The story-teller, precisely because not claiming any special wisdom, communicates it through the open-endness of story itself. A novel offers a personal vision, an interpretation of experience, which no one perhaps is in a position to claim. The novelist, on this view, is one who would offer to fix our horizon. Hence, for Benjamin, the rise of the novel was the decline of story. In his account, the true original of the novelist is not Cervantes, but the deluded benefactor of mankind, Don Quixote.[15]

Whether or not Benjamin's argument is convincing, its interest is as a cultural fact, as a straw in the wind, for, as the high modernist synthesis began to break up, one of the elements into which it dissolved was story. If *Ulysses* is modernist and *Finnegans Wake* postmodernist, their near contemporaries, *The Magic Mountain* and *Joseph and his Brothers*, are similar. The dissolution into an interrelated complex of stories is Mann's move towards a later mode of fiction. Such shifts in literary form are not merely formal, and the dissolution into story is closely linked with the thematic questions of foreignness and the inhabiting of belief. If the story-teller is generically a wanderer, so are the religious questors, the god-creators, Abraham, Jacob and Joseph. Mann's overall tale is one of growth towards a higher form of life, and, just as Joseph's monotheism is more evolved than the Pharoah's polytheism, so we implicitly understand that the Judeo Christian God is itself only one more phase in the evolution of human culture in its aspiration to the 'highest'. But, most importantly, this tolerant, relativistic sense of the interrelations between religions is shared by the characters. During his sojourn in Egypt, Joseph learns as well as teaches. Jacob's atavistic horror of Egypt contrasts with Joseph's capacity to adapt himself to Egyptian customs. When Joseph eventually marries and has children in Egypt, he trusts his God to appreciate his position, particularly since God is responsible for it, and he relies on 'God's large, worldly-wise freedom from prejudice' (*Joseph* p. 1008; *Joseph der Ernährer* p. 256).

This seems to be Mann's important motive. Just as the struggle to achieve the individual ego out of the mythical collective depends on maintaining a proper sense of relation to the collective, so too as an individual culture evolves it needs to understand its own individuality within a larger family of human cultures. Part of the charm of the book is the way in which Mann's post-Frazerian, comparative consciousness of the religions of the ancient Mediterranean world is attributed to the ancient peoples themselves. Far from being caught in cultic hostility, they have a diplomatic and intelligently comparative interest in each others' gods. The gradual invention of God in man's image, or the invention of humanity through the image of God, requires openness as well as faith, and even Jacob, who is so much less adaptable than Joseph, is capable of reconciling different points of view. As he reflects

the forms in which Israel worshipped the eternal God under the tree did not after all differ much from the cult of the children of Canaan – aside from all the offensive sporting and unseemliness. (*Joseph* p. 1146; *Joseph der Ernährer* p. 560)

And Jacob goes on to speculate that the old polytheistic gods may indeed
live on as separate persons within the one true God. The doctrine of the
Trinity arises from his reconciling his tribal belief with the general family
of human religions; and Jacob's sense of the many within the one echoes
the separate stories within Mann's narrative. The inhabiting of religious
tradition is embodied in the mobile horizon of its stories. Rather than a
single fixed horizon, there is a constant mutual adjustment and overlap-
ping. In Mann, as in Benjamin, story is a holistic form of understanding
which avoids totality or dogmatism.

Thomas Mann and Primo Levi: modern to postmodern

The Joseph tetralogy hovers consciously on the brink of postmodernism
without accepting it. Just as Jacob insists on the one God, so Mann does
not allow the integrity of his work to be completely dissolved into
multiplicity. In the Cervantes essay, too, Mann recognises this possibility
only in order to reject it. Any such 'dissolution of form' is a seductive
folly. And so, while enjoying the 'epic wit' of Cervantes in allowing Don
Quixote his dizzying detachment from the narrative frame, Mann goes
on to see this kind of technique as dangerous in the later romantic artists
who were his own significant forebears, and he ends by appealing to his
Joseph story as holding the proper balance. Using the term 'humour' for
what we would now call fictive self-consciousness, he says that the
romantics

came so dangerously near the ironic dissolution of form. It is well to be
constantly aware that this is the intimate pitfall of every technique that seeks to
combine the humorous with the realistic. From the comic touch of certain epic
means of producing reality to the word-plays and artifices of downright buffoon-
ery, faithful to form and yet amorphous, it is only a step. I do indeed give my
reader an unexpected opportunity of seeing with his own eyes Joseph, son of
Jacob, sitting by the well in the moonlight, and of comparing his bodily
presence, fascinating if also humanly incomplete as it is, with the ideal renown
that centuries have woven about his figure. But I hope that the humour of this
method of seizing the occasion to evoke reality may still deserve the honourable
name of art. ('Voyage' p. 442)

It is clear that, for Mann, postmodern relativity, when taken to the point
of *mise en abyme*, a self-consciousness which throws the meaning of the
work itself into question, represents no advance over the conscious
synthesis of modernist mythopoeia. He sees the possibility clearly
enough, but understands it as a temptation to relax the effort by which
the synthesis is maintained. As in Cervantes, the formal play does not

undermine our world, or our beliefs, but teaches us how to inhabit them. From this point of view, much postmodern self-consciousness, particularly when it claims a superior metaphysical insight to modernism, is tilting at windmills.

Cervantes was a presence throughout the successive phases of European fiction and it is not surprising to see in this transitional work of Thomas Mann a new Cervantes created by modernist and incipiently postmodern perception. But it seems more than chance that Walter Benjamin, the figure who best illuminates the significance of this shift in Mann, should be Jewish. For the Jewish tradition of story, evoked by Mann, doubtless lies behind Benjamin's perception too. Indeed, even in many Jewish novelists, such as Bernard Malamud, the centre of gravity is still closer to story than to novel and, not surprisingly, the next stage of the process can also be seen most clearly and positively in a Jewish writer. Primo Levi actively invites this when he recounts in *The Periodic Table* how, as a talented and resourceful Jew working in foreign captivity, he would shut himself away 'to read Mann's Joseph stories'.[16] In this connection, it is a telling coincidence that Levi should also recount, in his opening chapter, how his Piedmontese ancestors were descendants of those exiled Spanish Jews whose fate was shown by the Cervantes essay to be part of the creative thinking behind the Joseph tetralogy. These underground connections are appropriate, for Levi's extraordinary and admirable book, despite its great formal ingenuity, never for a moment seems to be excogitated from formalist concerns. Like all great formal innovation, it seems to arise inevitably from the experience it communicates. Whereas Mann's tetralogy was conceived before the war, Levi's book was a response to the Jewish experience of the Nazi years. The willful destruction of European Jewry was an event whose scale and horror notoriously resist artistic treatment while calling out for memory and response. Documentary, anecdote and essay are perhaps the forms which can best bear the weight of the experience involved. But, apart from his own admirable writings of a memorial and essayistic kind on this theme, Levi's *The Periodic Tale* is a subtle use of story and science to encompass this experience within a post-Auschwitz humanism.

Just as Levi refers to the Joseph novels as 'stories', so the staple of his own narrative is a series of stories held together, not by the mythic family relation seen in Mann, but arbitrarily by the invoked structure of the periodic table. By using the table of chemical elements as his structure Levi achieves several effects. The most strategic is a negative one: he avoids the personal interpretative horizon Benjamin objected to in the

novelist. His 'scientific' structure affirms a significant grasp of the world
while avoiding overall explanations, whether ethical, historical or metaphysical. This sceptical elusiveness applies not just in contrast to the
realist novel form, but to the mythopoeic form of modernist fiction. Like
many writers of his generation, he is deeply sceptical of myth. Where
Mann sought to preserve myth as a humanistic resource, and to resist its
hi-jacking by fascism, Levi's generation meets the very word with
suspicion. So too, just as the chemical elements, such as mercury and
uranium, often have mythic names but can be scientifically understood,
Levi treats myths as he would lumps of matter to be analysed. Hence, like
some of the great modernists discussed earlier, he replaces Promethean
ambition with an ideal of worldly cunning:

Prometheus had been foolish to bestow fire on men instead of selling it to them:
he would have made money, placated Jove, and avoided all that trouble with the
vulture. (*Periodic Table* p. 143; *sistema periodico* p. 147)

But, in his debunking of Prometheus in favour of a Ulyssean practicality,
Levi is not concerned to replace the myth by a better one so much as to
dissolve it into its elements. The debunking is humorously sceptical
rather than destructive, for in Levi the mythic is still something that
cannot be escaped. Even our words are essentially myths. They are
concentrations of historical experience which must be understood precisely because we have no choice but to use them. The considered weight
of his own historical experience allows him no cheaply generalised
deconstruction. His awareness of the dangerous potencies of words, as in
'*Bewältigung der . . . Vergangenheit* / overcoming of the . . . past' (*Periodic Table*
p. 217; *sistema periodico* p. 221), is an awareness of their necessary power.
Indeed, they are most dangerous when they lose their true power and
dwindle into cliché. From this point of view, his critical energy goes into a
kind of servicing of language, into keeping it usable. Yet this is too passive
and prophylactic an emphasis in the face of his creative achievement.

   I have said that he dissolved Mann's form, while keeping faith with
Mann's humanism, through story. Levi's separate stories act as precious
nuggets of experience produced by a chemist who looks even on excre-
ment as material from which a value can be extracted (*Periodic Table* pp.
180–1; *sistema periodico* p. 184). He implicitly thematises this in an image
that arises from his situation as a young captured partisan awaiting
execution when a fellow prisoner tells him of gold to be found in the local
river.

During those days, when I was waiting courageously enough for death, I harboured a piercing desire for everything, for all imaginable human experiences, and I cursed my previous life, which it seemed to me I had profited from little or badly, and I felt time running through my fingers, escaping from my body minute by minute, like a haemorrhage that can no longer be stanched. Of course, I would search for gold: not to get rich but to try out a new skill, to see again the earth, air, and water from which I was separated by a gulf that grew larger every day; and to find again my chemical trade in its essential and primordial form, the Scheidekunst, precisely, the art of separating metal from gangue. (*Periodic Table* p. 137; *sistema periodico* p. 141)

His image of the *Scheidekunst*, the separating of gold from dross, applies to his own combined activity as protagonist and story-teller running time through his fingers with an eye constantly alert to the precious grains of significance to be won from it. When he starts writing after the war the same image recurs:

It was exalting to search and find, or create, the right word, that is, commensurate, concise, and strong; to dredge up events from my memory and describe them with the greatest rigour and the least clutter. (*Periodic Table* p. 153; *sistema periodico* p. 158)

The full creative significance of this can be seen in the final episode of his post-war exchange with Dr Müller, his former director in the laboratory at Auschwitz. Quite apart from whether Levi has made up the entire episode, there is a subtle play with historical and fictional elements. Significantly he never meets Dr Müller again, so that this post-war Müller exists for him entirely on paper, as a rhetorical effect, and therefore in a manner akin to a fictional character. Indeed Levi is nervous of meeting the man in the flesh, given that the reality of the meeting must inevitably be incommensurate with its meaning for him. It might be possible to meet him, Levi says, if Müller himself shared this consciousness, or if he were so completely unaware as to be an object of simple contempt. But the real person will be incommensurable with his own significance; as Hannah Arendt discovered in coining the phrase 'the banality of evil'.[17] And, in seeking to understand Müller in advance of a possible meeting, Levi notes, he is constructing him like a fictional character. But the man who replies to his letter has none of the comfortable clarity of fiction. Indeed, Müller is himself a writer, a rival purveyor of fiction, because like other characters in *The Periodic Tale* he wishes to write himself an acceptable past. His letter was visibly the work of an inept writer; rhetorical, sincere only by half, full of digressions and far-fetched praise, moving, pedantic, clumsy: it defied any summary, all-encompassing judgement. (*Periodic Table* p. 219; *sistema periodico* p. 223)

This maintains the writerly and fictive image, even while enforcing the historical particularity of Müller as opposed to the stereotypes either of fiction or of German post-war remorse.

But, in a more telling sense again, the logic of this is that Müller *is* indeed a fictional character. Levi is initially uncertain whether the Müller who has written to him on business is 'his' Müller. The whole suspense of the situation focuses on this identification. It is a common name and, says Levi, 'there must be two hundred thousand Müllers in Germany' (*Periodic Table* p. 213; *sistema periodico* p. 217). But the whole question of identification is really a feint. If we momentarily anglicise the name Müller, it may recall Arthur Miller and his play *All My Sons* (1947). The play concerns a wealthy manufacturer's refusal to acknowledge the loss in action of his pilot son who may have been flying with faulty parts supplied by the father's own firm. The moment of illumination comes when the father recognises that it actually does not matter: the dead pilots were 'all my sons'. So too, the initial remark about the many Müllers in Germany acquires an opposite meaning by the end of the episode. In truth, Levi did not need to meet this individual because, as he might have said, 'they are all my Müllers.' But, where Arthur Miller used the structure of the well-made play to express his ethical logic, Levi uses his art of *Scheidekunst*. Treating all the elements throughout as ambiguously fictional or historical, he is able to catch the particle of truth which belongs to neither by itself. The historical Müller does effectively slip though his fingers, but Levi retains his meaning in the secret substance of fiction disguised as history. As with Alex Haley's *Roots* (1977), it is the thought that a real historical connection has been made which first compels us.[18] Conversely, García Márquez, in one of his early journalistic pieces, commented on the irony that Colombian readers were well known for seeking the originals of purely fictional characters, while they treated the painfully realistic novels of the contemporary Colombian *Violencia* as fictions.[19] Levi combines both recognitions. The force of the episode lies in the pursuit of the specific historical Müller, but the meaning, and the lingering after effect, come from this Müller having been transformed into a fiction, the representative case.

The dissolution of the categories of 'fact' and 'fiction' into meaning is reflected in the central use of the chemical table. While the arbitrariness of the periodic table as a narrative structure is an important strategic device, the table acquires a number of positive meanings as the book progresses. Most fundamentally, perhaps, it is a way of celebrating the material reality which Levi had devoted his life to understanding and which takes on an increasingly resonant significance. Sartre spoke of the Jewish commitment to reason as an appeal to the reality principle and therefore as an antidote to prejudice.[20] This thought is echoed by Levi (*Periodic Table* p. 42; *sistema periodico* p. 44). But there is something more radical again in Levi's invocation of the sheer material reality of the world as the narrative horizon. Natural science provides an even firmer ground than the general principle of reason.Yet, as has been seen in previous chapters, and as Levi himself makes clear, the world is in no simple sense open to the observation of modern science; it is only understood through human reason. And so Levi, too, exploits the necessarily interpretative and projective relation of science to the world, but he differs from the great modernists in that rather than raising the whole of science to a metaphorical status, as in Joyce's 'Ithaca' episode, Levi interweaves the literal and the metaphorical creating patterns of awareness which depend on our distinguishing the threads. He constantly invests the chemical elements with metaphorical significance while retaining their literal reference. These different levels of usage create sudden sparks across the gaps as Levi presents ethical and psychological insights in a neutral, scientific language of power. In a more literal sense than D. H. Lawrence, Levi tries to see human beings simultaneously as ethical identities and as carbon.[21]

He reveals a positive meaning for Nietzsche's notion of the 'will to power' as the basic principle of life behind the myth of humanity. It is literally vital for Levi to achieve an impersonal, non-humanistic viewpoint. Only by seeing human beings as elemental phenomena can he preserve his reason in the face of an unimaginable evil whereby he himself has been placed outside of the human. This elemental psychology is internalised as a strength in his friend Alberto's tough-minded advice:

You should never be disheartened, because it is harmful and therefore immoral, almost indecent. (*Periodic Table* p. 143; *sistema periodico* pp. 146–7)

This naturalistic conception of ethics is Nietzschean, but it takes its force from the way the language of human psychology throughout the book is continuous with that of natural process. Of course, the anti-human viewpoint is adopted for a human purpose, and lurking in the background here is a mythopoeic inversion of the relation of chemistry to alchemy. Like other modern writers, including García Márquez in *One Hundred Years of Solitude*, Levi invokes alchemy to suggest an age when science, not yet distinguished from magic, was associated with wisdom. It is neither possible nor desirable to recover the world of alchemy, but Levi seeks, like Nietzsche, to snatch an equivalent human meaning from within scientific nihilism. A modern invoking of alchemy is akin to modernist mythopoeia; except that, where modernist mythopoeia concentrates on the construction of a comprehensive horizon, and assimilates science to metaphor, Levi has the different realms constantly interweaving, mutually questioning and then suddenly exfoliating with a strange, complex insight which creeps up on us unawares, although with luminous clarity and logic once it arrives. Discussing the difficulty of secreting materials in prison-camp conditions, Levi reflects on the problem of containing liquids; a problem for industrial chemists, and for God:

This is the great problem of packaging, which every experienced chemist knows: and it was well known to God Almighty, who solved it brilliantly, as he is wont to, with cellular membranes, eggshells, the multiple peel of oranges, and our own skins, because after all we too are liquids. Now, at that time, there did not exist polyethylene, which would have suited me perfectly since it is flexible, light, and splendidly impermeable: but it is also a bit too incorruptible, and not by chance God Almighty himself, although he is a master of polymerization, abstained from patenting it: He does not like incorruptible things. (*Periodic Table* p. 141; *sistema periodico* p. 144)

Levi superimposes the meanings of 'corruptible' as 'biodegradable', 'mortal' and 'prone to evil'. God could have made us of plastic, at once insentient and durable, but the idea is not attractive and nor, one realises, is its spiritual equivalent, the absence of free will or an incapacity for evil. The image of God as industrial chemist poses the problem of evil in its classic, Judeo-Christian form, while secularising, and thereby reversing, it into a more universal recognition. For the problem of evil changes its nature outside of a theistic conception. It then becomes rather the problem of good. And how can there be good without evil? The human, like the humanistic, has no ultimate grounding, yet, as Zeitblom said, its values must be lived as absolute. A non-believing Jew, who does not have the option, as history showed, of ceasing to be a Jew, may draw on the culture of belief without the belief; a position akin to conscious mythopoeia. In this paragraph of Levi's, as a profoundly lived insight is sieved through his sceptical wit, a past culture becomes freshly available to the present in the inverted form of agnosticsm. Levi is a pre-eminent case of truth proved on the pulses and he also shows, like Cervantes and Mann, how freedom from doctrinal enclosure is the truest way of inhabiting a communal belief.

CHAPTER 6

Living with myth: Cervantes and the new world

While helping to inaugurate the tradition of European realist fiction, Cervantes' creative range encompassed the romance from his early *La Galatea* (1585) to the posthumously published *Persiles and Sigismunda* (1616). Indeed, it is a truism that even in *Don Quixote*, far from simply satirising the romances of chivalry, he was deviously adding to their number, and, Borges argues, the long-term reception of the book shows the irrepressibility of the mythopoeic imagination even in the most banal contexts of modernity: 'For myth is the beginning of literature, and the end.'[1] This footing in romance proved to be important for modern Latin American writers within the Hispanic tradition. Whereas Mann, a scion of northern Europe, was attracted principally to the tolerant Erasmian irony of Cervantes, later Latin American writers, such as Mario Vargas Llosa, Carlos Fuentes and Gabriel García Márquez, were to turn to him more specifically as a point of mediation between modernity and the marvellous, as a way back to the world of romance.

ALEJO CARPENTIER: RECOVERING THE MARVELLOUS IN *THE KINGDOM OF THIS WORLD*

The Cuban novelist, Alejo Carpentier, himself of mixed descent, was an important part of this story, as his works are constantly concerned with the historical interrelations of modern European and indigenous Latin American cultures. His first novel *Ecue-Yamba-O* (1933) was a critical and commercial failure leading to a long gap in his fictional output. The work was an attempt to get inside an indigenous cultural world by a sophisticated literary means, and Roberto Gonzalez Echevarría has pointed out that if there is a 'crack' between the two aspects this provides precisely the project for his future fiction.[2] For Carpentier's true subject was the boundary area between cultures, whether regional or historical, and his next novella, *The Kingdom of this World* (1949), developed this problematic with a concentrated power that he perhaps never surpassed, and which still seems to be underappreciated in the critical literature. In his Prologue to the novella, Carpentier mentions as a creative starting-point an incident from Cervantes' *Persiles and Sigismunda* concerning a man with the *lupina* sickness, the belief that he has changed into a wolf. Frederick de Armas has surveyed the extensive commentary on this episode turning on the question of whether Cervantes' narrative implies a belief in this possibility.[3] He points out that the narrative position is elusive, and we can rather say that, just as in the matter of 'curiosity' discussed in the preceding chapter, this is a case of what Hans Blumenberg would call 'epochal ambivalence' in passing from a residually magical to a scientific world view. Carpentier saw the whole of Latin America, in this sense, as a vast epochal amalgam, with its mixture of indigenous and African cultures along with modern intellectual culture. Oswald Spengler had been an influential figure for Carpentier's generation, and his idea that you could have cultural 'contemporaneity' independently of coincidence in historical time was suggestive.[4] On this view, Cervantes, as a writer of epochal transition, was a cultural 'contemporary' of modern Latin American writers. And we could say that Latin American writers of the mid- to late- twentieth century are in turn contemporaries of European modernism in so far as Latin America experienced the equivalent moment of self-inspection somewhat later; and, of course, after absorbing the European modernist movement itself. In effect, Latin America had its 'modernist' moment in a postmodern form, and the dissolution of Enlightenment universality was a key element in this.[5]

The Kingdom of this World, set in the French Caribbean colony of Santo Domingo in the years before and after the French Revolution, relates the historical past to the present not just in the content, but in the narrative form itself; as Carpentier signals in his important, if misleading, prologue. Having spent a decade or so in the Paris of the surrealists, Carpentier returned to the Caribbean and declared that, whereas the surrealists were merely in reaction to European rationalism, and were therefore essentially still part of it, in Latin America the surreal was real. In other words, instead of being a partial and reactive artistic movement, as it was Paris, in Latin America the surrealist impulse was the only way to reflect the extraordinary histories and landscapes of the region. Actually, the surrealist movement included a strong, and quite conscious, anthropological critique of Eurocentrism which Carpentier rather passes over in his account, and it would be more accurate to say that he was developing this aspect of surrealism to a new level of self-critical complexity.[6] Yet there was a difference in cultural context which he sought to highlight with the phrase *lo real maravilloso,* or 'the marvellous reality'. Carpentier's original phrase is already problematic, and the mischief has been increased by the common English transliteration of 'magical realism', which is not only more sentimental, but crucially deflects the focus from a quality of reality back on to the literary medium from which Carpentier's Spanish phrase had attempted to rescue it. His point was that the marvellous inhered in the reality rather than in the form. The mistranslation is cultural rather than merely 'linguistic'. It reflects the way the European tradition, in many instances, continued to implode into an empty formalism, such as the post-war 'new novel' in France, while much significant innovation in fictional form, in the latter part of the century, would come from the egregiously named 'third world'. Of course, Carpentier's 'marvellous reality' eventually became the 'magical realism' of the world publishing market, but, even as Carpentier used the phrase, it was already problematic, since, where fiction is concerned, the distinction between reality and form is largely in the mind. His prologue is best understood as a rhetorical flourish giving an important insight into his creative concerns, rather than as a literal analysis of his fictional world. For the underlying questions of truth, miracle and historical meaning are much more subtly thematised within the novel itself. As is often the case, the creative artist's true thinking is not in the abstract, but an intrinsic aspect of the work, and at a formal, rather than a simply thematic, level.

The novel covers the period of several slave rebellions and the reign of Henri Christophe, a former black cook, who built from slave labour the spectacular mountain-top palace of Sans Souci. By the end of the book this kingdom, too, has passed away, and the central figure, the former slave Ti Noel, now a hallucinating old man, lives to see the takeover of the land by mulatto developers. The novel compresses a highly selected history of the period into the lifetime of Ti Noel. But more than chronological compression is involved here, for the novel draws from the historical situation a complex question about the necessity and power of cultural belonging, or identity, as opposed to the universality of reason and justice. It contrasts with C. L. R. James' historical treatment of the same period in *The Black Jacobins* (1938). James likewise writes with an eye to the modern aftermath of his historical theme, and comments in his first edition on the inevitable liberation of black Africa; prophecies which by later editions were already coming true. James concentrates, however, on the heroic figure of the slave leader, Toussaint L'Ouverture, whose misfortune was, like a tragic latter-day Don Quixote, to believe literally the claims of the Revolution, and to go on believing in them when the Revolution itself had betrayed them. As the French Revolution was increasingly taken over by the interests of the new bourgeois commercial class, it still needed the legitimacy enshrined in its foundational myth of being a movement of all the people. The question of slavery sat right in the middle of this gap between principle and practice, while Toussaint, as a genuine figure of the Enlightenment, and acting on a more than sectarian interest, was the tragic hero on whom this betrayal was enacted. Where James tells a story of tragic, and still relevant, heroism, Carpentier tells a less personalised and heroic tale as he seeks to understand the confusions of cultural misperception. For the mutual misinterpretations of the different peoples have a bearing on the labyrinth of cultural relativism which was becoming more conscious and urgent in Carpentier's own day. The problem was there at the time of the events, of course, and is crucial to understanding them, but the full consciousness of it *as* a problem came at the time of the writing. As slavery, and now increasingly colonialism itself, had become unacceptable, so the underlying problems of cross-cultural understanding and judgement were becoming more, rather than less, salient. The power of Carpentier's narrative form is to see the unfolding of the historical events in the light of this problematic, yet without a reductively retrospective wisdom or explanation. On the contrary, the now manifest illusions and errors of the past serve to highlight the dilemmas of the present.

In the early part of the novel, the one-armed escaped slave, Mackandal, organises a successful insurrection, giving courage to his followers by telling them stories of the nobility of their African past; a motif later expounded by Frantz Fanon.[7] For the slaves, this is a more significant expression of common purpose than the talk of equality which also comes over the ocean from pre-Revolutionary France. When Mackandal is captured, his exemplary execution, by burning at the stake in the town square, is a highly theatrical affair, as the slaves are brought in from the whole area, while the white owners watch from the balconies.[8] The blacks are not unduly concerned since they expect Mackandal to escape, using his magical powers of metamorphosis to turn himself into a mosquito, and they are indeed, in their own minds, coming to witness the quite different spectacle of their masters' discomfiture. Their expectation of this is so clear that they actually 'see' it happen when the one-armed Mackandal wriggles from the rope in his agony and throws himself with a cry into the crowd. Virtually no one sees the soldiers throw him back into the fire, where he is almost instantly consumed, and the crowd shouts 'Mackandal sauvé' / 'Mackandal is saved.' They think they have seen what we would call a miracle, and in a sense they have. Between their perception of a miracle, and the narrative's rational account of the event, there is created a third possiblity which is not merely the sum of these two versions, if such an irrational number could be conceived, yet arises from both. For Mackandal at that moment is indeed metamorphosed, not into a mosquito, but into a myth: the moment at which his identity has been significantly transformed is not the moment of his death, but when he threw himself into the 'black waves' of the crowd. At that moment he lost his personal existence to become part of the collective consciousness; and the blacks' shout, based on their visual misperception, speaks a deeper truth. When a man becomes a mythical vehicle of collective values these are inevitably vulnerable to destruction through his possible human weakness; as indeed Mackandal's last cry may signify. But a dead man is invulnerable at least to certain kinds of destruction, and the death of Mackandal at his most mythopoeic moment protects his meaning forever. As a myth, as the expression of collective feeling and purpose, he is indeed saved. His people now call out his name, just as Yeats named the patriots of 1916 only after their mythic transformation. Published critics, as well as students, often find the interplay of perceptions in this book difficult to appreciate as a positive meaning. For example, one critic, whose very theme is myth, speaks of the rationalism confusedly undermining its mythopoeic and miraculous elements.[9] This shows how the modern readers' own rationalistic assumptions constantly get in the way; what is at stake is not perceptual reality, but meaning.

The theatricality of the occasion focuses the relation of perception and meaning: in theatre meaning does not lie in what literally happens; and Mackandal's performance in his public situation is fittingly symbolic and illusionistic, while being perceived and understood quite literally by his black audience. The French slave-owners are equally watching a theatrical meaning rather than a physical event. Since they have brought the slaves to witness an exemplary punishment, M. Lenormand de Mezy is struck by the blacks' apparent indifference to the suffering of one of their own kind, and, on their return home, he starts to rehearse a chamber lecture to his wife on this theme, erecting a scientific theory of race upon this misperception. But there is something more fundamental than misperception involved for him too. His comment on the slaves' indifference to the suffering of 'one of their own kind' is a classic instance of the failure of self-recognition analysed by Stanley Cavell

if a man sees certain human beings as slaves, isn't he . . . rather missing something about himself, or rather something about his connection with these people . . . When he wants to be served at table by a black hand, he would not be satisfied to be served by a black paw. When he rapes a slave or takes her as a concubine, he does not feel that he has, by that fact itself, embraced sodomy. When he tips a black taxi-driver . . . it does not occur to him that he might more appropriately have patted the creature fondly on the side of the neck. He does not go to great lengths to convert his horses to Christianity or to prevent their getting wind of it. Everything in his relation to his slaves shows that he regards them as more or less human – his humiliations of them, his disappointments, his jealousies, his fears, his punishments, his attachments.[10]

The theatricality of the occasion brings home Cavell's point. The punishment can only be exemplary if the slaves are M. Lenormand's own fellow creatures. A dog cannot be given a punishment exemplary for other dogs, each dog has to be beaten individually. Only human beings can be expected to respond to spectacle. The larger logic of the occasion, therefore, enforces the cultural contradiction underlying its specific inhumanity. Who actually is one of our own kind? Or, as the question was once famously posed, who is my neighbour? Yet the universalising force of this way of putting the question follows hard upon the recognition that the blacks have derived a highly effective unity and power from the possession of a specific cultural configuration of their own. This problematic of cultural identity versus universality of values is the central thematic concern of the work, and is expressed in the elusiveness of its narrative voice and premisses throughout. Despite, or rather because of, the apparent simplicity of the story, readers often find it judgementally disorienting without realising that it is part of the point. It is a testimony to Carpentier's true sophistication and his way of sneaking under, and unsettling, the likely assumptions of the reader. While all readers initially identify with the black slaves against their white masters, the more thoughtful reader already experiences an implicit dilemma, in that the sense of injustice depends on a universalist conception arising from the same European Enlightenment culture which is responsible for colonialism. At one level, the potential dilemma is removed by the evident divisions within European culture, and by its being presented under a tribalistic, rather than a universal, aspect. For example, the advanced wing of the Enlightenment looks on Reason as a 'goddess', while the churchgoing of the more conservative whites serves a tribal cult no less superstitious than any supposedly primitive religion. We are led, in other words, to see both black and white culture relativistically. Yet there remains an underlying problem in the consciousness of the modern reader, as opposed to any of the historical characters, that the absolute objection to slavery is a historical product, albeit a very belated one, of Enlightenment universalism. No reader would now accept that the evil of slavery was merely a relative value of modern Western culture; it cannot be perceived as other than universally evil.

Conversely, Franz Fanon stressed the importance of an heroic African past as a psychological resource, and therefore as an active political energy in the present. Yet he also saw the danger of having only this past to bring to the 'universal trysting place'.

This historical necessity in which the men of African culture find themselves to racialize their claims and to speak more of African culture than of national culture will tend to lead them up a blind alley. Let us take for example the case of the African Cultural Society . . . The aim of this society was . . . to affirm the existence of an African culture, to evaluate this culture on the plane of distinct nations and to reveal the inner motive forces of each of their national cultures. But at the same time this society fulfilled another need: the need to exist side by side with the European Cultural society, which threatened to transform itself into a Universal Cultural Society. There was therefore at the bottom of this decision the anxiety to be present at the universal trysting place fully armed, with a culture springing from the very heart of the African continent. Now, this society will very quickly show its inability to shoulder these different tasks, and will limit itself to exhibitionist demonstrations, while the habitual behaviour of the members of this Society will be confined to showing Europeans that such a thing as African culture exists, and opposing their ideas to those of the ostentatious and narcissistic Europeans.[11]

For Fanon, the relationship between specific cultural identity and universal values had become an urgent problem. It is not a question that admits of general or theoretical answers. It is rather a matter of learning to live with a problematic consciousness. The Mexican poet, Octavio Paz, in the essays that were to become *The Labyrinth of Solitude*, meditated on this question over the same years with a different emphasis, and perhaps a longer-term historical prescience. Unlike Fanon, he was considering a people who already had their independence, and he now saw a larger historical cultural shift taking place whereby history would return to being a meditation on humanity rather than the stories of individual cultures or nations. The Mexican, he declared, was now living on the world stage, so that whatever solutions were to be found to the Mexican's problems would, if they were effective, inevitably be of universal validity.

And mankind, too, has recovered its unity. All of today's civilizations derive from that of the Western world, which has assimilated or crushed its rivals. The decisions we make in Mexico now affect all men, and vice versa. The differences that separate the Communists and the West are much less profound than those that separated the Persians and the Greeks, the Romans and the Egyptians, the Chinese and the peoples of Europe. Communists and bourgeois democrats brandish opposing ideas, but those ideas have a common source and are phrased in a common language which both sides understand. The contemporary crisis is not a struggle between two diverse cultures, as the conservatives would have us believe, but rather an internal quarrel in a civilization that no longer has any rivals, a civilization whose future is the future of the whole world. Each man's fate is that of man himself. Therefore, every attempt we make as Mexicans to resolve our conflicts must have universal validity or it will be futile from the outset.[12]

During and after the Second World War the conflicting need for both an individual and a universal culture was becoming apparent, and Latin America was to play an important part in articulating this question, since the mixed heritage of the region continually enforced the problematic consciousness of both an indigenous loyalty and a European, or Enlightenment, formation. Carpentier's novel catches this whole problematic in an ingenious way for which the very brevity of the narrative is an important clue. Its historical compression arises in significant measure from the laconic economy with which the novel records the horrors it retells. The narrative tone is not a Flaubertian metaphysical detachment, nor even quite an historian's objectivity, it is rather the necessary posture of anthropological neutrality. Almost from the outset, in other words, we see how culture-bound all the responses of the participants are, so that the reader's response, too, is problematised. Whereas a book like *Uncle Tom's Cabin* (1852) mobilised sentiment against a contemporary evil, this novel, set consciously within the original post-Rousseau heyday of moral sentimentalism, reverses the emotional dynamic of such fiction: it exercises an anti-sentimental distancing to highlight a difficult ethical complex whose real bearing is in the reader's historical present; indeed, in the very act of reading. The studied neutrality of tone is an aspect of the novel's anthropological focus. Of course, we feel the evil of slavery and of the many acts of inhumanity. Yet we also see that such inhumanity is itself all too human, and universally so. When Henri Christophe becomes one of the cruellest rulers on the European model, he is showing us, whatever his intentions, that blacks are fully human too. A virtue that had no such potentiality for evil would be not only sentimental, but meaningless. In Primo Levi's pregnant formulation, God 'does not like incorruptible things'. The novel is not concerned with personal psychology so much as cultural structures.

Carpentier's probing of cultural relativity is enforced by his use of the 'marvellous' which acquires a tougher edge of meaning than one would suspect from the rousing simplicities of the prologue. In the first half of the story, the voodoo religion and beliefs of the black slaves are presented as cultural facts, so that, although our ethical solidarity is with them, we only understand them through the cultural assumptions of the modern West. There is a structural condescension here even while there is no human or tonal superiority. The same applies to the episode of Mackandal's execution in which the blacks' perception is made comprehensible in the rational terms of the assumed reader. In a later episode, however, the standpoint is reversed. When Henri Christophe's archbishop falls out of favour, he is publicly cemented into the wall (*Kingdom* pp. 76–80; *Reino* pp. 99–103). There is no doubt that he is dead. Yet during high mass the archbishop appears to Christophe whose physical collapse at the shock is the first stage of the collapse of his whole kingdom (*Kingdom* p. 81; *Reino* p. 106). The reader may infer that the apparition is a delusion of Christophe as he undergoes a heart attack, and that the narrative is merely adopting the legendary account, or Christophe's own perception, of the episode. But this rationalist recuperation is not offered by the text itself. Indeed, just as the Mackandal execution exemplifies Cavell's analytic point about the double-think of slavery, so this episode seems designed to exemplify Nietzsche's remarks on miracle:

Whoever wishes to test rigorously to what extent he himself is related to the true aesthetic listener or belongs to the community of the Socratic-critical persons needs only to examine sincerely the feeling with which he accepts miracles represented on the stage: whether he feels his historical sense, which insists on strict psychological causality, insulted by them, whether he makes a benevolent concession and admits the miracle as a phenomenon intelligible to childhood but alien to him, or whether he experiences anything else. For in this way he will be able to determine to what extent he is capable of understanding *myth* as a concentrated image of the world that, as a condensation of phenomena, cannot dispense with miracles. It is probable, however, that almost everyone, upon close examination, finds that the critical-historical spirit of our culture has so affected him that he can only make the former existence of myth credible to himself by means of scholarship, through intermediary abstractions. But without myth every culture loses the healthy natural power of its creativity: only a horizon defined by myth completes and unifies a whole cultural movement.[13]

Nietzsche and Carpentier share the note of diagnostic cultural challenge; the desire to probe in what spirit the rationalistic, scientific culture is being inhabited. Literal belief in miracle would mean that it was not being coherently inhabited at all, while absolute rejection of the fiction suggests a fetishising of the rationalistic principle. Aesthetic acceptance implies an understanding of the mythic flexibility and concentrated sense of purpose which would characterise any lived and effective culture. Reason can be deified, or given a narrowly positivistic value, or it can be seen as itself subject to culturally relativistic use. Its truth is not in question, so much as the value put on the truth claims it represents. That is the real function of the marvellous in this novel. To enforce its cultural relativity, Carpentier includes something that challenges recuperation by rationalistic explanation. In effect, this involves him in a systematic reworking of the historical novel form as it was developed by Walter Scott partly from late eighteenth-century gothic fiction and during the conservative British backwash to the French Revolution.

Much twentieth-century fiction on historical themes involves a critique, or a radical recasting, of Scott's realist narrative form, but Carpentier is an especially significant example in that he goes back to the historical period from which Scott's form evolved. He recasts the form as a way of recasting the history. In his first novel *Waverley* (1814) Scott wrote of the primitive landscapes and anarchic energies of the highlands. With the 1745 rebellion still within possible living memory, Scott's novel contained, and neutralised, this potentially dangerous charge by presenting such revolutionary impulses with romantic nostalgia as a vanished and impossible excess. The controlling form of the Scott novel was the balanced, rational, universalistic overview of Fielding who was, like Scott, a conservative man of the law; and who famously dismissed the 'marvellous' from his new province of writing and marginalised the Jacobite rebellion as the background to an episode in *Tom Jones* (1749). Carpentier reverses that process. Although he cannot step outside the terms of a victorious rationalism, nor would he wish to do so, he uses the black culture to highlight the historical relativity of the Enlightenment itself, its fetishising of its own criteria, and the danger of over-confident authority arising precisely from the genuineness of its claims to universality. In this respect, the thrust of Carpentier's critique brings him into the same territory as Adorno and Horkheimer's *Dialectic of Enlightenment* which was also composed over the middle decades of the century. From their left progressive standpoint, it was scandalous that the Enlightenment, in seeking to escape from myth, should be constantly engendering new forms of the mythic within itself. Hence Adorno turned to the idea of a 'negative dialectics' to suggest the function of modernist art, through its aesthetic self-consciousness, as a constant labour of demythologising. Carpentier suggests an opposite way of treating the same question. If the mythic is an inescapable aspect of culture, it should be consciously accepted, and the more so if it is a potential force for both liberation and self-knowledge. Furthermore, it may be that the very hostility to the mythopoeic is what makes it damaging. Yet Carpentier clearly is no more inclined than Adorno and Horkheimer to an obscurantist valorising of myth at the expense of Enlightenment, and like them he turns to the aesthetic, although without using the word, as the crucial mediating category. For the cultural relativity dramatised within his novel is constantly focused by mutual incomprehension specifically in the realm of art, and this in turn links the theme of cultural relativity to a definition of Carpentier's own narrative as a socially progressive act. The artistic theme of the novel is therefore crucial to its overall meaning. Carpentier uses the anthropological and historical context of the story to work out a meaning for art as a positive form of modern mythopoeia.

Once again the historical moment is pertinent. Alexander Baumgarten's *Aesthetic* (1750) was the first modern use of the word 'aesthetic' to denote a quasi-autonomous, specialised realm, and Carpentier's interest lies in the longer-term, modern consequences of this development of Enlightenment thought, and so, in a deceptively naturalised way, he derives from the incidents of the historical narrative an implicit running meditation on the nature of art. At the same time this meditation on art is embedded within non-artistic as well as artistic occasions, and thereby reflects his concern for the larger, anthropological meaning of art within the given culture. Hence there are episodes with specifically artistic motifs such as the declamations of French classical tragedy by Mademoiselle Floridor, the provincial actress whom M. Lenormand de Mézy brings back from France as his second wife. Then there are governing images such as the theatrical setting of the Mackandal execution. And, finally, there are incidents which, taken in isolation, have no artistic reference at all, but which are powerfully inflected by the larger context. When, for example, Henri Christophe's body is engulfed in a bath of drying cement from the building of his fortress palace he becomes a kind of statue, and the manner of his end picks up a theme of art as monumentalising and petrifying which runs throughout the book (*Kingdom* pp. 92–3; *Reino* pp. 120–1).

Indeed, Carpentier comes closest to the spirit of Cervantes not in his recovery of the marvellous, where he is working against the grain of his own cultural moment, but in his sophisticated exploration of aesthetic themes through apparently everyday incidents and absurd misunderstandings. The principal aesthetic misunderstanding between blacks and Europeans lies in the blacks' Quixotically literalistic responses to European artistic occasions. When the slaves hear Mademoiselle Floridor recite lines from Racine's *Phèdre* confessing the depraved desires and crimes of the lustful queen, they believe her to be confessing, if not rather boasting of, her own crimes (*Kingdom* pp. 47–8; *Reino* pp. 37–8). The ironies of this are richly multiple. As an insight into her own character it has some pertinence; only the tragic grandeur is inappropriate. But, more importantly, the play itself, as a supreme expression of French civilisation, invokes under rigorous aesthetic control its own barbarous 'other' which the narrative meanwhile has shown to be its true historical reality. The category of the 'savage' is a product of civilisation and an unconscious reflection of what that civilisation conceals within itself. In effect, the blacks' aesthetically naive response touches a truth which the aesthetic realm has only served to obfuscate.

Repeatedly, the art of the Europeans either obfuscates and idealises, or else it turns the living into an order of death. This latter motif begins with the very opening episode in which the artificial heads for displaying wigs in the barber's shop are visually rhymed with the severed heads of animals in the next-door butcher's window. Pauline Bonaparte comes to the Caribbean on a military ship reading the popular sentimental idealisation of the region in *Paul et Virginie* (1788) by Bernardin de Saint Pierre, a literary descendant of Rousseau. The art theme culminates in the Villa Borghese in Rome when Pauline Bonaparte's former masseur, Soliman, recognises her body by touch as one of the statues in the darkened upper storey of the building (*Kingdom* p. 101; *Reino* p. 130). The statue terrifies Soliman because he experiences it as a living corpse or as a deathly simulacrum of life; an uncanny sacrilege against life itself. The very accuracy of the reproduction in stone is what makes it so chilling. The blacks, by contrast, go in for a warmer kind of reproduction. While M. Lenormand, on their return from the performance of the Mackandal execution, lectures his wife on the inferiority of the negro race, Ti Noel begets twins on one of the kitchen maids in the stable. And the blacks likewise have artistic forms which are characterised by their non-separability from communal life. The picture frame, the museum, the theatre and the church all express the separation of the aesthetic and the religious domains in European culture from everyday life, but Mackandal's stories of Africa, or the ceremony in which the blacks prepare themselves for the uprising, are imaginative and ritual means for heightening and directing communal consciousness and feeling. Soliman's catatonic reaction in the Villa Borghese of drumming his heels on the floor, and thereby turning the whole empty space into a vast drum, echoes this earlier scene and recalls the different meaning of its art.

The black culture, therefore, exemplifies a positive possibility in art by which the aesthetic sophistication of European art is shown to have been won at a dangerous cost of sublimation and bad faith. Carpentier seeks to recover this in his own art even while writing within the European tradition. That is why the aesthetic theme is the most telling aspect of his critique. After all, the evils of slavery, however terrible, are rather old news by the mid twentieth century, and the critique by which we understand this is largely an internal function of the European Enlightenment. There is a danger here of self-fulfilling anachronism in the realm of moral feeling; of indulging the emotions of *ressentiment* both vicariously and in hindsight. But the possibilities and dangers of the aesthetic as a means of self-understanding, along with the problem of anthropological relativity, remained important unresolved questions for the mid twentieth-century reader. Art can be a means of ideological obfuscation or a means of understanding and communal purpose. In Adorno and Horkheimer's version of the dialectic of Enlightenment, there is only an unceasing struggle against the encroaching falsity of the mythic. Carpentier suggests a different model. Although we initially seem to have only an unsatisfactory choice between a voodoo religious cult or a deracinated aestheticism, his own narrative suggests we may recover a deeper mythopoeic root beneath the artistic tradition which produced Racine. As we provisionally inhabit a work of fiction, so we inhabit a world view, but this is far from being a position of empty relativism. The reader feels human solidarity with the blacks without sharing their magical world view, and inhabits the rationalist world view of the whites while not identifying with them humanly. The book incorporates the inescapability of critical perception into its narrative method in a way that dissolves any sense of criticism as some kind of separate activity which may be performed as an optional extra to the apprehension of the work or, for that matter, outside of everyday existence.

If the burden of Carpentier's title is to privilege the kingdom of this world over the kingdom of heaven, he also assimilates the latter in the mythopoeic spirit defined by the narrative. Heaven is abundantly exposed in the novel as the myth of a particular culture, as is appropriate to the Enlightenment setting. But the exposure has been exposed in its turn, and to expose the Christian heaven as myth, therefore, is not the conclusion but simply the first step towards understanding its possible meaning. Even universal truths are myths by virtue of their human use, by becoming foci of emotional conviction and effective action, and, since every truth has in that sense a mythopoeic potential, what matters is not the propositional truth so much as the human impact of the idea; and that is not simply a truth question. Which truth is it best to privilege and inhabit? Carpentier's objection to the Christian heaven is that it is a politically quietistic myth, but the same idealism and feeling put into the creation of an earthly kingdom based on universally humane values might be historically efficacious. His own story finally seeks, like Mackandal's stories at the beginning of the slave rebellion, to create an enlarged sense of possibilities and a focused sense of purpose. Carpentier's recovery of the marvellous is a vindication of his own art as mythopoeic; as an expression of utopian purpose in history. Just before the end of the story he puts a too directly utopian gloss on the phrase 'kingdom of this world' which acts as a simplifying chord, like the relative simplicity of his prologue, but the very final vision of the disintegrating Ti Noel honours the darker complexity of the narrative and reinforces the historical reality from which the utopian impulse continues to acquire its meaning.

MYTH AND FICTION IN GABRIEL GARCÍA MÁRQUEZ' *ONE HUNDRED YEARS OF SOLITUDE*

Carpentier's anthropological detachment and relativity with respect to myth is thematised within the fiction in such a way as to define the meaning of the fiction itself as a conscious, and progressive, form of mythopoeia. The categories are kept just sufficiently separate in the mind for the one to be able to redefine and reinforce the other. In *One Hundred Years of Solitude* (1968) Garcia Márquez uses fiction as a more distinct category again, and with a more sharply deconstructive edge, to dislodge myth by revealing it as myth. But the impact is still not debunking, or even unsympathetic. It is a highly seductive fiction designed to incorporate, rather than just expose, the seductive power of myth.

I have shown at length elsewhere how the fateful story of the Buendias is not a myth for us, but is told at the level of myth to reflect its meaning for them; and the key means of effecting this double implication is the Cervantean device of the fictitious foreign historian.[14] The deep structure of their lives, their collective inability to love outside the incestuous circle of the family, is experienced by them as an objective historical fate, but it is finally placed under the sign of fiction, and revealed as a self-created or illusory fate, with the discovery of Melquíades' parchments on which the whole story has been foretold. In contrast to the progressive mythopoeia of Carpentier, García Márquez presents myth as a dangerous psychic entrapment, yet he equally uses a mythopoeic method, in a homeopathic spirit, to reveal the condition from within. Its therapeutic quality lies in its accepting the self and the past rather than simply denying it, or 'overcoming' it in Primo Levi's sense. The Buendias are repeatedly imaged as sleep-walking through their lives after the insomnia sickness, and a rough awakening is not traditionally the way to deal with that condition. The mythic warp and weft of history and fiction in their experience is a whole cloth which is not just to be torn apart; it is now their historical truth and is rather to be acknowledged.

The popular note of the book is functional in this regard. Its almost excessive charm made it an immediate best-seller around the world, and in that respect it is highly accessible. Yet the book has remained elusive of interpretation in a way that reflects a tougher core. The enigma built into its central narrative device feels like a fictional game, and the reader is encouraged to regard it as such, yet it also focuses a more subliminal ambivalence about the whole story, which has after all encompassed serious political and historical resonances. Only gradually do we realise that the charm itself is strategic: the nostalgia of the Buendias, representing an emotional fixation in the history of the region at large, is relived both at the level of its seductive charm and at the level of a charming fiction. Readers tend consciously to focus on one or the other aspect, but it may be that the true triumph of its populism is to communicate its more complex impact subliminally. The overt and ludic resistance to analytic closure, the fictional self-consciousness, keeps its weightier and less formulated dimensions open too. This suggests that the fictitious historian device serves an opposite epochal need from Cervantes' use of it. The structure of foretold chronicle distinguishes the elements of created fiction, fatalistic myth and external history within a felt whole. Cervantes sought to distinguish the significance of fiction at a time when, as in Shakespeare's history plays, it shared with history a common function of moral exemplarity, and his levels of narrative mediation highlight the question in an open-ended, locally ingenious way. By contrast, García Márquez' device has the tightly enclosed logic of the Moebius strip or an Escher drawing. In its circular labyrinth we recognise that history and fiction cannot be separated, and bringing this mythic recognition to consciousness, rather than seeking a positivist denial of it, is the truly liberating act.

If the late twentieth-century boom of Latin American fiction is a Spenglerian 'contemporary' of earlier European and American modernism, it involves difference as well as parallels; and not least because it had digested that earlier achievement. García Márquez might be seen as critically reworking both the brooding fatalism of *Nostromo* and the optimism of *The Rainbow* in *One Hundred Years of Solitude*, or the perverse, culturally programmed self-destructiveness of *Tess of the d'Urbevilles* in *Chronicle of a Death Foretold* (1981). Carlos Fuentes' Quetzalcoatl novel, *Change of Skin* (1967) revisits the territory of *The Plumed Serpent* in an entirely different mode. The difference centres around myth. Much of this later fiction is critical of inherited and mythic forms, and yet sees the necessity of immersing itself in the destructive element. It commonly uses myth against myth, rather than reject the category. Typically, it has a more a relativistic and local awareness of myth in contrast to the universalism of the modernists. The quaint localism of the Genesis myth in *One Hundred Years of Solitude*, for example, is quite unlike the burden of ontological grounding it assumes in *The Rainbow*. García Márquez' regional inflection mocks the very idea of grounding and origin. And so fiction becomes an important term prising apart, in consciousness if not in experience, the categories of history and myth. So too, Cervantes has become a usable forebear in the latter part of the century in a way he was not for the modernists. Their Nietzschean acceptance of myth is replaced by a Cervantean problematics of emotional projection, and it was prescient of Thomas Mann to combine these two figures as the modernist synthesis was breaking up. Fuentes similarly combines them in the narration of *Change of Skin*, but it is now the mad Nietzsche who dominates. It is as if Cervantes' job were to be done again, dispelling the modern power of the mythopoeic as he once dispelled the medieval power of the marvellous.

One Hundred Years of Solitude is the summative example of this, and, if Carpentier's mid-century form is epochally post-modernist in its critical relativity, in its having left the synoptic ambition of high modernism behind, García Márquez' novel is postmodernist in the more specific generic sense that drops the hyphen. Its unaffected populism, and its fictional self-consciousness placing the whole history *en abyme*, are hall-marks of this. Yet its play with unreality is no merely fictional game. In his long and varied career as a journalist, Garcia Márquez played obsessively on the word 'world' as he ruminated on the strange unreality of the geo-political order he was often reporting to a local or regional readership.[15] An important gift of his journalism to his major novel was an ability to present the power of unreality in the contemporary world. In this respect he is a contemporary of Thomas Pynchon.

CHAPTER 7

Living without myth: deconstructing the old world

The Latin American writers just considered effect a critique of myth from the inside. Their myths are regionally specific rather than arising from the sheer fact of conscious being in the world, which was the characteristically modernist implication, and they see the necessity of understanding them diagnostically, yet, by the same token, they also see them as part of an historical identity. Their way of being half inside and half outside their myths allows them to make positive literary use of mythopoeic possibility, even if this has occasionally led to sentimental readings which miss their actual toughness and complexity. But the directly mythopoeic aftermath of European and American modernism has been characteristically different.

The disintegration of the realist mode in fiction after about 1880 did not arise, as is sometimes claimed, from some literalistic naivety in the form itself, but from the increasingly evident lack of a cultural consensus to underwrite it. Systems of belief which we do not share are thereby exposed, in the market-place, debunking sense, as myths. The modernist generation found a radical solution to this. Rather than naturalise their own projected significances within the narrative texture, they made the inescapable foundation in shared belief and values fully conscious. Myth itself became the most fundamental kind of truth claim. What distinguishes modernist mythopoeia, therefore, is not just the central use of myth, but its according to myth the ultimate metaphysical value. Myth was a mediating term between history and fiction in the modernist decades. By the latter part of the century, however, as trust in the mythic continued to fall, or the absence of common beliefs and values became more evident, so the relations of history and fiction became consciously problematic. They lost their common term without being separable.

The history/fiction debate through the late sixties and onwards was therefore culturally significant even if it was often intellectually factitious. The point is not that you can have a history without any fictional or narrative dimension, or a fiction with no reference or relevance to the historical world. Neither form is likely ever to be pure, in fact, but that does not stop it being clear as a category and intention. There is no problem in principle, only in practice; and at the level of practice the problem is banal since it is of the essence in putting these principles into practice. That is what the principles are for. The sense of scandal arises from confusing these two levels of the question. But such a confusion was what Thomas Pynchon sought meaningfully to achieve. It is not, in other words, the sheer mixture of genres that matters; as is evident from innumerable, quite unproblematic, varieties of historical fiction since Scott. Pynchon makes the distinction matter, while also making it impossible to draw. His paranoiac fiction creates not just a bureaucratic, but an epistemological, catch 22. In that respect *Gravity's Rainbow* is an implosion or inversion of modernist mythopoeia. Much as Salman Rushdie speaks of a character who has lost his religious faith as having a 'god-shaped hole' inside him, Pynchon presents the historical world as a myth-shaped whole surrounding us all. Yet it is also now, of course, a black hole consisting not of mere emptiness of meaning, but of a terrifying and unanswerable complex of questions into which all inter- pretation is sucked.

More specifically, Pynchon shows a particular transformation of the mythopoeic that may occur when an attempt is made actively to eradicate myth, or to try living without it. The mythopoeic in Pynchon is like the alligators in the New York sewers in his earlier novel *V*: these grow and multiply precisely because of the attempt to destroy them or drive them underground. But to see the alligators themselves as a myth is to use the word in too loose a way. The alligators are not a myth, but something else created perhaps by the absence of myth. If the sleep of reason produces monsters, so perhaps does the sleep of myth. Pynchon's world, after all, is not the sleep of reason, but a world of reason in insomniac overdrive in the early hours, and in this respect it represents a larger North American literature of paranoia going back at least to Joseph Heller's *Catch 22* (1962). In that respect, Pynchon's paranoia is an inverse parallel to the insomnia sickness in García Márquez' *One Hundred Years of Solitude*, whereby the Buendias passed from a world of myth to the world of history. They think they can cope without their dream selves, but they are only the more completely and unconsciously governed by these psychic structures in their waking lives. Hence García Márquez' humorously therapeutic use of myth in telling the story of their unconscious. Paranoia, too, is significantly reflected in a particular mode of fiction best defined by a non-fictional analogue which is itself an epochal reflection.

As a way into this it is worth pausing on Pynchon's own thematising of fiction, story-telling and myth. In his book on Pynchon, Tony Tanner quotes the passage from *V* in which Benny Profane, with his friend Angel, creates alligator stories to impress a girl he has just met.

Together on the stoop they hammered together a myth. Because it wasn't born from fear of thunder, dreams, astonishment at how the crops kept dying after harvest and coming up again every spring, or anything else very permanent, only a temporary interest, a spur of the moment tumescence, it was a myth rickety and transient as the bandstands, and the sausage-pepper booths of Mulberry Street.[1]

Tanner goes on to comment how the 'old myths no longer work' and ends his chapter with the following comment:

When all the 'scaffolds' are down, perhaps – *perhaps* – something new and regenerative may appear. Meanwhile in the fragmenting, self-disassembling, declining world that Pynchon's novel depicts for us it is clear that no one possesses what Fausto Maijstral wishes for his daughter: 'a single given heart, a whole mind at peace. That is a prayer, if you wish.' It is a prayer that we should all wish to pray.

Tanner accepts the narrator's comments seeing Benny's stories as a kind of debased myth representative of the contemporary cultural condition. In broad terms this seems fair enough, although it also reduces Pynchon's ironic presentation to a propositional banality, while the actual narrative context gives a significant further twist to these remarks. The passage is introduced as follows:

'What do you guys do?' Lucille said.
I tell tall stories to girls I want to screw, Profane thought. He scratched his armpit. 'Kill alligators' he said.
'Wha.'
He told her about the alligators; Angel who had a fertile imagination too, added detail, colour. (*V* p. 128)

Within the terms of the narrative the alligators are not, as Tanner alleges, a myth, whether old style or new, since they are indeed the creatures Profane and his friends hunt for a living. Strictly speaking, Profane and Angel are not actually creating a myth, but presenting the truth as a tall story. It is hardly surprising that Lucille does not know whether to believe what a Joyce character would call the 'allegators'.

Walter Benjamin and Thomas Mann already reflected a postmodern shift whereby story, rather than either myth or novelistic realism, became the fundamental model of fictional truth. For Pynchon's postmodernism another form, the tall story, is the implicit model. The tall story, which has a venerable history in the American tradition, is significantly different from either myth or folk-tale, and it has taken on some distinctive contemporary forms. If we think in terms of the tall story rather than myth we invoke a different set of questions. The present discussion, therefore, is not a foot-note to the debate on history and fiction, but is concerned with a related question concerning the emotional chemistry of reception: what difference, if any, does it make to a reader's or listener's response if a story is believed to be true rather than fictional? What if the difference seems all-important but we cannot actually tell? This question was an important one in the early days of European fiction when authors such as Defoe and Richardson systematically equivocated on it. I have written at book length on that topic in relation to the subsequent development of the European novel, and one of the reasons the subject required extended treatment was that the problematic relations of literalistic and fictional belief were to disappear as a problem as they were absorbed into the implicit contractual understanding of realist fiction.[2] But this problematic continued to have a significant afterlife within realist fiction, and, as realism disintegrated, it came once again to the surface. In the mid century, realism, after being sustained in a new form by the modernist synthesis, dissolved once again into its eighteenth-century elements.

Richard Steele's *Spectator* paper of Monday, March 10th 1712 consists of a rather banal cautionary tale about the dangers of London life for innocent girls from the provinces, in the form of a letter from an unknown correspondent signing herself Octavia. But Steele introduces it with a brief suggestion that the letter is not a fiction:

It is often said, after a Man has heard a Story with extraordinary Circumstances, it is a very good one if it be true: But as for the following Relation, I should be glad were I sure it were false. It is told with such Simplicity, and there are so many artless Touches of Distress in it, that I fear it comes too much from the Heart.[3]

The device here is reminiscent of Primo Levi's invoking of the 'real' Müller. Steele judges that the story will have an impact despite its banality if it is believed to be true. Indeed, once it is taken as true, its commonplace nature will actually work in its favour. And to convince the reader that the story is indeed true, Steele appeals to the 'artless' touches of distress in the writing of the letter. But by this time Steele's logic has developed a significant circularity. On the one hand, the impact of the story is seen to depend in some measure on the belief in its being a real letter from an unfortunate woman, while on the other hand we can only infer its literal truth from intrinsic, or literary, qualities in the writing. In other words, the appeal to an extra-literary consideration has an affective value for the reader, yet is itself ultimately a textual device. Without changing the letter itself, Steele has wrapped it up in an equivocation as to its status. Steele's device has a benign circularity making it easy to pass over. Any literalistic belief on the reader's part will only enhance the ethical impact of the tale. But equivocation with literal and fictional belief becomes central again in the mid-twentieth century both as a problem and as a device. Of course, the cultural context is very different, and the break-down into these elements has taken many forms, including Norman Mailer's combinations of journalism, essay, autobiography and fiction. In Mailer's case, the overriding motive of political and cultural commentary linked him predominantly to the history/fiction question. He mixes these elements, but does not significantly equivocate about them as such. In contrast, Pynchon's active equivocation is a reversal of Steele's harmless circularity in passing off the fictional as real, for Pynchon presents history, with vicious circularity, as a tall story. It may be significant, however, that Steele's story concerns the dangers of city life in an early phase of modern urbanisation for, in addressing itself to the dangers peculiar to entering a city environment, it points to the true formal analogue of Pynchon's fiction which is neither history, nor fiction, nor myth, but a particular form of tall story that has come to be known as 'urban legend'.

In *The Vanishing Hitchhiker: American Urban Legends and their Meanings* J. H. Brunvand defined urban legend as a predominantly adolescent form essentially distinct from folk-tale or myth and even from the tall story as normally understood.[4] It differs from folk-tale in that the legend is always told as having actually happened to someone at two or three removes from the speaker. It does not occur, implicitly or explicitly, under the formula of 'once upon a time', for in most cases it would, like Steele's letter, have little impact if it did. The legend of the foreign substance in the Coca-Cola can, for example, has little intrinsic narrative value. Myth, folk-tale or fiction all have intrinsic significances which are not dependent upon their literal veracity. But what gives the urban legend its distinctive character is that it is pointless without the belief in its literal truth. Hence the importance, as Brunvand notes, of a kind of naive artistry designed to make it seem veridical, as in Steele's 'artless Touches of Distress', or, more importantly, an introductory comment, like Steele's, affirming the literal truth of what follows. This also distinguishes urban legend from the tall story as normally understood. For the tall story, as in Benny Profane's case, is known by its narrator to be exaggerated or false, and is indeed a kind of individual narrative pyrotechnics such as Angel goes on to supply, whereas urban legend is a collective possession passed on artlessly and in good faith as true. But the twist in Benny's case is that the alligators, which are real in his world, are fictions created by Pynchon from the classic material of urban legend; the pet alligator, flushed down the toilet, which started to breed in the sewers. Benny tells as a tall tale what Pynchon's narrative presents as reality in the form of urban legend. It is a *mise en abyme* whereby the simple-minded paranoia of urban legend is developed into a sophisticated mode of fiction.

Brunvand's definition of urban legend as a distinct form helps to distinguish between the self-conscious mythopoeia of the Joycean era and the postmodern equivocation in *Gravity's Rainbow* (1974) as to the historical status of its narrative material. For Pynchon's early, overt use of the legendary form hints at the underlying fictional posture which is more completely merged with history in the later novel. Indeed, it is helpful to return to the modernist period to illustrate the distinction between myth and legend by an occasion when they significantly overlap. In *The Great War and Modern Memory* Paul Fussell takes issue with a claim in Bernard Bergonzi's *Heroes' Twilight* that the experience of the trenches dispelled conventionally literary effects, such as mythic allusion, from the poetry of combatants.[5] Fussell demonstrates, by contrast, the extraordinary literariness of responses to the war by many soldiers; so much so, he argues, that the war itself then took on a mythic meaning partly informed by literary structures such as an inverted pastoralism. He goes on to observe that the peculiar conditions of life at the front with thousands of men living in a continuous series of trenches across the European continent, in conditions of both boredom and danger, and largely deprived of real information about what was happening to them, produced the most fertile, primordial ground for the creation of myth. Yet Fussell also emphasises the often ironic uses of literary convention in the poetry of the war and in that respect comes close to acknowledging

Bergonzi's point. The whole question can be seen more sharply if the two critics are understood as referring to three essentially different objects under the same name: primary myth, the literary use of myth and urban legend.

One of Fussell's specific examples of such war-time myth creation is the widespread story of the Canadian soldier believed to have been crucified in no-man's-land.[6] But this has all the characteristics of urban legend rather than of myth. What is confusing is simply that the paranoic legend has adopted the most prestigious mythic model in our culture as its subject-matter. But, in using this traditional material, the modern legend is precisely not creating it; it is rather perhaps consuming it, and thereby transforming it into something else. The new element lies in the telling of it as a real event, which transforms it into an image of extraordinary cruelty. For Christ's crucifixion, however horrifying, was not extraordinary in its historical moment, and his being executed like a common criminal is an essential part of the Christian myth. Christ's crucifixion, after all, as the Frenchman put it, was only *son boulot*, his job. Hence, whether it is viewed as history or as myth, the original crucifixion does not have the same impact. Urban legend, by contrast, depends on a maximum stretching, without breaking, of the tension between the horror or unusualness of the event and the belief that it has really happened. The legend of the boyfriend murdered on a date, or the baby-sitter in the house with a child-murderer, are classic instances and it is clearly the same frisson that characterises the story of the crucified soldier. The outcome is that the Christian archetype has been significantly transformed in its emotional impact, if not in its abstractly definable meaning. The myth has itself become the material of an atrocity legend, and the superimposition of the two, while initially confusing, actually helps to enforce the distinction.

Yet, while enforcing the distinction, the legend of the crucified soldier also brings out the significant points of affinity between the two forms. For, although legend is independent of myth, it seeks to occupy the same ground, and where they meet the mythopoeic is therefore displaced, or transformed, by legend. In the present case, the crucified soldier is a grotesque reversal of the Christian myth, and that in a sense, as Fussell argues, makes it into a new myth. But, in so far as the original myth is now being experienced through the medium of urban legend, much as Benny Profane wrapped the truth in a tall story, the mythopoeic has rather been dissolved into the paranoic mode of urban legend. And the further consequence is that, whereas myths and folk-tales are long-term

cultural sedimentations with a usually sustaining meaning, urban legends are the sprouting products of more immediate situations of anxiety.
One assumes they die with their situation, as did the story of the crucified
soldier. In this respect urban legend does not need to parody an original
myth, or even be hostile to it, in order to undermine it. Its own nature is
already more intrinsically corrosive than parody. Of course, the Christian myth is so powerful and transhistorical that it survives the local effect
of being made into the material of urban legend. But what about more
secular and historical myths such as nationhood, democracy and legal
justice which are Pynchon's characteristic territory?

It may be significant that Brunvand interprets the paranoia of urban
legend as the product of a specifically adolescent sub-culture, while
Pynchon presents it as the likely outcome of any honest attempt to
understand the true workings of modern society. In suggesting that
urban legend is a predominantly adolescent form, Brunvand sees it as
the naive expression of anxieties arising from the insecurity of limited
experience combined with increased responsibility. But the adult populations of modern societies are also required to shoulder the responsibili-
ties of citizenship and of wealth creation while being restricted with
respect to information and the exercise of power. The modern electorate
must behave like an adult, but it cannot expect to be treated like one;
which puts it in the classic dilemma of the adolescent. In the public,
rather than the personal, sphere, a condition of adolescence is imposed
on a wide scale. These are the classic conditions for political rumour and
anxiety; the structure of feeling that Pynchon has both used and thematised. The paranoic response does not, therefore, require an active
conspiracy; everyday politics, exacerbated by the information and opinion industries, is enough. Pynchon has focused this psychological formation as a significant and intelligible piece of historical reality in its own
right. There is in fact a progression from *V* and *The Crying of Lot 49* into
Gravity's Rainbow. No longer a literary fantasy, the conspiracy in *Gravity's
Rainbow* is completely identified with a central set of events in modern
history: the establishment of a fascist state in Nazi Germany; the taking
over of German rocket technology by the allies after the war; and the
subsequent development of the space program as a prestige symbol for
the US economy. *Vineland* goes on to do for the American seventies and
eighties what *Gravity's Rainbow* did for the forties to the sixties. In fact, the
assimilation of fiction to history in the shift from the German *Rakete*
(rocket) to the American 'racket' is so close that Dale Carter has been
able, without overt irony, to write an impressively documented history of

the same subject making central use of the novel as if it were simply a work of history.[7]

In respect of the political problem of knowledge Pynchon could be the subject of a further chapter to Hugh Kenner's *The Stoic Comedians*. Kenner's authors all saw the encyclopaedic spread of knowledge as a debasing of knowledge itself and a loss of its potentially progressive political value. Pynchon's inflection of the encyclopaedia theme is neatly caught by Eigenvalue's remarks to Stencil, the questing hero of *V*:

> In a world such as you inhabit, Mr. Stencil, any cluster of phenomena can be a conspiracy. So no doubt your suspicion is correct. But why consult me? Why not the Encyclopaedia Brittanica? It knows more than I about any phenomena you should ever have interest in.[8]

Eigenvalue's remarks are a nice play on Nietzsche's point concerning the ambiguity of what the encyclopaedia 'knows'. Whereas the classic critique of modernity stressed the atomistic isolation of the encyclopaedia's contents, and therefore its failure to be real knowledge for life, this passage stresses their unknowable interconnections and the impossibility of separating yourself from what you know even when you actually suspect this of being somehow fake or untrue. There is no social or mental space outside this condition.

So too, *Gravity's Rainbow* contrasts diametrically with Joyce's synthetic encyclopaedism. Pynchon's encyclopaedic use of different disciplines takes the form of a labyrinth rather than a maze. Its system, that is to say, is not one from which the reader is expected to emerge, or within which there is a vantage-point *sub specie temporis nostri* from which to contemplate the whole. It is significant in this regard that its scientific allusions and discourse are characteristically literal rather than metaphorical; although they are of course given metaphorical expansions such as the use of chemical process as the model of social process etc. Like the use of science in *The Periodic Table*, this stands in contrast to the typically metaphorical use of science in modernism, where the writers wanted to affirm the radical metaphoricity of science itself. But, in Pynchon's case, the way the ambiguity has started to matter again is a linguistic correlative of the overriding paranoic equivocation between fiction and historical fact. Of course, all language, in Nietzsche's sense, is metaphorical. This is no bad thing in itself, and, as Paul Ricoeur has indicated at length, it is the condition of original thought in more areas than poetry. Something of the same recognition, albeit by ironic inversion, is evident in the following passage from *V*:

Manhood on Malta thus became increasingly defined in terms of rockhood. This had its dangers for Fausto. Living as he does much of the time in a world of metaphor, the poet is always acutely conscious that metaphor has no value apart from its function; that it is a device, an artifice. So that while others may look on the laws of physics as legislation and God as a human form with beard measured in light-years and nebulae for sandals, Fausto's kind are alone with the task of living in a universe of things which simply are, and cloaking that innate mindlessness with comfortable and pious metaphor so that the 'practical' half of humanity may continue in the Great Lie, confident that their machines, dwellings, street and weather share the same human motives, personal traits and fits of contrariness as they. (*V* p. 305)

But the note of barely controlled hysteria in the passage suggests how the recognition of radical metaphority can also be vertiginous; as it was in Nietzsche's essay. As Nietzsche insisted, there is no Archimedian point of literal meaning, such as Fausto imagines, from which to control the metaphorical. In *Gravity's Rainbow* the problem of language as radically metaphorical, which has been inserted as a narrative aside in V, becomes a pervasive premiss of the narrative.

This points to the most radically significant perhaps of those intermediate 'zones' in which most of the action of *Gravity's Rainbow* takes place. Pynchon's way of bringing the 'literal' terms of one field into 'metaphorical' conjunction with those of another seems to generate a comparable anxiety about the nature of meaning in important areas; as for example complex social processes which fall outside direct observation. Or as he puts it: 'here in the Zone categories have been blurred badly.'[9] Hence there is an epistemological, as well as a political, dimension to the suggestion in *Gravity's Rainbow* that society may have passed a point of complexity where it is now beyond possible control. Such a vision, whether one takes it literally or metaphorically, has a chilling effect. Whether, that is, it describes the political facts or the political feeling, the feeling is in any case a significant cultural, and therefore political, fact.

It is hard to get a critical purchase on *Gravity's Rainbow*, or to assess its vision of modern history; and quite properly so since that is part of its point. None the less, some reflections on its power and limitations arise from the present discussion and bear on the fortunes of myth in the late twentieth century. Taken in isolation, *Gravity's Rainbow* might suggest that paranoia is a product of history, but the logic of the creative progression from the earlier novels, as suggested above, is rather that the paranoia is primary; that the psychological structure of urban legend is the governing and a priori form. This may not be a matter to be decided definitively, or one on which even the author himself could necessarily give a decisive view, but it makes a crucial difference to how we ultimately value the novel, even accepting that this is precisely its studied effect and what makes it a pertinent mirror of its time.

From one point of view, the novel constitutes, by its very mode as well as by its subject-matter, a significant reflection of the contemporary world. In embodying and thematising a widespread psychological formation, it encapsulates a contemporary dilemma. At the same time, the adolescent provenance of urban legend is a reminder of how this fictional model seems to involve a necessary measure of partaking in the condition in question, and a relative absence of inner experience. It shares the adolescent's capacity to project his or her own inner state directly and critically on to the social world. In the departure from modernist mythopoeia a force of self-critique is significantly lost. One would not ask for a return to the Jamesian theatre of consciousness, but Pynchon's characterisation is clearly of the era in which we speak of 'subjects' rather than 'selves'; the flattening of myth into paranoia goes with an absorption of the self into the black whole. In this respect, the novel's internal logic conceived in the mode of urban legend is self-fulfilling in a way that is also unsatisfying. The departure from mythopoeia in the modernist, Nietzschean, self-responsible sense goes with a two-dimensional incapacity to create a significant horizon of value within which to pose any self-critique. I have already remarked that Tanner's extrapolated commentary on contemporary cultural conditions, while flattening the fictional texture of the episode from *V*, is not essentially out of keeping with Pynchon's implication. Tanner has perhaps expressed directly a reductiveness which Pynchon's method, by its sheer energy and ingenuity, constantly evades but cannot finally avoid. And equally, of course, the mode of urban legend stands in contrast to the sustaining value of story as seen in Levi or Carpentier. Indeed, Brunvand records that urban legend came to notice when ethnologists and folklorists followed rural black populations into the American cities in the mid twentieth century, and found that their old folklore had been replaced by this new urban form. Once again, the new form has consumed the old.

I am not sure to what extent this is a limiting criticism of Pynchon or a positive appreciation of his meaning. I suspect it is at least partly the former, but his elusiveness and humour make it hard to decide, and certainly he does not seem to be the dupe of his own paranoic vision. His novel is rather a constant attempt to hold this in an objective focus without letting it settle into a mere object, a fixed interpretation from a self-confident ideological standpoint. Peter Sloterdijk has commented on the broader modern significance of the cynical laughter to which Thomas Mann refers in *The Magic Mountain*.[10] Mann himself seeks to overcome this with humanistic irony and comedy; the original impulse of the novel, it may be remembered, was as a comedic answer to *Death in Venice*. Pynchon no longer aspires to be the ironic but humanistic 'lord of counterpositions', yet there is still a comic race against cynicism which, like the long, furious ride on the railway of the underground rocket factory (*Gravity's Rainbow* pp. 310–13), allows a non-cynical laughter to keep barely ahead whatever sinister possibilities may be closing in.

Neither folktale, nor the classic forms of modernist mythopoeia found in Joyce or Mann, claimed an objective standard of truth or value: that is why modernism consciously based itself on myth. But they do affirm an intrinsic standard, which is also why modernism based itself on myth. As I have repeatedly emphasised, the question of value should not be confused with that of truth, but urban legend depends crucially on the question of truth while myth encapsulates the question of value. The meaning or value of myth is not tested by whether it can be mapped on to the world, but by whether the world ought to be mapped on to it. That is as true of Thomas Mann's affirmation of eros over thanatos as it is for the more traditional case of the Christian resurrection. There are those, however, like Fredric Jameson, who claim that the political is the ultimate horizon of human value.[11] I believe this claim is incoherent, and therefore weightless; or true only in an empty sense. Of course everything is political in that politics is the necessary arena of conflict and consensus, but that does not mean that values are, or can be, derived from politics. In that respect politics is like the encyclopaedia, it includes everything, but is not itself a mode of understanding or guidance. This is one of those obvious truths which is so obvious as to be overlooked, and so true that you can safely afford to overlook it. Or safely at least in the sense that the reality of implicit values will not go away just because you deny them, or cannot account for them. Your world does not disappear because you deny its existence. And, similarly, no one could ever test what it would be like for this to be true; for politics to be indeed the ultimate horizon of human meaning. Unless one useful way of thinking about Pynchon is that he presents as epochal reflection what Jameson presents as truth claim. Pynchon shows what it might actually be like to live in a world where such a two-dimensional reality actually pertained, and where it would be natural to believe in the allegators.

IDEOLOGY AND CONFIDENCE: FLIGHTS OF FANCY IN ANGELA
CARTER'S '*NIGHTS AT THE CIRCUS*'

The case of Pynchon suggests that curious things may happen to the
mythopoeic imagination when it is suppressed or denied. Hans Blumenberg's *Work on Myth* argues that attacks on myth are one of the important
modes through which it continually transforms itself and survives.[12] The
attack on myth is a form of *work* on myth, and the alligators who multiply,
like the return of the repressed, in the urban underworld of the New
York sewers are like some new mutation of the mythopoeic imagination.
In that respect it is useful to see urban legend in continuity with
modernist mythopoeia with which it shares some structural similarities.
One similarity is that Pynchon's paranoia is not merely a personal or
psychological state: it reflects a general structural condition. It maintains
the holism of myth, and with that its conscious inability to claim a
privileged or objectively grounded viewpoint. Although there is no
escape from the paranoic condition, it is at least named and recognised
as such. Angela Carter's *Nights at the Circus* is also an attack on inherited
myths, but its standpoint is the opposite of Pynchon's conscious paranoia. The central image of her novel is not the mystery below the surface,
but a heroine whose capacity for flight gives both herself, and the reader,
a confident overview. The novel's confidence arises not from a claim to
knowledge of the historical specificities central to a book like *Gravity's
Rainbow*, but from an ideological understanding that works irrespective
of these. It rests on an analysis of cultural forms rather than on historical
evidence at the level of fact, and it derives from this a certain unassaila-
bility, yet its standpoint is problematic in a way that has a representative
value for a great deal of late twentieth-century literature; and of thinking
about literature.

Ideological critique is safe for the individual practitioner in the sense
that the efficacy of the implicit world of values from which it arises is not
put in jeopardy by their being consciously denied. But, at another level, it
is unsafe in a way that Carter exemplifies. The narrative structure,
devised for good and effective internal purposes, necessarily carries a
further implication which partly undermines the central project. This is
a book which, by setting ideological critique against both myth and other
traditional cultural formations, actually reveals internal difficulties about
ideological critique itself. This is not a disagreement with the broadly
feminist outlook of the novel; on the contrary, the problem arises
precisely in relation to worthy causes.

The book is sceptical of almost all inherited wisdom, and particularly as this is enshrined in such venerable forms of mystification as folk-tale, myth and literary classics by male writers. At the same time it wishes not just to dismiss such forms, but to assimilate their narrative power while exploring their possible meanings, or non-meanings, in a spirit of sceptical irreverence. So the central motif of the winged woman inverts the myth of Leda and the swan, while Carter's 'sleeping beauty' is a freak exhibit crying in her unknown dreams. Most of Carter's characters, and no doubt many of her readers, are in something like the position she ascribes to the human inhabitants of the Siberian forest on hearing a Schubert song:

if the fauna and flora of the Siberian forest responded as the Thracian forest once did to the music of Orpheus, the human forest-dwellers were deaf to the mythic resonances, since these awoke no echoes in their own mythology.[13]

The great myths of the culture are no longer felt to be theirs. There is much humour and pathos in the glancing inversions of such allusions throughout the book, and it is partly reminiscent of Carpentier's *The Kingdom of This World* in its eventual gathering of folk magic into a utopian political purpose. At the same time, it is questionable whether mythic and folkloric meaning can be read from a standpoint of consistently demystifying scepticism. Bruno Bettelheim objected to readings of the stepmother figure as misogynist because he thought this figure was part of a folk-tale structure which includes the lost real mother. Stepmother stories negotiate for young children the necessary trauma of separation from the mother.[14] On this reading, the two figures correspond to what are sometimes known as the good and bad breasts. At the same time, it is now a widespread fact of culture that such elements are *perceived* as misogynistic. That is the level, one of ideological interpretation, with which Carter is concerned, and it is the narrative handling of the committed viewpoint which I wish to consider more closely.

The book has two aspects: a successful thematic or psychological core along with a questionable historical frame. The dilemma is that Carter needs to separate these, but they are not separable. The successful centre of the book concerns the issue of confidence. Carter develops this theme by gradually reversing the normal meaning of the expression 'confidence trick' to show that acquiring or instilling self-confidence may be, legitimately, a kind of trick. Set exactly at the turn of the century, the novel tells of a circus 'aerialiste', Sophie, known principally by her stage name of 'Fevvers', who fascinates a male reporter, Walser, when he comes to interview her for his series of Great Humbugs of the World. The central narrative device is that her wings are actually real, although for professional purposes she must keep up the pretence that they are artificial. The novel is a fable of achieved female self confidence, and the secret sources from which confidence comes. Belief in oneself has to be distinguished both from mere self-deception and from external questions of historical or factual truth. The world of the circus, involving both danger and illusion, encompasses all these points. For the book demonstrates how confidence frequently depends not on strict truth and sobriety so much as on illusionism and panache. Sophie has confidence from the outset, while Walser, who comes initially to expose her but stays to fall in love with her, is the one who must acquire it in two different, but related, senses: he needs to learn true confidence in himself as well as confidence, or belief, in her. She largely conducts his education, but does this, in the best traditions of the *Bildungsroman*, largely unknowingly to him, and in the latter part of the book he is actually separated from her, so that he is equally educated by events and is not merely her creature, while she in her turn is temporarily knocked off her perch to undergo uncertainty and humiliation. During this period he acquires his other important mentor, the Siberian shaman.

The shaman is to some extent a professional sham-man, but he is not himself a sham, like his sinister counterpart Herr M. who had obliged Mignon, before her circus days, to participate in his exploitative illusionism. For the shaman is the prototypical artist and community psychologist. He orchestrates illusions only for the welfare of his community, and it is he who enacts the central reversal of the usual meaning of the expression 'confidence trick'.

The Shaman was most certainly *not* a humbug. His was the supreme form of the confidence trick – others had confidence in him because of his own utter confidence in his own integrity. He was the doctor and the midwife of the village, the dream-reader and the fortune-teller, the intellectual and the philosopher, to boot; he also conducted weddings and burials. Furthermore, he negotiated with and interpreted the significance of those natural forces to which the circumstances of their lives made them especially vulnerable. (*Nights* p. 263)

Confidence is a psychological necessity, yet it is also a trick; if it eventually has an effect on the external world it is through an enabling transformation of the self. Even while drawing upon the numinous figure of the shaman, then, who is her most serious approach to the mythopoeic, Carter enforces a deconstructive reading of him as trickster

in the everyday illusionist, rather than the anthropological, sense. Furthermore, it is the same principle which ultimately justifies the ostentatiously tricksy texture of the novel itself, for the act of narration is also
made into a purposefully illusionistic performance.

This is effected from the opening section of the novel as Fevvers, like
Wilhelm Meister, narrates to her prospective lover the story of her early
life; and thereby provides a double, or merged, voice for the narrative as
a whole. For Carter, unlike Goethe, is not ironising Fevvers here so
much as using her to define the significance of the narrative manner at
large. Sophie is not just a narrating character, we might say, but a way of
characterising the narration. Other magic children in contemporary
fiction, such as Oskar in *The Tin Drum* and Saleem in *Midnight's
Children*, have first-person control of their respective narratives. Sophie
does not, but the manner of the narration continues to bear the stamp of
her personality, of her ambiguous illusionism, and of her initial impact
on Walser as surrogate reader. At the end of the novel she resumes her
narrative to Walser, encompassing within it their new and unpredicted
selves.

But a more specific connection between the act of narration and the
confidence theme is to be seen in Sophie's wings. The wings are a bold
and comic symbolism hardly requiring solemn explication, but they are
also the stalking-horse for an implicit linking of sexuality and narrative.
Some remarks from Karen Blixen's *Out of Africa* throw light on the
gendered specificity of the wings:

Denys Finch-Hatton and I went with Mr. Bulpett for a picnic to the top of the
Ngong Hills on his seventy-seventh birthday. As we sat up there we came to
discuss the question of whether, if we were offered a pair of real wings which
could never be laid off, we would accept or decline the offer.

Old Mr. Bulpett sat and looked out over the tremendous big country below
us, the green land of Ngong, and the Rift Valley to the west, as if ready to fly over
it at any moment. 'I would accept,' he said, 'I would certainly accept. There is
nothing I should like better.' After a little time of thought he added: 'I suppose
that I should think it over, though, if I were a lady.'[15]

Fantasies of flight may be common to both sexes, but a set of wings seems
a particularly unwelcome appendage for a woman; and even more so for
a 'lady'. The dream of flight, which Freud saw as expressing a feeling of
sexual confidence, seems in Sophie's case to go with a particular phy-
sique and personality. At the outset of the novel, the wings have
masculine overtones. In the circus poster she is depicted with 'tremendous red and purple pinions' and is described as a Helen who evidently

'took after her putative father, the swan, around her shoulder parts' (*Nights* p. 7). This woman with the appearance of a 'voluptuous stevedore' (*Nights* p. 15) is by no means unattractive to Walser, although in the first instance her masculine manner is unnerving to him. Filled with the contents of her 'ejaculating' champagne bottles, he is embarrassingly obliged to urinate, the physiological alternative to a virile condition (*Nights* pp. 12, 52). But he is none the less attracted, and, as he is increasingly able to accept this response positively in himself, so the masculine associations of the wings fade after the opening encounter. Both Walser and Sophie are freed from the merely conventional in their sexual responses.

The crucial aspect of the wings, however, in the sexual sphere, is not that they make her masculine, which they do not, but that she cannot lie on her back. A curious feature of our culture is the widespread view, among both men and women, that sexual congress with the man on top is an expression of male domination. I take it that with different assumptions one could as well see the same posture as an image of the woman being serviced. In other words, the widespread reading of this sexual posture is a symptom of the culture rather than an intrinsic feature of the posture itself. None the less, the perception is a cultural fact, and Carter seems to take it as another cultural given to be overturned; although her reversal, I would have thought, actually rests on an acceptance of the banal stereotype. The novel, which began with Sophie's seductive narration to Walser, ends with a sexual consummation in which she takes the initiative and remains in benign control. The sexualised wings have indeed become an analogue of Sophie's, and therefore of Carter's, narrative. Sophie, as an artist of narrative challenges the most famously winged artist in modern literature, Joyce's Stephen Dedalus, by whom artistic creation was given a distinctly masculine stamp. Sophie, too, has survived by 'exile and cunning' (*Nights* p. 285) having tempted 'the fate of Icarus' (*Nights* p. 32). Sophie's sexuality links her twin performances as aerialiste and narrator in both of which she exercises a female fascination and mystery. The key point here, of course, is that she indeed exercises them, that they are chosen and controlled, even while exploiting traditional mystifications of the female and feminine.

As aerialiste she must preserve her mystery. The apparent authenticity of her wings is crucial to her public appeal, yet if they were actually known to be genuine she would become a mere freak. In this sense her very authenticity is a fake; or, as her rival performers put it, 'she was cheating' (*Nights* p. 156). Her narration is likewise a controlled use of illusion to protect, rather than to hide, the truth. The following passage from her account to Walser of her early life suggests the effect of the technique.

'Imagine me, sir, tripping in nothing but Ma Nelson's shawl into that drawing-room where the shutters were bolted tight, the crimson velvet curtains drawn, all still simulating the dark night of pleasure although the candles were burned out in the crystal sconces. Last night's fragrant fire was but charred sticks in the earth and glasses in which remained only the flat dregs of dissipation lay where they had fallen on the Bokhara carpet. The flimsy light from the farthing dip I carried with me touched the majesty of the swan-god on the wall and made me dream, dream and dare.

'Well-grown though I was, yet I had to pull a chair to the mantelpiece in order to climb up and take down the French gilt clock that stood there in a glass case. This clock was, you might say, the sign, or signifier of Ma Nelson's little private realm. It was the figure of Father Time with a scythe in one hand and a skull in the other above a face on which the hands stood always at either midnight or noon, the minute hand and the hour hand folded perpetually as if in prayer, for Ma Nelson said the clock in her reception room must show the dead centre of the day or night, the shadowless hour, the hour of vision and revelation, the still hour in the centre of the storm of time.

'She was a strange one, Ma Nelson.'

Walser could well believe it. (*Nights* p. 29)

It is appropriate that her first flight should require the removal of the patriarchal figure of time, since the mature Sophie's gravity-defying suspensions in mid-air, like the Russian sequence of the novel, will be as much a conquest of time as of space. And the parallel suggests that the real interest here lies not in the content so much as in the manner of the narration which is an apparent flight of fancy matching her apparently fancied flights.

In this regard, the opening phrase 'Imagine me, sir' takes on a pregnant double reference. Most straightforwardly, she is asking him to exercise his imagination in recreating the past events from her life, but she is also, more subtly, insinuating that, as far he is concerned, she herself, both then and now, is something that has essentially to be imagined. After the titillating detail of her wearing only a shawl, she continues her story in a parodic imitation of popular fiction of the period. We, along with Walser, have no choice but to accept the events as authentic, although the manner signals a fictional or stylistic perform-ance. This is the same wrapping of truth within apparent illusion as characterises her aerial performances, and it gives a double point to the remark at the end of the quoted passage when we are told 'Walser could well believe it', for this now has a dual reference echoing her opening phrase. Most immediately, his belief refers to the statement *about* Ma Nelson, a figure in Sophie's tale. Yet the 'it' in which he believes now implicitly subsumes the larger question that Walser, or the reader, might have asked about the truth of the whole tale. He has got drawn into believing the tale despite, or perhaps because of, her teasing manner and, as we later discover, she is in fact significantly deceiving him here on the matter of her virginity and her sexual availability; as it turns out her 'inaccessibility' was indeed 'legendary' (*Nights* p. 19). The parodic aura of innocence and moralism in the passage is a double bluff; it is part of a genuine deception at the heart of their relationship, and it is sustained until the end of the novel.

In effect, Sophie's wrapping the truth in a tall tale has the opposite meaning, eventually at least, to Benny Profane's alligator stories. Where Benny created uncertainty, Walser gets drawn into Sophie's story, and as he does so he does not just suspend disbelief in the narrated events, but develops a different order of belief in her. Out of the narrative 'relation' of events there arises a quality of relation*ship*; trust in a person rather than belief in facts. One might say, in general, that true trust in another lies not in the belief that they will always tell you the whole truth, but in your implicit reliance on their editing it. Carter, however, gives this theme a stronger, more active formulation, in the sphere of sexual attraction. Walser starts from a position of absolute distrust in interviewing her as a candidate for his collection of 'Great Humbugs of the World' and the development of their relationship suggests that a continuing measure of uncertainty is vital to trust. Where there is knowledge there is no need for faith, nor any virtue in it. And so, even at the end, Walser is still not sure enough of Sophie to call her by her real name. Her artfulness is designed throughout to accomplish the mystery of trust and to affirm a trust in mystery. In British usage the term 'fancy' refers to sexual attraction as well as to the merely imagined or illusory. The semantic complex in this word perhaps reflects a popular recognition of the connection between these aspects of love: imagination and the confidence to follow a whim. Certainly, the trick of confidence Sophie performs *within* Walser is achieved by the external confidence tricks she performs on him until he finally recognises what it means to fancy her. In sum, the multiple theme of confidence as enacted in the manner of the narrative is the strong point of the book, even for readers not completely charmed by the local play of narrative wit. If flight is a common fancy it remains something that even Sophie, born with wings, has to learn. Any art, including that of having a fully human self, has to be acquired. The narrative bravura is ultimately justified by its internal meaning as a moment by moment flight of the ego without other support.

The confidence theme is the positive psychological core of the novel, but Carter makes clear that it is conditional upon a remove from real history. The opening of the Russian section refers explicitly to the violent world of 'authentic history to which this narrative . . . does not belong' (*Nights* p. 97). In that respect, the novel is indeed a work of magical realism, rather than what Carpentier meant by the marvellous in reality. In other words, while full of earthiness and streetwise shrewdness, the narrative bravura distinguishes itself from the larger historical process from which it increasingly diverges into its own carnivalesque time. Carter holds apart what Carpentier and Pynchon, in their various ways, combine as, respectively, the marvellous and the paranoic. The larger public history is held in suspension for the sake of this internal, psychological action. None the less, the confidence theme *within* the narrative, and the confidence *of* the narrative, are closely intertwined in a way that remains problematic in so far as Sophie's performance is also Carter's.

Some readers, not necessarily male, find the intended charm of the book highly resistable, and I believe it is worth identifying the reason more precisely since the questions raised go beyond a critical reading of this novel. When Angela Carter died in 1992 in the middle of a flourishing career her loss was keenly felt by many readers, not just personally, but as a public voice. An essay by John Bayley in *New York Review of Books* in April of that year gave a critically balanced summary of her fiction which her more committed readers did not find satisfactory and it drew a quick rejoinder from Hermione Lee indicating what Carter meant to such readers.[16] The nub of the problem is that, although her work is full of overt scepticism about inherited wisdom of all sorts, and even about much of the conventional wisdom of contemporary feminism, it none the less exudes a cosy knowingness with respect to the right-thinking values of her assumed audience. The problem is not with the views, but with the spirit in which they are held. At one level Bayley's review simply showed that he was not one of the charmed circle. But we do not have merely to leave the work, undiscussably, to its different readerships, for the structure of the book actually focuses this doubleness. By facing in two directions at once, as it were inwards and outwards, the narrative structure reflects a characteristically contemporary form of emotional anachronism.

A familiar feature of postmodern fiction is to use different epochs from the past as all equally available, as if in a vast theatrical repertory. The mythopoeic spatialising of history, which characterised much earlier modernist literature, has lost its critical and corrective function with respect to nineteenth-century historicism and dwindled into an endless permutation of film sets. This can be used quite appropriately where there is a lightness of touch. Two novels of the eighties exemplify this. Jeanette Winterson's *The Passion* (1987) and Rose Tremaine's *Restoration* (1989) both use a period setting to tell a story of personal emotions for which the period is not essential and indeed the very emphasis on period, combined with the magical elements of the narrative, make this clear. *Restoration* catches this in the very title as the restoration period is the occasion for a tale of personal recovery. Similarly, both novels play on the physical organ of the heart in a non-realistic way to concretise the central metaphor of their emotional themes. Historical realism is ostentatiously not the point of these books, and both are successful within their own premisses. In broad generic terms, Angela Carter's *Nights at the Circus* is very similar to these novels, but its ambition is different and the outcome is more problematic. The novel thematises, and yet embodies, a dilemma which is, if not peculiar to our time, then especially urgent within it.

The novel places itself on a midnight hour between centuries and is explicitly, as has been seen, a fantasy tale falling outside of history. So too, Sophie's first attempts at flight, which lead to the central fantasy of the book, also take place at this timeless hour, and her mid-air suspensions are conquests of time as well as space. The same spirit is at work in respect of the literary past, as can be seen by comparing her allusions to *Wilhelm Meister's Apprenticeship* with Jean Rhys' use of *Jane Eyre* in *Wide Sargasso Sea* (1966). The power and pathos of Rhys' novel arise from its genuinely moving inside the world of its original. It is an internal reinterpretation of its predecessor whereby a possible tragic logic is derived from the already existing situation, and the Rochester figure is not so much criticised as, more chillingly, understood. Carter, by contrast, turns Goethe's Mignon into something deliberately opposed to the original.

Mignon's song is not a sad song, not poignant, not a plea. There is a grandeur about her questioning. She does not ask you if you know that land of which she sings because she herself is uncertain if it exists – she knows, oh! how well she knows it lies somewhere, elsewhere, beyond the absence of the flowers. She takes the existence of that land and all she wants to know is, whether you know of it too. (*Nights* p. 249)

This is not a conceivable internal possibility of Goethe's Mignon. On the contrary, this new Mignon's song is an image of the novel's own utopianism as a confidently controlled and assertive fantasy, embracing what is not yet real and rejecting the past. By the time she sings this song, as set to its later Schubert setting, Mignon has already recovered her personal wholeness as the original Mignon was never able to do. In literary-historical, as well as historical, terms, the novel creates its own utopian space outside the known past.

The narrative premisses are clear and coherent. But the trouble is that a weight of public history is inevitably being drawn upon too. In affirming the necessary self-confidence of the individual Carter sees, rightly enough, that there is a cultural historical dimension to the question. Language itself embodies the subliminal, acculturated ways in which women have traditionally been undervalued, and the individual woman has therefore to be thought of, and to think of herself, in a collective aspect. Confidence depends upon both solidarity and ideological understanding, but there are problems in thinking of *oneself* in this way. Internally to the narrative Carter is self-questioning, or is quietly critical regarding postures to which she is sympathetic. So the generalised manhating of Sophie's best friend, Lizzie, or the extreme sexual separatism of the female prisoners after their escape from the panopticon, are viewed with irony. Above all, she rejects the sexual puritanism to be found in some brands of feminism. Yet in its relation to external history the book merely accepts a feminist reading as its emotional premiss. The narrative as a whole depends on the reader being one of a right-thinking community. The book is of the era of 'consciousness raising' and offers, in its internal structure, an implicit analysis of that well-meaning phrase in which the state of consciousness that is to be attained is already defined by the initial project. Once the book is perceived in this way, its elements of magic and earthy realism become too much a series of rhetorical gestures, slightly wearisome in their archness. For some readers Sophie's last laugh remains unpersuasive, and, even after the self-conscious twists of the trickery theme, there is something of the humbug about her after all.

The point, however, is not to break this delicately constructed novel upon a curmudgeonly wheel; nor is the objection to Carter's feminist solidarity as such; indeed I assume the general necessity for this. The point is rather that the novel is an articulated instance of a characteristically contemporary dilemma which, as the period setting suggests, can be understood as a form of emotional anachronism. By imaginatively stepping outside of time, Carter effects an emotional co-option of the past by the present. There is no easy answer to this problem. Active beings must have memory and purpose, which means that their emotions are always in response to other times. Yet, although the emotions of the past are a vital aspect of the present, they must also be kept distinct so as not to become an emotional slush fund free from critical accounting. In one of his 'Skirmishes of an Untimely Man' (*Twilight of the Idols* p. 92) Nietzsche suggested that, while a liberation struggle may bring out heroic and admirable qualities, once 'liberal institutions' have been achieved the same emotional forms become inauthentic; a form of *ressentiment*.[17] They are qualitatively defined by their relation to their moment. For our own day, however, Nietzsche's model is too simple. Even such apparently clear-cut cases as the independence of former colonies, an event marked by ritual on a particular date, is likely to usher in only the ambiguous and indefinite twilight of cultural and economic neo-colonialism. It is not always easy to say, therefore, when domination has truly given way to liberation, and in more gradual areas of socio-cultural change, such as racial prejudice, there is clearly a long interregnum. In that respect, Nietzsche's two-stage model needs to be modified into a three-stage one. A first state of genuine domination is characterised by the fact that the dominant group, and perhaps many of the dominated, are not conscious of it as being such. This is followed by a period of 'oppression' when the condition is explicitly recognised and, in practice, since the third state, that of complete liberation, is rarely achieved, it is this second condition that presents the difficulty. This state is liable to an inextricable mixture of the authentic and the inauthentic, and many citizens of the late twentieth century find it a daily dilemma.

I am, of course, speaking here of the educated classes in Western societies. Clearly, there are orders of oppression and deprivation in the world to which these emotional niceties are irrelevant. But in this limited context, the question of emotional authenticity, and its effect on personal, social and working relations, is of some importance. Since the perception of being oppressed is relative not only to one's own past, but also to other groups, or perhaps even individuals, with a claim to be perceived in a similar way, the conscious state of being a member of an oppressed group is difficult to maintain in a spirit that does not become self-serving or emotionally bullying. In the British context, for example, the emphasis on minorities and gender from the seventies to the eighties has accompanied an occlusion of class. While it may be vital to remember them, it is impossible to inherit either the guilt or the suffering of one's forebears except through the conduct or circumstances of one's own life. Such feelings on behalf of a group usually escape, at least in their own perception, the charge of self-indulgence, but part of the evil of prejudice against groups lies precisely in the generalised perception of the individual, and this aspect is preserved even as the evaluations are reversed. Thoughtful citizens of the late twentieth century live within this condition of emotional anachronism. Carter's novel exemplifies the difficulty of doing so; the continuous balancing act that is required.

Carter's confident revisionary play with mythic and folkloric material typifies a larger contemporary shift from myth to ideology as the favoured term for designating the totality of a world view. Myth is a problematic term, but it wears its problems on its sleeve; ideology, by contrast, is a fatally confidence-breeding term. Terry Eagleton and Fredric Jameson have both criticised the postmodern spirit for its critical emptiness, its relativistic drifting with the contemporary consumerist culture.[18] I have no quarrel with this criticism although, as is evident from the present argument, and, as they would agree, there is also a worthwhile literature answering to such a generic description. Carter's novel, with its narrative magic and its playful use of the historical period as a kind of backdrop to its psychological theme, is formally open to this generic description, but that is actually its strength. The real objection is rather to the collective self-assurance underlying the novel's whimsy, and that has a quite different origin. It arises from the confident privileging of the political as the ultimate horizon of value, or of the ideological as the basic criterion of criticism; a development which both Eagleton and Jameson have continually promoted. There is a widespead assumption that by understanding someone's ideology you can encompass them intellectually and thereby take possession of them critically. Some primitive tribes are said to believe that enemies who discover their real names will have power over them. We have a comparable superstition, a superstition rising from reason itself, in believing that you have complete intellectual insight or critical power over a complex form of life by reducing it to its ideological configuration. Adapting Adorno and Horkheimer, this may be the truest form in which mythopoeia lives on in our time and as a continuing product of Enlightenment.

PART IV

Conclusion: ideology, myth and criticism

The positive sense of 'mythopoeia' drawn from the practice of several modernist writers recognises the subjectivity of every world view. In affirming the necessary 'horizon' of the self, Nietzsche acknowledged, indeed highlighted, the measure of arbitrariness in world-making, and yet this was far from being an empty relativism such as a purely theoretical account might suggest. Every world view is inescapably an object, as well as a means, of critical judgement; whether consciously or unconsciously, and whether by disagreement or acquiescence. This truth is disguised by the fact that people absorb their native culture long before the problem, if it is one, can be brought to consciousness; and the totality of the culture never could be brought fully into consciousness anyway. Wittgenstein's 'form of life' and Michael Polanyi's 'tacit dimension' both point to this truth.[1] To some degree, an unconscious acquiescence in one's native culture is not only inescapable, but desirable. For, even if all implicit values and commitments could be raised to critical consciousness at the same time, such a feat would be paralysing, like Funes' stupendous feat of total memory and perception in Borges' story. You can, however, be conscious of *having* a world view, even if you cannot be fully conscious *of* the world view as such, and when Nietzsche's horizon image is linked to an aesthetic model it makes this recognition emblematically self-conscious and enforces a sense of responsibility and inner attention to the dangers of dogmatism.

The aesthetic dimension is crucial. Colin Falck has argued a somewhat parallel case that literature is the modern form of myth.[2] His argument, however, depends on accepting the ultimately poetic notions of myth which were prevalent in the early decades of the century.[3] It is, of course, true that several modernist writers accepted the scientific claims of this early anthropology. That does not make them completely vulnerable when that anthropology is outdated, any more than the discarded cosmology or humours theory of Chaucer deprive him of his intrinsic meaning. But these writers have in any case left something more subtly resilient which it has perhaps taken further changes in world outlook to make apparent. Rather than modern man being able to recover the mythopoeic relation to nature and the self proposed by Cassirer and others, it is necessary to see that this conception was itself a myth, an unconscious example of modern mythopoeia. And Cassirer himself, after taking time out at the end of his life to diagnose the damaging 'myth of the (modern fascist) state', went on to develop the aesthetic dimension of his philosophy of symbolic forms; a task pursued after his death by Suzanne Langer.[4] Nietzsche understood, along with many of the next literary generation, that there is no primordial point of origin or grounding except by fiat for which the aesthetic is the closest analogy. Even the Greeks took the cult of Dionysus from *other* peoples and adopted it in a secondary or artistic spirit.[5] Only by virtue of that artistic transformation did it became the Dionysian of Nietzsche's interpretation. In the modern context, the aesthetic recognition, when properly understood, obviates futile and distracting questions of grounding and focuses attention on questions of intrinsic value. The modernist literary use of myth on which I have been concentrating is an emblem of this recognition. Falck's study strictly requires brackets around the word 'truth' in its title, and another layer of recognition in its argument.

Over the latter part of the century, however, 'myth' has given way to 'ideology' as the favoured term to denote the implicit structure of a world view. The shift from myth to ideology represents a vital gain in demystification, and it would be senseless to argue simply for a recovery of the earlier term. What does matter is to recover its meaning and see that an over-exclusive focus on ideology is a reduction of the properly mythopoeic consciousness of modernism. A host of commentators has observed that ideology critique is logically parasitic in that it has to stand upon an implicit world of values. It is also historically parasitic in that the recognition of living within implicit understandings was partly imbibed from the literature and thought of modernism, which therefore represents the unconscious of ideology critique. And, owing to this suppression of ancestry, the attention to 'ideology' now acts as a means of ideological foreclosure. Unlike the mythopoeic self awareness, it typically offers to expose false consciousness in others; it is not designed to promote awareness of its own implicit dimension, except through the circularity of 'consciousness raising'.

Three broad historical phases can be distinguished here. The original nineteenth-century Marxist development of ideological consciousness was a vital and liberating recognition within a period wedded to organicist conceptions often lending themselves to conservative interpretation. Language reflected unconscious or underlying structures which could therefore be exposed through it. In the modernist era there grew up a sense that language actually governed, or was a complete index of, reality. The modernist desire to 'purify the language of the tribe' was partly based on this belief, and it had a decisive impact on the academic study of literature. Orwell's political critiques of English usage are products of the same period. But modernism was a period of epochal transition; still honouring the unconscious aspect of tradition and the greatness of past achievement. Most modernist writers, for example, thought it vital to distinguish the 'major' from the 'minor' authors of the past. For these writers, therefore, and for the critical tradition they inaugurated, the governing power of language never settled into intra-linguistic literalism. Language was a vital index of forms of life, but neither the form nor the life were reducible to language. In the sixties and onwards, however, came a new sociological rather than properly critical spirit. Here the notion of 'greatness' is rejected in the name of Raymond Williams' demystifying insistence that 'culture is ordinary', and ideological critique is now thought fully to reveal the world of the writer in question.[6] Its unconscious is, or can be, exposed. This new phase of intra-linguistic literalism is exercised by readers often explicitly hostile to the experience of aesthetic wonder.

The point is exemplified in the new use of the term 'gender'. A purely linguistic, grammatical term has replaced the word 'sex' as a way of referring to sexual difference. The point, quite properly, is to demystify this difference as being a socio-cultural product rather than a purely natural category. This is part of an important and necessary social change, and a new self-understanding, but it has itself now become a reverse dogma. The word 'essentialism' is a shibboleth, a possibility that falls outside discussion, like heresy in old-fashioned Catholic education, although the fact is that none of us know what the proportions of nature and nurture, of sexuality and gender, actually are. All things answer to their moments, and the very term 'ideology' now brings with it a damaging increase in the spurious confidence whereby sociologically minded commentators feel they have a ready-made, as it were objective, standpoint by which to judge the author. Not, that is to say, a critical standpoint deriving from a body of experience to weigh against the author's, and which of course seeks to be objectified and evidential, but a set of general criteria that obviates the need for this. I have noted the reductive view of modernism offered by Fredric Jameson arising from his desire to see the 'political' as the ultimate horizon of meaning in literary texts. In dismissing the 'myth' of personal identity, it was Jameson himself who proved to be most susceptible to myth creation in his own work-a-day, pejorative sense of the word, for, while clearly riding on the confidence of orthodoxy, Jameson carefully nurtured, for himself and his assumed readers, the flattering consciousness of being an embattled minority. This was not Jameson at his best, but it is hard to see how he could disown the position taken, and I have dwelt on this moment for its representative nature which his remarks assume and reflect. Much academic criticism at any time is derivative, and it is pointless to object to the average quality, but this makes it especially important that the influential and admired examples, particularly as offered to students, should not themselves be reductive ones. Some decades ago, in the wake of modernism, Northrop Frye's system of mythopoeic literary classification arose from an attempt, using myth as a common term, to make a connection between literature and life, but the system itself became a barrier to the critical interaction of literature and life once a generation of Frye-influenced academics was able to use it as a ready-made system. Myth certainly deserved to get a bad name in literary critical as well as political usage, but ideological critique has suffered the same kind of reduction. The truly mythopoeic conception, on the other hand, throws the reader back on to the imaginative experience as primordial in a way that the modernist writers understood. Curiously enough, just as this recognition has been obscured by ideological interest groups within the literary disciplines, it has been discursively recovered by other lines of thought which have more recently argued the primordial value of poetry or narrative in the ethical life. The repressed always returns, but not in quite the same form. In the present case, the lost recognition has returned as a philosophical theme rather than as a critical practice, and it would perhaps not please some recent writers to find that they were actually rediscovering the position of F. R. Leavis who derived it directly from Eliot and Lawrence.[7]

Exclusively ideological reading loses the internal critical dynamic of literature itself. In fact, an unstated *ressentiment* against literature, and criticism, often underlies it. Such a hostility to criticism may be seen in the following passage chosen once again for its typicality as expressed in its confidently synoptic style:

The ideological function of 'organic' works of art depends on a balance between an internal semantic plenitude that escapes simple fixations and ideological demarcations that enclose the work of art from external considerations. Countless books on aesthetics developed in line with the institution of art as autonomous give testimony to this point. The autonomous work of art simultaneously permits ideological exclusions and the subjective experience of fullness.[8]

The author has a point, of course, but the word 'aesthetic' as usual rests on a false opposition; while the counterposing of 'ideological' and 'subjective', along with the reductive understanding of 'autonomous', exclude the real problem, and the true sphere of criticism, by a black and white dualising. The word 'subjective' confines to mystified naivety precisely the internal standpoint from which the 'ideological' aspect might properly be tested. Some aesthetic exclusions are justified and many are necessary; they are intrinsic to the possibility of art and are often formalised as genres. By the same token, criticism must question the legitimacy of every exclusion; the basic aesthetic contract of the work in question. In works of literature with claims to serious attention, a given world view is experimentally inhabited, while criticism involves both understanding the world view and assessing its habitability.

In this respect, ideology can be a false clue. To put the point in a practical way, there are Marxist saints and Marxist brutes, as well as Christian saints and Christian brutes. This means not just that these personal qualities happen to be combined with the given ideological outlook, but that the individual in question actively lives the ideology. The life gives the meaning to the ideology and the ideology itself may tell you little of what you most need to know about the person. Nor is this to set the notion of 'ideology' against that of the 'individual', or 'subjectivity', for the values of the individual are, as values, never merely individual. What literary mythopoeia signals is not so much transhistorical as intrinsic value; or rather it engages the question of value as such. So too, it is the fundamental encounter with value and commitment that is really involved in the notion of artistic greatness, for not all works that can be characterised as art have such a primordial kind of importance. The belief that all people should be equal politically and before the law does not entail the manifest absurdity that they are equal in talent and *virtu*, and, in the same way, one may believe that 'culture is ordinary' without thinking all its manifestations are of equal significance. To strip away mystified values is the beginning, not the end, of the problem, and the notion that all values are mystified would be evidently self-defeating if it could be brought fully into consciousness. The mythopoeic conception of literary meaning is one that keeps this recognition in focus. It recognises the limits of an ideological understanding even if, by definition, there can be no discursive encompassing of what is left out. This recognition was a powerful element in modernist literature, and Jameson and Said show a sure instinct in seeking to suppress it.

What is at stake is how to handle the unconscious of the text. The conviction of understanding, or of having a technique for understanding, this unconscious tends to be projective; it leads the critic to infer a complete system and to see historical evils as necessarily entailed by a given ideological viewpoint. You may not think you have a given attitude, but the ideological critic knows better. So that, for example, Heidegger's collusion with the Nazi state is the product of his philosophy, and any acceptance of aspects of that philosophy is tainted too. There are, of course, important questions at stake in the relations between the thought and the life, but ideological literalism short-circuits the very terms of the necessary discussion. To live within a given ideological form is not necessarily to accept all the consequences that other of its inhabitants, or of its opponents, may see in it; and nor does this mean that such implications have merely been suppressed. On the contrary, while ideological critique seeks typically to expose the 'unconscious' of imaginative literature, this literature is itself, as David Parker has observed, frequently the unconscious of the critique.[9] Or, one might say, criticism is the unconscious of theory. Criticism is always concerned to detect the unconscious of the text, but it will not truly do so if it imagines it has a privileged Archimedian point from which to do so. To deny this Archimedian point is not to say that life always escapes ideology, only that ideology cannot be assumed to encompass it. None the less, Jacques Derrida, who is not known for his conservative softness on the notion of the self, remarks more forcibly that 'there is no ethico-political decision, that must not pass through the proofs of the incalculable and of the undecidable, otherwise everything would be reducible to calculation.'[10] This working sense of the limits of political reason in explaining its own motivations is encapsulated in the mythic self-consciousness.

The conception of literature represented by modernist mythopoeia was a way of recognising the whole of which ideology and subjectivity are aspects. It is the converse of what Peter Sloterdijk has called 'enlightened false consciousness'.[11] It is not vulnerable to the charges of ideological naivety implied by such terms as 'subjectivity' or 'essentialism' because its internal scepticism encompasses the relevant critique. In accepting the necessity of the responsible self, it does not assume an essence, but neither does it make any reductive counter-assumptions about the purely social construction of the self. Living with suspended judgements in such matters is its fundamental posture, even while expressing the values and convictions of an individual or community. For, of course, it in no way follows that mythopoeic writers had no convictions, or that they were always right or wise in the ones they held. Therein, as I have indicated in specific instances, lies a world of activity for criticism; although I have made that point in a largely parenthetical way since what is at stake here are the more general premises of criticism.

The meaning of the mythopoeic conception is to present the products of literary or artistic imagination as primordial constatations of value. That is the point of the analogy with archaic mythopoeia. From the standpoint of modernity, the relevant emphasis is that, rather than literature *being* 'myth', it is myth which clarifies the nature of literature. The mythopoeic conception is a strong understanding of literary meaning as a holism admitting of no judgemental criterion other than the completeness of the reader's own experience. The work presents a form of life for critical understanding. Nietzsche remarked, quite correctly, that life itself cannot be judged: overall judgements of life are meaningless in themselves and have a merely symptomatic value *vis à vis* the person who makes them.[12] But an individual life, or any particular form of life, can be judged; indeed it cannot but be judged whether implicitly or explicitly, although there is a great difficulty in isolating it for judgement; of establishing the bounding line. Literature is the most vital means of making the material of such judgements interpersonally available. And that is what criticism responds to, in the only way it properly can, holistically and without shortcuts. Of course, good critics do this whether or not they say, or believe, it is what they do; and to that extent the question is inconsequential. But it matters how we conceive of what we do, and the search for an ideologically defined vantage-point, rather than a personal authority and judgement, promotes mischievous mirages. The slowly dawning recognition of this came to an important culmination in the literature of the early twentieth century with the awareness of living, inescapably, within a worldview. That is why modernist mythopoeia, when properly understood, remains exemplary for anyone who might want to know what literature and criticism are, and why they matter.

Notes

INTRODUCTION

1. See 'The Uncanny' in *The Complete Psychological Works of Sigmund Freud* ed. and trans. James Strachey, 24 vols. (London, Hogarth Press, 1966–74) vol. XVII, PP. 217–56.
2. *Essays of Three Decades* trans. H. T. Lowe-Porter (London, Secker and Warburg, 1947) p. 422.
3. *Doctor Faustus* trans. H. T. Lowe-Porter (Harmondsworth, Penguin, 1968) p. 47; *Doktor Faustus* (Frankfurt, Fischer, 1947) p. 63.
4. See *The Republic* Bk. III, 414b. The phrase commonly rendered as 'great lie' is translated as 'magnificent myth' in *The Republic* ed. and trans. Desmond Lee (Harmondsworth, Penguin, 1955) p. 181. See translator's note p. 177.
5. Ezra Pound was arrested for treason in 1945 because of his war-time radio broadcasts in support of Mussolini's régime. He was held for some months in a cage in Pisa and was subsequently confined to St Elizabeth's mental asylum in New Jersey for twelve years.
6. See especially Alasdair MacIntyre *After Virtue* (rev. ed., London, Duckworth, 1985) and Richard Rorty *Contingency, Irony and Solidarity* (Cambridge University Press, 1989).
7. See 'How Primordial is Narrative?' in *Narrative in Culture* ed. Cris Nash (London, Routledge, 1992) pp. 172–98.
8. Nietzsche gave the collective title *Untimely Meditations* to four early essays: 'David Strauss, Confessor and Writer' (1873), 'Schopenhauer as Educator' (1874), 'The Uses and Disadvantages of History for Life' (1874) and 'Richard Wagner in Bayreuth' (1976). See *Untimely Meditations* trans. R. J. Hollingdale, (Cambridge University Press, 1983).
9. The argument of this book assimilates the following previously published material: *Primitivism* (London, Methuen, 1972); 'Myth, Art and Belief' in *Context of English Literature 1900–1930* ed. Michael Bell (London, Methuen, 1980) pp.19–43; 'Narration and Action: Goethe's 'Bekenntnisse Einer Schönen Seele' and Angela Carter's *Nights at the Circus*', *German Life and Letters* 45/1 (January 1992) 16–32; 'Mythic Fences and European Neigh-

bours: the Pertinence of Modernist Mythopoeia' *New Comparison* 16 (1993) 98–108; 'Novel, Story and the Foreign: Cervantes, Thomas Mann and Primo Levi' in *Cervantes and the Modernists: the Question of Influence* ed. Edwin Williamson (London and Madrid, Tamesis, 1994) pp. 85–102; 'D. H. Lawrence and Thomas Mann: Unbewusste Brüderschaft' *Etudes Lawrenciennes* 10 (1994) 187–97.

I MYTH IN THE AGE OF THE WORLD VIEW

1. *The Question Concerning Technology and Other Essays* ed. and trans. William Lovitt (New York, Harper and Row, 1977) p. 130.
2. See especially George Berkeley (1685–1753) *The Principles of Human Knowledge* (1710, 1734) and David Hume (1711–1776) *Enquiry Concerning Human Understanding* (1748).
3. Fichte's (1762–1814) principal work was the *Science of Knowledge* (1st version, 1794).
4. See J. G. Herder (1744–1803). His most relevant works were *Travel Diary* (1769), *Treatise on the Origin of Language* (1772), *The Spirit of Hebrew Poetry* (1777), *Ideas for a Philosophy of the History of Mankind* (1784–91).
5. (1770–1831) See *Lectures on the Philosophy of History* delivered biennially 1822/3 to 1830/1. trans. J. Sibree (London, Bohn, 1858).
6. See George W. Stocking *Victorian Anthropology* (New York, The Free Press, 1987).
7. 'There are two paths to life: one is the regular one, direct and honest. The other is bad, it leads through death . . .' *The Magic Mountain* trans. H. T. Lowe-Porter (Harmondsworth, Penguin, 1952) p. 596; *Der Zauberberg* (Berlin and Frankfurt, Fischer, 1964) p. 547.
8. (1883–1969) *Die Psychologie der Weltanschauungen* (Heidelberg, Springer, 1954)
9. (1880–1936) *The Decline of the West* (Vienna and Leipzig, 1918–23)
10. (1857–1913) *Cours de Philosophie Positive* (Paris, Bachelier, 1830–42)
11. Nietzsche recognises this personal vision, rather than argument, in 'Schopenhauer as Educator'. *Untimely Meditations* pp. 141, 182.
12. 'Preface' to *The Nigger of the 'Narcissus'* (London, Gresham, 1925) p. x.
13. Wolfgang Iser *The Fictive and the Imaginary: Charting Literary Anthropology* (Baltimore and London, Johns Hopkins University Press, 1993).
14. Ibid. pp. 155–7.
15. *The Question Concerning Technology* p. 132.
16. *The Ruins, or a Survey of the Revolutions of Empires* (London, T. Allman, 1835).
17. Nietzsche's attack on Christianity pervades his work, but see especially *Towards a Genealogy of Morals* (1887). Joyce, Lawrence, Pound and Yeats all shared something of this view.
18. See 'Introduction' to Cunningham, Andrew and Nicholas Jardine *Romanticism and the Sciences* (Cambridge University Press, 1990) pp. 1–9.
19. Friedrich Schlegel (1772–1829) *Dialogue on Poetry and Literary Aphorisms* trans. Ernst Behler and Roman Struc (Pennsylvania State University Press, 1968).

Quotations from reprinted text in *The Rise of Modern Mythology 1680–1860* ed. Burton Feldmann and R. D. Richardson (Bloomington, Indiana University Press, 1972) p. 300.

20. *The Grammar of Science* (London, Walter Scott, 1892).
21. Arthur Eddington 'Introduction' to *The Nature of the Physical World* (Cambridge University Press, 1928) pp. xi–xix.
22. *Magic Mountain* p. 218; *Zauberberg* pp. 201–2.
23. (1669–1744) *The New Science* 1st edn 1725. Rev. trans. of 3rd edn (1744) Thomas Goddard Bergin and Max Harold Fisch (Ithaca NY, Cornell University Press, 1968).
24. Karl Marx *Capital* orig. pub. 1889. Freud especially *The Interpretation of Dreams* (1900); *Five Lectures on Psychonalysis* (1910); *Totem and Taboo* (1930) and *Civilization and its Discontents* (1930) in *Complete Works* vols. IV–V; VOL. XI, PP. 3–56; VOL. XXI, PP. 59–145.
25. *The Birth of Tragedy out of the Spirit of Music* trans. Walter Kaufmann (London, Vintage, 1957) p. 112.
26. *Rise of Modern Mythology* p. 301.
27. Max Müller (1823–1900) saw myth as a 'disease of language': *Comparative Mythology* (1856), *Contributions to the Science of Mythology* (1897); Edward B. Tylor (1832–1917) had a universalist evolutionary theory of culture: *Researches into the Early History of Mankind and the Development of Civilisation* (1865), *Primitive Culture* (1871); Andrew Lang (1844–1912) saw folklore as an insight into ancient myth: *Myth, Ritual and Religion* (1887).
28. The Golden Bough 1st edn, 2 vols. 1890; 2nd edn 3 vols. 1900; 3rd edn 12 vols. 1915; Abridged version (1922).
29. See John B. Vickery *The Literary Impact of the Golden Bough* (Princeton University Press, 1973). For the continuing afterlife of Frazer see Marc Manganaro *Myth, Rhetoric and the Voice of Authority: A Critique of Frazer, Eliot, Frye and Campbell* (New Haven and London, Yale University Press, 1992).
30. *Collected Poems* (London, Macmillan, 1950) p. 211.
31. Ezra Pound *Collected Shorter Poems* (London, Faber and Faber, 1952) p. 208.
32. *Rise of Modern Mythology* p. 310.
33. Ibid. p. 312.
34. J. J. Winckelmann (1717–68) 'On the Imitation of the Painting and Sculpture of the Greeks' (1755) in Winckelmann: *Writings on Art* sel. and ed. David Irwin (London, Phaidon, 1972) p. 72.
35. *Rise of Modern Mythology* p. 322.
36. ' "Reason" in language! Oh what a deceitful old woman! I fear we are not getting rid of God because we still believe in grammar.' *Twilight of the Idols* trans. R. J. Hollingdale (Harmondsworth, Penguin, 1968) p. 36.
37. Leszek Kolakowski *The Presence of Myth* trans. Adam Czerniawsky (University of Chicago Press, 1989) p. 26; Peter Sloterdijk *Critique of Cynical Reason* trans. Michael Eldred (London and New York, Verso, 1988) pp. 34–5; Charles Taylor *The Sources of the Self: The Making of Modern Identity* (Cambridge University Press, 1989) pp. 339–40.

38. For the significance of this phrase in relation to the question of modernity and world views see Owen Barfield *Saving the Appearances: a Study in Idolatry* (New York, Harcourt Brace, 1965).
39. See 'Attempt at a Self-Critique' in *Birth of Tragedy* pp. 19–20, 24.
40. See Immanuel Kant *Critique of Judgement* 1st edn 1790. trans. J. H. Bernard (New York, Hafner, 1972) p. 55.
41. Peter Alan Dale's *In Pursuit of a Scientific Culture* (Madison Wn. and London, University of Wisconsin Press, 1989) is an excellent account of the gradual nineteenth-century recognition of the ultimately aesthetic basis of science. He locates this in G. H. Lewes, George Eliot's consort, as well as in Friedrich Lange, whose *History of Materialism* (1866) strongly influenced Nietzsche. In his conclusion, however, criticising the twentieth-century inheritance of this tradition, he seems to scant its critical implications (pp. 280–5). Alan Megill in *Prophets of Extremity: Nietzsche, Heidegger, Foucault, Derrida* (Berkeley and London, University of California Press, 1985) takes a similar view as does Robert Pippin's *Modernism as a Philosophical Problem* (Oxford, Blackwell, 1991), see pp. 102–3.
42. See 'The Study of Poetry' *Essays in Criticism* 2nd Series (London, Macmillan, 1891) p. 5.
43. 'If it could be shown that the world really is an aesthetic phenomenon, then we would have to concede that in his essentials Nietzsche was right.' Megill, *Prophets* p. 102.
44. Iser, *Fictive and the Imaginary* p. 163.
45. Jorge Luis Borges, Labyrinths ed. Donald A. Yates and James E. Irby (Harmondsworth, Penguin, 1970) pp. 87–95; *Obras Completas de Jorge Luis Borges* ed. Carlos V. Frias (Buenos Aires, Emecé, 1974) pp. 485–90.
46. For a useful study of this topic see James Longenbach *Modernist Poetics of History* (Princeton University Press, 1987).
47. *Untimely Meditations* pp. 64–5.
48. Ibid. p. 66.
49. Ibid. p. 93.
50. Ibid. p. 63.
51. As a starting-point see Patrick Bridgwater *Nietzsche in Anglo-Saxony* (Leicester University Press, 1972). For an admirable survey of the German thought that needs to be brought to the Anglophone context, see Karl-Heinz Bohrer ed. *Mythos und Moderne* (Frankfurt, Suhrkamp, 1983). It is indicative that this volume has not been translated into English.
52. The question of a 'new mythology' has been pursued especially by Manfred Frank in many publications including *Der Kommende Gott* (Frankfurt, Suhrkamp, 1982).
53. 'What then is truth? A movable host of metaphors, metonymies, and anthropomorphisms . . .' 'On Truth and Falsehood in a Non-moral Sense' in *Philosophy and Truth: Selections from Nietzsche's Notebooks of the Early 1870's* trans. and ed. Daniel Breazale (New Jersey and London, Humanities Press, 1990) p. 84.

54. *The Rule of Metaphor* trans. Robert Czerny et al. (London, Routledge and Kegan Paul, 1978) p. 285.
55. Theodor Adorno and Max Horkheimer *Dialectic of Enlightenment* trans. John Cumming, 2nd edn (London, Verso, 1986) pp. 43–80.
56. Taylor, *Sources of the Self, passim.*

2 VARIETIES OF MODERNIST MYTHOPOEIA

1. *Collected Poems* 2nd edn (London and New York, Macmillan, 1950) p. 392.
2. 'Passion and Cunning: an Essay on the Politics of W. B. Yeats' in Norman A. Jeffares ed. *In Excited Reverie* (London and New York, Macmillan and St Martin's Press, 1965) pp. 207–78.
3. *Explorations* (London, Macmillan, 1962) p. 239.
4. Mary Ellen Thuente *W. B. Yeats and Irish Folklore* (Dublin, Gill and Macmillan, 1980).
5. *On the Study of Celtic Literature* (London, Smith and Elder, 1861).
6. 'The Celtic Element in Literature' in *Essays and Introductions* (New York, Macmillan, 1961) 173–88.
7. *Concordance to the Poems of W. B. Yeats* ed. Stephen Maxfield Parrish (Ithaca NY, Cornell University Press, 1963) pp. 219–23, 548.
8. John Quinn lent him Thomas Common's selection *Nietzsche as Critic, Philosopher, Poet and Prophet* (1901).
9. See Otto Bohlmann *Yeats and Nietzsche* (London, Macmillan, 1982).
10. *A Winter's Tale* Act iv, sc. 4, l. 97.
11. Jacques Derrida 'Eating Well: on the Calculation of the Subject, an Interview with Jacques Derrida' in *Who Comes after the Subject?* ed. Eduardo Cadova et. al. (London, Routledge. 1991) p. 108.
12. *A Vision* (New York, Macmillan, 1937) pp. 25, 8.
13. As in the contrasting moods of Schiller's 'Ode to Joy' (1786) or Wordsworth's 'Surprised by Joy' (1813).
14. *Essays and Introductions* p. 164.
15. *Yeats* (New York, Oxford University Press, 1970) p. 439.
16. 'Yeats: the Problem and the Challenge' in *Lectures in America*, with Q. D. Leavis (London, Chatto and Windus, 1969) pp. 59–81.
17. Lawrence and Pound responded strongly to John Burnet's *Early Greek Philosophy* (1892). The whole thrust of Heidegger's work was a recovery of the pre-Socratic life world.
18. Lilian Feder *Ancient Myth in Modern Poetry* (Princeton University Press, 1971); Daniel Albright *The Myth against Myth: a Study of Yeats' Imagination in Old Age* (London, Oxford University Press, 1972).
19. *Astrophil and Stella* I, L. 14. *The Poems of Sir Philip Sidney* (Oxford, Clarendon Press, 1962) p. 165.
20. *Myth against Myth* p. 174.
21. *Twilight of the Idols* p. 103.
22. *Explorations* p. 434.

23. Ibid. p. 435.
24. *Ulysses* ed. Walter Gabler (Harmondsworth, Penguin, 1986) p. 644.
25. Richard Ellman *'Ulysses' on the Liffey* (London, Faber, 1972).
26. *Magic Mountain* p. 496; *Zauberberg* p. 453.
27. In a later phase these two tendencies are exemplified respectively in S. L. Goldberg *The Classical Moment* (London, Chatto and Windus, 1961) and Colin McCabe *James Joyce and the Revolution of the Word* (London, Macmillan, 1979).
28. *Literary Essays of Ezra Pound* ed. T. S. Eliot (New York, New Directions, 1968) p. 399.
29. Richard Ellmann *James Joyce* (New York and London, Oxford University Press, 1965) p. 533.
30. See Fritz Senn 'Esthetic Theories' *James Joyce Quarterly* 2 (Winter 1965) 134–6.
31. Steven Marcus *The Other Victorians* (London, Weidenfeld and Nicolson, 1966).
32. See William M. Schutte *Joyce and Shakespeare* (Hamden Conn., Archon Books, 1971).
33. Virgina Woolf 'Modern Fiction' in *The Common Reader* (London, Hogarth Press, 1925) pp. 184–95; D. H. Lawrence to Edward Garnett *The Letters of D. H. Lawrence* vol. ii, ed. James T. Boulton and George Zytaruk (Cambridge University Press, 1981) p. 183.
34. Thomas S. Kuhn *The Structure of Scientific Revolutions* (Chicago and London, Chicago University Press, 1962).
35. *Literary Essays* p. 400.
36. *Magic Mountain* p. 218; *Zauberberg* pp. 201–2.
37. *Birth of Tragedy* p. 91.
38. Letter to Carlo Linati, 21 September 1920. *Letters of James Joyce* vol. i, ed. Stuart Gilbert (New York, Viking, 1957) pp. 146–7.
39. 'Spatial Form in Modern Literature' in *The Widening Gyre: Crisis and Mastery in Modern Literature* (New Brunswick, NJ, Rutgers University Press, 1963) pp. 3–62.
40. 'The Making of *The Magic Mountain*' *Atlantic* January 1953. Reprinted in *Magic Mountain* (New York, Random House, 1955) p. 723.
41. *Birth of Tragedy* p. 137.
42. *Literary Essays* p. 406.
43. Matthew Arnold Preface to *Poems, a New Edition* (1853).
44. *Untimely Meditations* p. 79.
45. *Essays of Three Decades* p. 423.
46. *Tractatus Logico-Philosophicus* trans. D. F. Pears and B. T. McGuinness (London, Routledge and Kegan Paul, 1961) pp. 150–1.
47. 'It is what human beings *say* that is true and false; and they agree in the *language* they use. That is not agreement in opinions but in form of life.' *Philosophical Investigations* trans. G. E. M. Anscombe (Oxford, Blackwell, 1958) p. 88.

48. Colin Falck *Myth, Truth and Literature* (Cambridge University Press, 1980).
49. This was the underlying point of Leavis' critique of Charles Snow in *Two Cultures? The Significance of C. P. Snow* (London, Chatto and Windus, 1962) and a principal burden of *The Living Principle: 'English' as a Discipline of Thought* (London, Chatto and Windus, 1975).
50. Ferdinand de Saussure *Cours de Linguistique Générale* (Lausanne, Payot, 1916).
51. *Untimely Meditations* p. 71.
52. *Crime and Punishment* trans. David Margashack (Harmondsworth, Penguin, 1966) pp. 428–9.
53. *Untimely Meditations* pp. 72–3.
54. Ibid. p. 74.
55. *Labyrinths* p. 229; *Obras Completas* p. 667.
56. *Untimely Meditations* pp. 75–6.
57. Ibid. p. 79.
58. Hugh Kenner *Flaubert, Joyce and Beckett: the Stoic Comedians* (London, W. H. Allen, 1964).
59. Theodor Adorno *Negative Dialectics* trans. E. B. Ashton (London, Routledge and Kegan Paul, 1973).
60. *Twilight of the Idols* p. 26.
61. James Boswell *Life of Samuel Johnson* (New York and London, Oxford University Press, 1953) p. 947.
62. *Who Comes After the Subject?* pp. 96–119.
63. Anthony J. Cascardi *The Subject of Modernity* (Cambridge University Press, 1992).
64. In Hal Foster ed. *The Anti-Aesthetic: Postmodern Culture* (London, Pluto, 1985) pp. 114–15.
65. Lawrence *Letters* II, p. 183.
66. *The Philosophy of Symbolic Forms* 3 vols., trans. Ralph Manheim (Newhaven, Yale University Press, 1953–5).
67. Lucien Lévy-Bruhl *Primitive Mentality* trans. L. A. Clare (New York and London, 1923).
68. Ernst Cassirer *The Logic of the Humanities* trans. Clarence Smith Howe (Newhaven, Yale University Press, 1961) p. 53.
69. Cassirer's project was continued by Suzanne K. Langer in *Philosophy in a New Key: a Study in the Symbolism of Reason, Rite and Art* 3rd edn (Cambridge Mass. and London, Harvard University Press, 1957) and *Feeling and Form* (London, Routledge, 1953).
70. *Twilight in Italy and Other Essays* ed. Paul Eggert (Cambridge University Press, 1994) p. 107.
71. *Logic of the Humanities* pp. 76–7.
72. Michael Bell *D. H. Lawrence: Language and Being* (Cambridge University Press, 1992) especially pp. 51–96.
73. Ibid. *passim*.
74. Émile Benveniste argued that linguistic form can only be analysed in relation to its meaning and therefore from the level of the sentence, or the

complete utterance. See 'The Levels of Linguistic Analysis' in *Problems in General Linguistics* trans. Mary Elizabeth Meek (Great Gables Fla., University of Miami Press, 1971) pp. 101–11.

75. *On the Way to Language* trans. Peter D. Herz (New York, Harper and Row, 1971) p. 98.

76. *Gesamtausgabe* vol. 29/30, *Die Grundbegriffe der Metaphysik* (*The Fundamental Concepts of Metaphysics*) ed. Friedrich Wilhelm von Hermann (Frankfurt-am-Main, Vittorio Klostermann, 1983) and vol. 54, *Parmenides* ed. Manfred S. Frings (1982). My translations.

77. *Study of Thomas Hardy and Other Essays* ed. Bruce Steele (Cambridge University Press, 1985) p. 191.

78. 'I have been reading Frazer's *Golden Bough* and *Totemism and Exogamy*. Now I am convinced of what I believed when I was about twenty – that there is another consciousness than the brain and the nerve system: there is a blood-consciousness which exists in us independently of the ordinary mental consciousness, which depends on the eye as its source and connector.' Letter to Bertrand Russell, 8 December 1915. Letters II, p. 470.

79. 'Hadrian' was Lawrence's preferred title restored in *England, My England and Other Stories* ed. Bruce Steele (Cambridge University Press, 1990).

80. *Fantasia of the Unconscious and Psychoanalysis and the Unconscious* (London, Heinemann, 1961) p. 229.

81. *Fundamental Concepts* pp. 284–94.

82. *Women in Love* ed. David Farmer, Lindeth Vasey and John Worthen (Cambridge University Press, 1987) pp. 263–4.

83. *The Complete Poems of D. H. Lawrence* ed. Vivian de Sola Pinto and Warren Roberts 2 vols. (New York, Viking, 1964) vol. I, pp. 349–51. Derrida seems to miss the point of the bracketed human viewpoint in criticising Heidegger's account of the animal as 'poor in world'. *Who Comes After the Subject?* pp. 112–13.

84. *England, my England and Other Stories* p. 138. Hereafter *EME*.

85. *Fundamental Concepts* pp. 295–306.

86. Ibid. pp. 304–5.

87. *Parmenides* p. 237.

88. Ibid. p. 153.

89. *Women in Love* p. 189.

90. *You Just don't Understand: Women and Men in Conversation* (London, Virago, 1991).

91. *Fundamental Concepts* p. 338.

92. *Parmenides* p. 166.

93. Janice Hubbard Harris *The Short Fiction of D. H. Lawrence* (Rutgers University Press, 1984) pp. 125–9.

94. *Parmenides* pp. 154–5.

95. E. T. (Jessie Wood, née Chambers) *A Personal Record* (London, Cape,1935) p. 198.

96. '*Cavelleria Rusticana*, by Giovanni Verga' in *Phoenix: the Posthumous Papers of*

D. H. Lawrence ed. Edward D. McDonald (London, Heinemann, 1936) p. 248.

97. *The Rainbow* ed. Mark Kinkead-Weekes (Cambridge University Press, 1989) p. 77.

98. *Phoenix* pp. 249–50.

99. Ibid. p. 313.

100. *Mythology and Humanism: The Correspondence of Thomas Mann and Karl Kerenyi* trans. Alexander Gelley (Ithaca NY, Cornell University Press, 1975) p. 37.

101. *Women in Love* p. 186.

102. Ibid. p. 189.

103. Michael Ragussis *The Subterfuge of Art: Language and the Romantic Tradition* (Baltimore, Johns Hopkins University Press,1978).

104. *Women in Love* p. 486.

105. Freud and the Future' in *Essays of Three Decades* pp. 411–28.

106. See *Psychoanalysis and the Unconscious and Fantasia of the Unconscious.*

107. 'die Geburt des Ich aus dem mythischen Kollectiv'. See 'Joseph und Seiner Brüder: Ein Vortrag' *Gesammelte Werke* (Frankfurt, Fischer, 1960) vol. XI, p. 665.

108. *Rainbow* p. 10.

109. I developed this distinction in *Primitivism* (London, Methuen, 1972).

110. *On the Way to Language* p. 124.

111. See the chapters 'Spoon' and 'Gilbert Licks the Spoon' in *Mr Noon* ed. Lindeth Vasey (Cambridge University Press, 1984) pp. 15–33.

112. See Bell *Language and Being* pp. 72–4.

3 COUNTERCASES: T. S. ELIOT AND EZRA POUND

1. See, for example, Pound's remark 'We are governed by words, the laws are graven in words, and literature is the sole means of keeping these words living and accurate' *Literary Essays* p. 409.

2. *Tractatus* p. 115. I am partly assimilating this remark to Wittgenstein's later thought.

3. *The Cantos of Ezra Pound* (New York, New Directions, 1970) p. 526.

4. *Dial* 75 (1923) p. 483.

5. *The Waste Land* lines 225, 231, 233–4.

6. Quoted in J. Margolis *T. S. Eliot's Intellectual Development* (Chicago and London, Chicago University Press, 1973) p. 142.

7. *Selected Essays of T. S. Eliot* (London, Faber and Faber, 1951) p.145.

8. Ibid. pp. 390–1.

9. Ibid p. 336.

10. *The Living Principle: 'English' as a Discipline of Thought* (London, Chatto and Windus, 1975).

11. *Selected Essays* pp. 471–91.

12. Ibid. 269–71.

13. *On Poets and Poetry* (New York, Farrar, Straus and Giroux, 1943) pp. 249–64.

14. Ibid. p. 299.

15. Michael North *The Political Aesthetic of Yeats, Eliot and Pound* (Cambridge University Press, 1991) pp. 91–3.
16. *Literary Essays* p. 341.
17. Kathryne Lindberg *Reading Pound Reading: Modernism after Nietzsche* (New York and Oxford, Oxford University Press, 1987).
18. *The Spirit of Romance* (London, Peter Owen, 1952) p. 92.
19. Ibid. p. 16.
20. *Literary Essays* p. 431.
21. *Reading Pound Reading* pp. 100–5.
22. On this latter point see Ian Bell *Critic as Scientist: the Modernist Poetics of Ezra Pound* (London, Methuen, 1981).
23. *Language and Being* pp. 165–207.
24. *Nietzsche* (London, Fontana, 1978) pp. 21, 69.
25. *Phoenix II Uncollected, Unpublished and Other Prose Works by D. H. Lawrence* ed. Warren Roberts and Harry T. Moore (London, Heinemann, 1968) p. 567.
26. *Dialectic of Enlightenment* pp. 43–80.
27. *Philosophical Investigations* p. 223.
28. Jakob Taubes 'Zur Konjunktur des Polytheismus' in *Mythos und Moderne* ed. Karl-Heinz Bohrer (Frankfurt-on-Main, Suhrkamp, 1983) especially pp. 456–61. The aesthetic nature of modern mythopoeia is recognised by several contributors to Bohrer's volume.
29. Frobenius developed the use of this term particularly in *Erlebte Erdteile* 6 vols. (Frankfurt, 1925).
30. 'I Gather the Limbs of Osiris' in *Ezra Pound: Selected Prose, 1909–1965* ed. William Cookson (London, Faber, 1973) p. 71.
31. Leon Surette *A Light from Eleusis* (Oxford, Clarendon Press, 1979) pp. 132–3. On the impersonal creativity of the paideuma, see *Erlebte Erdteil*. vol. IV *Paideuma* pp. 142–9.
32. *The Chinese Written Character as a Medium for Poetry* (San Francisco, City Lights, 1969).
33. *Literary Essays* p. 4.
34. Peter Ackroyd *Ezra Pound and His World* (London, Thames and Hudson, 1980) p. 24.
35. *Selected Essays* pp. 27–9.
36. 'E. P. America's Wandering Jew' *Paideuma* 9 (1980) 461–80.
37. Daniel Bornstein *The Postromantic Consciousness of Ezra Pound* (Victoria BC, English Literary Studies, University of Victoria, 1977).
38. *Spirit of Romance* p. 228.
39. P. Bekker *Musikgeschichte als Geschichte der musikalischen Formwandlung* (Stuttgart, Berlin, Leipzig, 1926).
40. Mann put a disclaimer at the beginning of the book.
41. See 'Nature' in *The Collected Works of Ralph Waldo Emerson*, ed. Alf. R. Ferguson (Harvard University Press, 1971) vol. I, p. 7.
42. Quoted in *The Waste Land: A Facsimile and Transcript of the Original Draft* ed. Valerie Eliot (London, Faber, 1971) p. xxiii.

43. I speak of the effect of the poem. Peter Nicholls has pointed out the personal associations of the text in ' "A Consciousness Disjunct": Sex and the Writer in Ezra Pound's Hugh Selwyn Mauberley' *Journal of American Studies* 28 (1994), 61–5. For a broader argument parallel to mine, see Peter Nicholls 'LOST OBJECT(S): Ezra Pound and Italy' in *Ezra Pound and Europe* ed. Richard Taylor and Claus Melchior, (Amsterdam and Atlanta Ga., Rodopi, B. V., 1993) pp. 165–75.
44. *Spirit of Romance* p. 218.
45. *Literary Essays* p. 86.
46. *Pablo Neruda: Antologia Poetica* ed. Hernan Loyola (Madrid, Alianza, 1991) vol. II, P. 313.
47. 'There was a Boy' lines 24–5. *The Poetical Works of William Wordsworth* rev. ed. Ernest de Selincourt (London and New York, Oxford University Press, 1936) p. 145.
48. *Pound's Cantos* (Baltimore and London, Johns Hopkins University Press, 1992) pp. 179–90.
49. See bibliography.
50. See Peter Nicholls *Ezra Pound: Politics, Economics and Writing* (London, Macmillan, 1984) especially pp. 161–81.
51. Pound wrote a chamber piece *Le Testament* in 1926.

4   THE POLITICS OF MODERNIST MYTHOPOEIA

1. This was a principal theme in the correspondence of Mann and Kerenyi. See *Mythology and Humanism*.
2. *Culture and Imperialism* (London, Vintage, 1994) pp. 225–20.
3. *Selected Essays* p. 16.
4. *Rainbow* pp. 9–48.
5. Ibid. p. 91.
6. Ibid. p. 413.
7. *Heart of Darkness* ed. Robert Kimbrough (New York, Norton, 1963) p. 7.
8. 'An Image of Africa: Racism in Conrad's *Heart of Darkness*' in Chinua Achebe *Hopes and Impediments: Selected Essays 1965–1987* (London, Heinemann, 1988) pp. 1–13.
9. *Ulysses* pp. 271–2.
10. See, for example, Elie Kedourie *Nationalism* 4th expanded edn (Oxford, Blackwell, 1993); Ernest Gellner *Nations and Nationalism* (Oxford, Blackwell, 1983); Homi K. Bhabbha ed. *Nation and Narration* (London, Routledge, 1990).
11. Letter to Witter Bynner 13 March 1928. *The Letters of D. H. Lawrence*, vol. VI, eds. James T. Boulton and Margaret Boulton with Gerald M. Lacy (Cambridge University Press, 1991) p. 321.
12. *Phoenix* p. 31.
13. *Charles Dickens, a Critical Study* (London, 1898).

5 THE BREAK-UP OF MODERNIST MYTHOPOEIA

1. *Joseph and his Brothers*, trans. H. T. Lowe-Porter (New York, Knopf, 1948). German references to *Joseph und seine Brüder*, 4 vols., *Gesammelte Werke* ed. Peter de Mendelssohn (Frankfurt, Fischer, 1983). Original publication dates: *Die Geschichten Jaakobs* (Berlin, Fischer, 1933); *Der Junger Joseph* (Berlin, Fischer, 1934); *Joseph in Ägypten* (Vienna, Bermann-Fischer, 1936); *Joseph der Ernährer* (Stockholm, Bermann-Fischer, 1943).
2. *Essays of Three Decades* pp. 428–64.
3. *Thomas Mann y "Don Quixote": ensayos de literatura comparada* (Barcelona, Gedisa, 1990) pp. 247–49.
4. *Mythology and Humanism* p. 46.
5. Especially 'Pierre Menard, Author of the Quixote', 'Partial Magic in the Quixote', 'Parable of Cervantes and the *Quixote*' in *Labyrinths* pp. 62–71, 228–31, 278.
6. I discuss this closely in 'How Primordial is Narrative?' in *Narrative in Culture* ed. Cris Nash (London, Routledge, 1992) pp. 172–98.
7. *Cervantes y los casticismos españolas* (Madrid, Alianza, 1966).
8. Letter to Irita van Doren, 28 August 1951, *The Letters of Thomas Mann* sel. and ed. Richard and Clara Wilson (Harmondsworth, Penguin, 1975) p. 445.
9. *Don Quixote de la Mancha* trans. Charles Jarvis, ed. E. C. Riley (New York and London, Oxford University Press, 1992) pp. 313–16; *Don Quixote de la Mancha* ed. Martín de Riquer (Barcelona, Juventud, 1972) pp. 330, 332–3.
10. *Imagined Communities* (Thetford, Verso, 1983) especially pp. 28–40.
11. (Baltimore, Johns Hopkins University Press, 1966).
12. *Labyrinths* pp. 62–71; *Obras Completas* pp. 445–50.
13. See. p. 204 note 107.
14. See E. M. Forster *Aspects of the Novel* (London, Edward Arnold, 1927) pp. 40–1 and Boris Eichenbaum 'The Theory of the "Formal Method"' in *Russian Formalist Criticism* trans. and ed. Lee T. Lemon and Marion J. Reiss (Lincoln, University of Nebraska Press, 1965) pp.119–22.
15. *Illuminations* trans. Harry Zohn, ed. and intro. Hannah Arendt (London, Fontana, 1973) pp. 83–107.
16. *The Periodic Table* trans. Raymond Rosenthal (London, Abacus, 1986) p. 73; *Il sistema periodico* (Turin, Einaudi, 1975) p. 77.
17. Hannah Arendt *Eichmann in Jerusalem, a Report on the Banality of Evil* rev. edn (Harmondsworth, Penguin, 1977).
18. A black American, Haley claimed to have traced his ancestry back, through slave records, to an African village.
19. *Obra Periodistica* ed. Jaques Gilard (Barcelona, Bruguera, 1982) vol. III *Entre Cachacos*, pp. 892–3.
20. *Anti-Semite and Jew* trans. George J. Becker (New York, Schocken, 1948).
21. Letter to Edward Garnett, 5 June 1914. *Letters* II p. 182.

6   LIVING WITH MYTH: CERVANTES AND THE NEW WORLD

1. *Labyrinths* p. 278; *Obras Completas* p. 799.
2. Roberto Gonzalez Echevarría, *Alejo Carpentier: the Pilgrim at Home* (Ithaca NY, Cornell University Press, 1977) especially pp. 84–5.
3. Frederick de Armas, 'Metamorphosis as Revolt: Cervantes' *Persiles y Sigismunda* and Carpentier's El reino de este mundo' Hispanic Review 49, 1981, 297–316.
4. On the Latin American influence of Spengler see Echeverría *Pilgrim at Home* pp. 56–61.
5. This question has been much discussed recently as in Santiago Colás *Postmodernity in Latin America* (Durham Calif. and London, Duke University Press, 1994) and *The Postmodernism Debate in Latin America: Boundary II* special issue ed. John Beverley and José Oviedo, v. 20/3. Fall 1993.
6. See James Clifford's chapter 'On Ethnographic Surrealism' in *The Predicament of Culture: Twentieth-Century Ethnography, Literature and Art* (Cambridge Mass. and London, Harvard University Press, 1988) pp. 116–51. The surrealists mounted a rival exhibition to the colonial *Exposition* in Paris 1931, showing Catholic images as European fetishes.
7. Frantz Fanon *The Wretched of the Earth* trans. Constance Farrington (Harmondsworth, Penguin, 1967) p. 169.
8. *The Kingdom of this World* trans. Harriet de Ornis (Harmondsworth, Penguin, 1975) pp. 30–2; *El reino de este mundo* (Barcelona, Seix Barral, 1983) pp. 39–42.
9. Barbara Webb *Myth and History in Caribbean Fiction* (Amherst, University of Massachusetts Press, 1992) pp. 30–1.
10. Stanley Cavell *The Claim of Reason* (Oxford, Clarendon Press, 1979) p. 376.
11. *Wretched of the Earth* pp. 172–3.
12. Octavio Paz *The Labyrinth of Solitude* trans. Lysander Kemp (Harmondsworth, Penguin, 1985) p. 161.
13. *Birth of Tragedy* p. 135.
14. See Michael Bell *Gabriel Garcia Márquez: Solitude and Solidarity* (London, Macmillan, 1994) esp. pp. 40–69.
15. Ibid. pp. 52–7.

7   LIVING WITHOUT MYTH: DECONSTRUCTING THE OLD WORLD

1. Tony Tanner *Thomas Pynchon* (London, Methuen, 1982) p. 55.
2. *The Sentiment of Reality: Truth of Feeling in the European Novel* (London, Unwin, 1983).
3. *The Spectator*, ed. Donald F. Bond (London, Oxford University Press, 1965) vol. III, p. 178.
4. J. H. Brunvand *The Vanishing Hitchhiker: American Urban Legends and their Meanings* (New York and London, Norton, 1981).
5. *The Great War and Modern Memory* (New York and London, Oxford University

Press, 1975) p. 131; Bernard Bergonzi *Heroes' Twilight* (London, Constable, 1965).

6. *Great War and Modern Memory* pp. 117–18.
7. Dale Carter *The Final Frontier: the Rise and Fall of the American Rocket State* (London, Verso, 1988).
8. *V* (New York, Bantam, 1964) p. 140.
9. *Gravity's Rainbow* (London, Picador, 1975) p. 303.
10. *Critique of Cynical Reason* pp. 530–38.
11. See *The Political Unconscious: Narrative as a Socially Symbolic Act* (London, Methuen, 1981).
12. *Work on Myth* trans. Robert M. Wallace (Cambridge Mass. and London, MIT Press, 1985).
13. (London, Picador, 1984) p. 268.
14. Bruno Bettelheim *The Uses of Enchantment* (London, Thames and Hudson, 1976) pp. 114, 226.
15. *Out of Africa* (London, Putnam, 1964) p. 204.
16. John Bayley 'Fighting for the Crown' *New York Review of Books* 39/8 (23 April 1990) 1–13; Hermione Lee 'Angela Carter's Profane Pleasures' *Times Literary Supplement* 4655 (19 June 1992) 5–6.
17. *Twilight of the Idols* p. 92.
18. Terry Eagleton 'Capitalism, Modernism and Postmodernism' in *Modern Criticism and Theory* ed. David Lodge (London and New York, Longman, 1988) pp. 384–98. Jameson 'Postmodernism and Consumer Culture' in *The Anti-Aesthetic: Postmodern Culture* ed. Hal Foster (London, Pluto, 1985).

CONCLUSION: IDEOLOGY, MYTH AND CRITICISM

1. See Michael Polanyi *The Tacit Dimension* (London, Routledge and Kegan Paul, 1967) and Wittgenstein *Philosophical Investigations*.
2. See bibliography.
3. For a sharp critique of this see K. K. Ruthven *Myth* (London, Methuen, 1976) p. 74.
4. Ernst Cassirer *The Myth of the State* (New Haven, Yale University Press, 1946). Langer *Philosophy in a New Key* and *Feeling and Form*.
5. *Birth of Tragedy* p. 39.
6. See 'Culture is Ordinary' in *Resources of Hope*, ed. Robin Gable (London, Verso, 1989) pp. 3–18.
7. On the general theme see David Parker's chapter 'The Ethical Unconscious' in *Ethics, Theory and the Novel* (Cambridge University Press, 1994) pp. 43–52.
8. Jochen Schulte-Sasse, Foreword to Peter Bürger *Theory of the Avant-Garde* trans. Michael Shaw (Manchester University Press, 1984) p. xxxix.
9. 'Evaluative Discourse: the return of the repressed', Parker *Ethics, Theory and the Novel* pp. 7–31.
10. *Who Comes after the Subject?* p. 108.
11. Sloterdijk *Critique of Cynical Reason*. This phrase is central to his analysis and is

the opposite of modernist mythopoeia as defined by Karl Jaspers, 'Whoever seeks in this book a direct answer to the question of how to live, will seek it in vain . . . The book is only meaningful to those who experience life as a personal, irrational, inescapable responsibility.' Foreword to *Die Psychologie der Weltanschauungen* (my trans.).

12. *Twilight of the Idols* p. 30.

Select bibliography

Achebe, Chinua, *Hopes and Impediments: Selected Essays 1965–1987* (London, Heinemann, 1988).

Ackroyd, Peter, *Ezra Pound and his World* (London, Thames and Hudson, 1980).

Adorno, Theodor, *Negative Dialectics* trans. E. B. Ashton (London, Routledge and Kegan Paul, 1973).

Adorno, Theodor and Max Horkheimer, *Dialectic of Enlightenment* trans. John Cumming (London & New York, Verso, 1986).

Albright, Daniel, *The Myth against Myth: a Study of Yeats' Imagination in Old Age* (London, Oxford University Press, 1972).

Allison, David B., ed. *The New Nietzsche: Contemporary Styles of Interpretation* (New York, Dell Publishing, 1977).

Almeida, Hermione de, *Byron, Joyce through Homer* (Basingstoke, Macmillan, 1981).

Anderson, Benedict, *Imagined Communities* (Thetford, Verso, 1983).

Arendt, Hannah, *Eichmann in Jerusalem: a Report on the Banality of Evil* rev. edn (Harmondsworth, Penguin, 1977).

Armas, Frederick de, 'Metamorphosis as Revolt: Cervantes' *Persiles y Sigismunda* and Carpentier's *El reino de este mundo*' *Hispanic Review* 49 (1981), 297–316.

Arnold, Matthew, *On the Study of Celtic Literature* (London, Smith and Elder, 1861).
Poetry and Criticism of Matthew Arnold ed. A. Dwight Culler (Boston, Houghton Mifflin, 1961).

Barfield, Owen *Saving the Appearances: a Study in Idolatry* (New York, Harcourt Brace, 1965).

Bekker, p. *Musikgeschichte als Geschichte der musikalischen Formwandlung* (Stuttgart, Berlin and Leipzig, 1926).

Bell, Ian, *Critic as Scientist: the Modernist Poetics of Ezra Pound* (London, Methuen, 1981).

Bell, Michael, *Primitivism* (London, Methuen, 1972).
The Sentiment of Reality: Truth of Feeling in the European Novel (London, Unwin, 1983).
D. H. Lawrence: Language and Being (Cambridge University Press, 1992).
Gabriel Garcia Márquez: Solitude and Solidarity (London, Macmillan, 1994).

Bell, Michael, ed. *Context of English Literature 1900–1930* (London, Methuen, 1980).

Benjamin, Walter *Illuminations* trans. Harry Zohn and intro. Hannah Arendt
     (London, Fontana, 1973).
Benveniste, Emile, 'The Levels of Linguistic Analysis' in *Problems in General
     Linguistics* trans. Mary Elizabeth Meek (Great Gables Fla., University of
     Miami Press, 1971).
Bergonzi, Bernard, *Heroes' Twilight: a Study of the Literature of the Great War*
     (London, Constable, 1965), rev. edn (Manchester, Carcanet, 1996).
Berlin, Isaiah, *The Magus of the North: J. G. Hamann and the Origins of Modern
     Irrationalism* (London, J. Murray, 1993).
Berman, Marshall, *All that is Solid Melts into Air: the Experience of Modernity* (New
     York, Simon and Schuster, 1982).
Bernstein, Michael A., *The Tale of the Tribe: Ezra Pound and the Modern Verse Epic*
     (Princeton University Press, 1980).
Bersani, Leo, *A Future for Astynax: Character and Desire in Literature* (Boston, Little
     Brown, 1976).
Bettelheim, Bruno, *The Uses of Enchantment* (London, Thames and Hudson,
     1976).
Beverley, John and José Oviedo, eds. *The Postmodern Debate in Latin America:
     Boundary II* special issue, 20/3 (Fall 1993).
Bhabha, Homi K. *Nation and Narration* (London, Routledge, 1990).
Birenbaum, Harvey, *Between Blake and Nietzsche: The Reality of Culture* (London,
     Bucknell University Press, 1992).
Blixen, Karen, (Isak Dinesen) *Out of Africa* (London, Putnam, 1964).
Blumenberg, Hans, *The Legitimacy of the Modern Age* (London, MIT Press, 1983).
     Work on Myth (London, MIT Press, 1985).
Bohlmann, Otto, *Yeats and Nietzsche: An Exploration of Major Nietzshean Echoes in the
     Writings of W. B. Yeats* (London, Macmillan, 1982).
Bohrer, Karl-Heinz, ed. *Mythos und Moderne* (Frankfurt, Suhrkamp, 1983).
Bond, Donald F. ed. *The Spectator* (London, Oxford University Press, 1965).
Bornstein, Daniel, *The Postromantic Consciousness of Ezra Pound* (Victoria, BC,
     English Literary Studies, University of Victoria, 1977).
Boswell, James, *Life of Samuel Johnson* (New York and London, Oxford University
     Press, 1953).
Bradbury, Malcolm and James McFarlane, eds. *Modernism 1890–1930* (Harmon-
     dsworth, Penguin, 1976).
Brantlinger, Patrick, *Rule of Darkness: British Literature and Imperialism, 1830–1914*
     (Ithaca and London, Cornell University Press, 1988).
Brennan, Timothy, *Salman Rushdie and the Third World: Myths of the Nation*
     (London, Macmillan, 1992).
Bridgwater, Patrick, *Nietzsche in Anglo-Saxonny* (Leicester University Press,
     1972).
Brunvand, J. H., *The Vanishing Hitchhiker: American Urban Legends and their Meanings*
     (New York and London, Norton, 1981).
Bürger, Peter, *Theory of the Avant-Garde* trans. Michael Shaw (Manchester Uni-
     versity Press, 1984).

Burnet, John, *Early Greek Philosophy* (London, A. and C. Black, 1920).

Carter, Dale, *The Final Frontier: the Rise and Fall of the American Rocket State* (London, Verso, 1988).

Cascardi, Anthony J., *The Subject of Modernity* (Cambridge University Press, 1992.

Casillo, Robert, *The Genealogy of Demons: Anti-Semitism, Fascism, and the Myths of Ezra Pound* (Evanston, Northwestern University Press, 1988).

Cassirer, Ernst, *Language and Myth*, trans. by Suzanne K. Langer (New York, Dover Publications, 1953).

The Logic of the Humanities trans. Clarence Smith Howe (Newhaven, Yale University Press, 1961).

The Philosophy of Symbolic Forms trans. Ralph Manheim. Vol. I *Language*, vol II *Mythical Thought*, vol. III *The Phenomenology of Knowledge* (Newhaven, Yale University Press, 1953–5–7).

Castro, Americo, *Cervantes y los casticismos españolas* (Madrid, Alianza, 1966).

Cavell, Stanley, *The Claim of Reason* (Oxford, Clarendon Press, 1979).

Chace, William, *The Political Identities of Ezra Pound and T. S. Eliot* (Stanford University Press, 1973).

Chiari, Joseph, *The Aesthetics of Modernism* (London, Vision Press, 1970).

Clifford, James, *The Predicament of Culture* (Cambridge Mass., London, Harvard University Press, 1988).

Colás, Santiago, *Postmodernity in Latin America* (Durham Calif. and London, Duke University Press, 1994).

Connor, Steven, *Theory and Cultural Value* (Oxford, Blackwell, 1992).

Cook, Albert S., *Myth and Language* (Bloomington, Indiana University Press, 1980).

Craig, Cairns, *Yeats, Eliot, Pound and the Politics of Poetry* (London, Croom Helm, 1982).

Cunningham, Andrew and Nicholas Jardine, *Romanticism and the Sciences* (Cambridge University Press, 1990).

Dale, Peter Alan, *In Pursuit of a Scientific Culture* (Madison Wis. and London, University of Wisconsin Press, 1989).

Derrida, Jacques, 'Eating Well: on the Calculation of the Subject, an Interview with Jacques Derrida' in *Who Comes After the Subject?* ed. Eduardo Cadova, Peter Conner and Jean Luc Nancy (London, Routledge, 1991).

Diamond, Cora, *The Realistic Spirit: Wittgenstein, Philosophy and the Mind* (Cambridge, Mass. and London, MIT Press, 1991).

Echevarría, Roberto Gonzalez, *Alejo Carpentier: the Pilgrim at Home* (Ithaca NY, Cornell University Press, 1977).

Eliade, Mircea, *The Myth of the Eternal Return* (London, Routledge,1955).

Eliot, T. S., *Selected Essays of T. S. Eliot* (London, Faber and Faber, 1951).

On Poets and Poetry (New York, Farrar, Straus and Giroux, 1943).

Ellmann, Richard, *Ulysses on the Liffey* (London, Faber, 1972).

James Joyce (New York and London, Oxford University Press, 1965).

Emerson, Ralph Waldo, *The Collected Works of Ralph Waldo Emerson* ed. Alf. R. Ferguson, vol. I (Boston, Harvard University Press, 1971).

Fairhall, James, *James Joyce and the Question of History* (Cambridge University Press, 1993).

Falck, Colin, *Myth, Truth and Literature* (Cambridge University Press, 1989).

Fanon, Frantz, *The Wretched of the Earth* trans. Constance Farrington (Harmondsworth, Penguin, 1967).

Feder, Lilian, *Ancient Myth in Modern Poetry* (Princeton University Press, 1971).

Feldmann, B. and R. D. Richardson, *The Rise of Modern Mythology 1680–1860* (Bloomington, Indiana University Press, 1972).

Fichte, J. G., *The Science of Knowledge: with First and Second Introductions* ed. and trans. Peter Heath and John Lachs (Cambridge University Press, 1982).

Forster, E. M., *Aspects of the Novel* (London, Edward Arnold, 1927).

Forster, John B., *Heirs to Dionysus* (Princeton University Press, 1981).

Foster, Hal, ed. *The Anti-Aesthetic: Postmodern Culture* (London, Pluto, 1985).

Frank, Joseph, *The Widening Gyre: Crisis and Mastery in Modern Literature* (New Brunswick NJ, Rutgers University Press, 1963).

Frank, Manfred, *Alfred Schuler: Zur Funktion des Mythos in der Moderne* (Berlin, 1978).
Der Kommende Gott (Frankfurt, Suhrkamp, 1982).
Gott im Exil (Frankfurt, Suhrkamp, 1988).

Frazer, James, *The Golden Bough: a Study in Magic and Religion* ed. Robert Fraser (London and New York, Oxford University Press, 1992).

Freud, Sigmund, *The Complete Psychological Works* ed. and trans. James Strachey, 12 vols. (London, Hogarth Press, 1966–74).

Frobenius, Leo, *Erlebte Erdteile* 6 vols. (Frankfurt, 1925).

Fussell, Paul, *The Great War and Modern Memory* (London, Oxford University Press, 1975).

García Márquez, Gabriel, *Obra periodistica*, ed. Jacques Gilard, vol. III, *Entre Cachacos* (Barcelona, Bruguera, 1982).

Geertz, Clifford, *The Interpretation of Cultures: Selected Essays* (London, Fontana Press, 1993).

Gellner, Ernest, *Nations and Nationalism* (Oxford, Blackwell, 1983).

Girard, René *Deceit, Desire and the Novel* (Baltimore, Johns Hopkins University Press, 1966).

Gissing, George, *Charles Dickens: a Critical Study* (London, 1898).

Goldberg, S. L., *Agents and Lives* (Cambridge University Press, 1993).
The Classical Moment (London, Chatto and Windus, 1961).

Gould, Eric, *Mythical Intentions in Modern Literature* (Princeton University Press, 1981).

Guthke, Karl S., *Die Mythologie der Entgotterten Welt* (Göttingen, 1971).
Der Mythos der Neuzeit (Berne and Munich, Francke, 1983).

Habermas, Jurgen, *The Philosophical Discourse of Modernity* (Cambridge, Mass., Harvard University Press,1987).

Harris, Janice Hubbard, *The Short Fiction of D. H. Lawrence* (New Brunswick NJ, Rutgers University Press, 1984).

Hegel, G. W. F., *Lectures on the Philosophy of History* trans. J. Sibree (London, Bohn, 1858).

Heidegger, Martin, *On the Way to Language* trans. Peter D. Herz (New York, Harper and Row, 1971).

The Question Concerning Technology and Other Essays trans. William Lovitt (New York, Harper and Row, 1977).

Gesamtausgabe vol. 29/30 *Die Grundbegriffe der Metaphysik* ed. Wilhelm von Hermann (Frankfurt-on-Main, Vittorio Klostermann, 1983) and vol. 54, *Parmenides* ed. Manfred S. Frings (1982).

Herring, Phillip, *Joyce's Uncertainty Principle* (Princeton University Press, 1987).

Herrnstein Smith, Barbara *Contingencies of Value: Alternative Perspectives for Critical Theory* (Cambridge, Mass., Harvard University Press, 1988).

Hiller, Susan, *The Myth of Primitivism: Perspectives On Art* (London, Routledge, 1991).

Hubner, Kurt, *Die Wahrheit des Mythos* (Munich, Beck, 1985).

Hutcheon, Linda, *A Poetics of Postmodernism: History, Theory, Fiction* (London, Routledge, 1988).

Huyssen, Andreas, *After the Great Divide: Modernism, Mass Culture, Postmodernism* (Bloomington, Indiana University Press, 1986).

Iser, Wolfgang, *The Fictive and the Imaginary: Charting Literary Anthropology* (Baltimore and London, Johns Hopkins University Press, 1993).

Jameson, Fredric, *The Political Unconscious: Narrative as a Socially Symbolic Act* (London, Methuen, 1983).

'Postmodernism and Consumer Culture' in *The Anti-Aesthetic: Postmodern Culture* ed. Hal Foster (London, Pluto, 1985).

Jan Mohammed, Abdul, *Manichean Aesthetics: The Politics of Literature in Colonial Africa* (Amherst, University of Massachusetts Press, 1983).

Jarroway, David, *Wallace Stevens and the Question of Belief* (Baton Rouge & London, Louisiana State University Press, 1993).

Jaspers, Karl, *Die Psychologie der Weltanschauungen* 4th edn (Heidelberg, Springer, 1954).

Jeffares, Norman A. ed. *In Excited Reverie* (London and New York, Macmillan and St Martin's Press, 1965).

Joyce, James, *Letters of James Joyce* vol. I, Stuart Gilbert (New York, Viking, 1957).

Kant, Immanuel, *Critique of Judgement* 1st edn trans. J. H. Bernard (New York, Hafner, 1972).

Kayman, Martin A., *The Modernism of Ezra Pound: the Science of Poetry* (Basingstoke & London, Macmillan, 1986).

Kearney, Richard, 'Utopian and Ideological Myth in Joyce' *James Joyce Quarterly* 28 (1991), 873–8.

Kedourie, Elie, *Nationalism* 4th expanded edn (Oxford, Blackwell, 1993).

Kenner, Hugh, *Flaubert, Joyce and Beckett: The Stoic Comedians* (London, W. H. Allen, 1964).

Kiely, Robert, ed. *Modernism Reconsidered* (Cambridge MA and London, Harvard University Press, 1983).

Kipperman, Mark, *Beyond Enchantment: German Idealism and English Romantic Poetry* (Philadelphia, University of Pennsylvania Press, 1986).

Kirk, G. S., *Myth: Its Meaning and Functions in Ancient and Other Cultures* (London, Cambridge University Press, 1970).

Kolakowski, Leszek, *The Presence of Myth* (University of Chicago Press, 1989).

Koppen, Irwin, *Thomas Mann y "Don Quixote": ensayos de literatura comparada* (Barcelona, Gedisa, 1990).

Kuhn, Thomas S., *The Structure of Scientific Revolutions* (Chicago and London, Chicago University Press, 1962).

Lange, Friedrich, *The History of Materialism* (London, Routledge, 1925).

Langer, Suzanne K., *Feeling and Form* (London, Routledge, 1953).

Langer, Suzanne K., *Philosophy in New Key: A Study in the Symbolism of Reason, Rite and Art* 3rd edn (Cambridge Mass. and London: Harvard University Press, 1957).

Lawrence, David Herbert, *Fantasia of the Unconscious and Psychoanalysis and the Unconscious* (London, Heinemann, 1961).

The Letters of D. H. Lawrence vol. II, ed. George Zytaruk and James T. Boulton (Cambridge University Press, 1981).

Phoenix: The Posthumous Papers of D. H. Lawrence ed. Edward D. McDonald (London, Heinemann, 1936).

Phoenix II: Uncollected, Unpublished and Other Prose Works by D. H. Lawrence ed. Warren Roberts and Harry T. Moore (London, Heinemann, 1968).

Study of Thomas Hardy and Other Essays ed. Bruce Steele (Cambridge University Press, 1985).

Twilight in Italy and Other Essays ed. Paul Eggert (Cambridge University Press, 1994).

Lawrence, Karen, *The Odyssey of Style in 'Ulysses'* (Princeton University Press, 1981).

Leavis, F. R. with Q. D. Leavis, *Lectures in America* (London, Chatto and Windus, 1969).

Two Cultures? The Significance of C. P. Snow (London, Chatto and Windus, 1962).

Lemon, Lee T. and Marion Reiss, trans. and ed. *Russian Formalist Criticism* (Lincoln, University of Nebraska Press, 1965).

Levenson, Michael, *A Genealogy of Modernism* (Cambridge University Press, 1984).

Modernism and the Fate of Individuality (Cambridge University Press, 1991).

Levi-Strauss, *The Savage Mind* (Chicago and London, University of Chicago Press, 1966).

Levy-Bruhl, Lucien, *Primitive Mentality* trans. L. A. Clare (New York and London, 1923).

Lindberg, Kathryne V., *Reading Pound Reading: Modernism after Nietzsche* (Oxford University Press, 1987).

Lodge, David, ed. *Modern Criticism and Theory* (London and New York, Longman, 1988).

Longenbach, James, *Modernist Poetics of History: Pound, Eliot and the Sense of the Past* (Princeton University Press, 1987).

Lovibond, Sabina, *Realism and Imagination in Ethics* (Oxford, Blackwell, 1983).

Lowry, Shirley Park, *Familiar Mysteries: The Truth in Myth* (New York, Oxford University Press, 1982).

Lyotard, Jean-François, *The Postmodern Condition: A Report on Knowledge* trans. Geoff. Bennington and Brian Massumi (Manchester University Press, 1984).

MacIntyre, Alasdair, *After Virtue* (London, Duckworth, 1981).

Makin, Peter, *Pound's Cantos* (Baltimore and London, Johns Hopkins University Press, 1992).

Malpas, J. E., *Donald Davidson and the Mirror of Meaning: Holism, Truth, Interpretation* (Cambridge University Press, 1992).

Manganaro, Marc, *Myth, Rhetoric and the Voice of Authority: A Critique of Frazer, Eliot, Frye and Campbell* (Newhaven and London, Yale University Press, 1992).

Manganaro, Marc, ed. *Modernist Anthropology: From Fieldwork To Text* (Princeton University Press, 1990).

Mann, Thomas and Karl Kerenyi *Mythology and Humanism: the Correspondence of Thomas Mann and Karl Kerenyi* trans. Alexander Gelley (Ithaca NY, Cornell University Press, 1975).

Essays of Three Decades trans. H. T. Lowe-Porter (London, Secker and Warburg, 1947).

Gesammelte Werke vol. XI, (Frankfurt, Fischer, 1960).

The Letters of Thomas Mann sel. and ed. Richard and Clara Wilson (Harmondsworth, Penguin, 1975).

Marcus, Steven, *The Other Victorians* (London, Weidenfeld and Nicolson, 1966).

Margolis, John, *T. S. Eliot's Intellectual Development* (Chicago and London, Chicago University Press, 1973).

McCabe, Colin, *James Joyce and the Revolution of the Word* (London, Macmillan, 1979).

McGee, Patrick, *Telling the Other: The Question of Value in Modern and Postcolonial Writing* (Ithaca, Cornell University Press, 1992).

Megill, Allan, *Prophets of Extremity: Nietzsche, Heidegger, Foucault, Derrida* (Berkeley and London, University of California Press, 1985).

Meisel, Perry, *The Myth of the Modern* (New Haven and London, Yale University Press, 1987).

Meyer, Theo, *Nietzsche und die Kunst* (Tübingen, Francke, 1992).

Michel, Ernst, *Der Weg zun Mythos: Zur Wiedergeburt der Kunst aus dem Geist der Religion* (Jena, 1919).

Nagel, Thomas, *The View from Nowhere* (New York and London, Oxford University Press, 1986).

Nash, Cris, ed. *Narrative in Culture* (London, Routledge, 1992).

Nehamas, Alexander, *Nietzsche: Life as Literature* (Cambridge MA and London: Harvard University Press, 1985).

Nicholls, Peter, *Ezra Pound: Politics, Economics and Writing; a Study of the Cantos* (London, Macmillan, 1984).

' "A Consciousness Disjunct": Sex and the Writer in Ezra Pound's *Hugh Selwyn Mauberley*' *Journal of American Studies* 28 (1994) 61–5.

'LOST OBJECT(S): Ezra Pound and Italy' in *Ezra Pound and Europe* ed. Richard Taylor and Claus Melchior (Amsterdam and Atlanta Ga., Rodopi, B. V., 1993), pp. 165–75.

Nietzsche, Friedrich, *The Birth of Tragedy out of the Spirit of Music* trans. Walter Kaufmann (New York, Random House, 1957).

Twilight of the Idols trans. R. J. Hollingdale (Harmondsworth, Penguin, 1968).

Untimely Meditations trans. R. J. Hollingdale (Cambridge University Press, 1983).

Philosophy and Truth: Selections from Nietzsche's Notebooks of the Early 1870's trans and ed. Daniel Breazale (New Jersey and London, Humanities Press, 1990).

Nolan, Emer, *James Joyce and Nationalism* (London, Routledge, 1995).

North, Michael, *The Political Aesthetic of Yeats, Eliot and Pound* (Cambridge University Press, 1991).

Nussbaum, Martha, *The Fragility of Goodness: Luck and Ethics in Greek Tragedy and Philosophy* (Cambridge University Press, 1986).

Love's Knowledge: Essays on Philosophy and Literature (New York and Oxford, Oxford University Press, 1990).

Orr, Leonard, ed. *Yeats and Postmodernism* (Syracuse and London, Syracuse University Press, 1991).

Parker, David, *Ethics, Theory and the Novel* (Cambridge University Press, 1994).

Paz, Octavio, *The Labyrinth of Solitude* trans. Lysander Kemp (Harmondsworth, Penguin, 1985).

Pearson, Karl, *The Grammar of Science* (London, Walter Scott, 1892).

Pippin, Robert, *Modernism as a Philosophical Problem* (Oxford, Blackwell, 1991).

Plato, *The Republic* ed. and trans. Desmond Lee (Harmondsworth, Penguin, 1955).

Polanyi, Michael, *The Tacit Dimension* (London, Routledge and Kegan Paul, 1967).

Popper, Karl, *The Myth of the Framework: In Defence of Science and Rationality* (London, Routledge, 1994).

Pound, Ezra, *The Spirit of Romance* (London, Peter Owen, 1952).

Literary Essays of Ezra Pound ed. T. S. Eliot (New York, New Directions, 1968).

The Chinese Written Character as a Medium for Poetry (San Francisco, City Lights, 1969).

Ezra Pound: Selected Prose: 1909–1965 ed. William Cookson (London, Faber, 1973).

Quinones, Ricardo, *Mapping Literary Modernism: Time and Development* (Princeton University Press, 1985).

Rabaté, Jean-Michel, *Joyce Upon the Void: The Genesis of Doubt* (London: Macmillan, 1991).

Ragussis, Michael, *The Subterfuge of Art: Language and the Romantic Tradition* (Baltimore, Johns Hopkins University Press, 1978).

Reiss, Timothy J., *The Discourse of Modernism* (Ithaca and London, Cornell University Press, 1982).

Reynolds, Mary T., *Joyce and Dante: The Shaping Imagination* (Princeton University Press, 1981).

Ricoeur, Paul, *The Rule of Metaphor* trans. Robert Czerny, Kathleen McLaughlin and John Castello (London, Routledge and Kegan Paul, 1978).

Righter, William, *Myth and Literature* (London, Routledge and Kegan Paul, 1975).

Robertson, Richie, 'Primitivism and Psychology: Freud, Nietzsche, Thomas Mann' in Peter Collier and Judy Davies, eds. *Modernism and the European Unconscious* (Cambridge University Press, 1990), pp. 79–93.

Rorty, Richard, *Objectivity, Relativism and Truth* (Cambridge University Press, 1981).

Contingency, Irony and Solidarity (Cambridge University Press, 1989).

Ruthven, K. K., *Myth* (London, Methuen, 1976).

Said, Edward, *Culture and Imperialism* (London, Vintage, 1994).

Sartre, Jean Paul, *Anti-Semite and Jew* trans. George G. Becker (New York, Schocken, 1948).

Saussure, Ferdinand de, *Cours de Linguistique Générale* (Lausanne, Payot, 1916).

Schutte, William M., *Joyce and Shakespeare* (Hamden Conn., Archon Books, 1971).

Schwartz, Sanford, *The Matrix of Modernism: Pound, Eliot and Early Twentieth-Century Thought* (Princeton University Press, 1985).

Sebeok, Thomas A., ed. *Myth: A Symposium* (Bloomington, Indiana University Press, repr. 1972).

Seiden, Morton Irving, *W. B. Yeats: the Poet as Mythmaker* (New York, Cooper Square, repr. 1975).

Senn, Fritz, 'Esthetic Theories' *James Joyce Quarterly* 2 (Winter, 1965), 134–6.

Sidney, Philip, *The Poems of Sir Philip Sidney* (Oxford, Clarendon Press, 1962).

Simpson, David, *Romanticism, Nationalism and the Revolt against Theory* (Chicago & London, University of Chicago Press, 1993).

Sloterdijk, Peter, *Critique of Cynical Reason* trans. Michael Eldred (London and New York, Verso, 1988).

Stanford, W. B., *The Ulysses Theme: A Study of the Adaptability of a Traditional Hero* (Oxford, Basil Blackwell, 1963).

Stern, Peter, *Nietzsche* (London, Fontana, 1978).

Stocking, George, *Victorian Anthropology* (New York, The Free Press, 1987).

Street, Brian, *The Savage in Literature: Representations of 'Primitive' society in English fiction 1858–1920* (London, Routledge and Kegan Paul, 1975).

Surette, Leon, *A Light from Eleusis* (Oxford, Clarendon Press, 1970).

Tannen, Deborah, *You Just Don't Understand: Women and Men in Conversation* (London, Virago, 1991).

Tanner, Tony, *Thomas Pynchon* (London, Methuen, 1982).

Taylor, Charles, *The Sources of the Self: the Making of Modern Identity* (Cambridge University Press, 1989).

The Ethics of Authenticity (Cambridge MA. and London: Harvard University Press, 1991).

Thompson, William Irwin, *The Imagination of an Insurrection: Dublin, Easter 1916, a Study of an Ideological Movement* (New York, Oxford University Press, 1967).

Thuente, Mary Ellen, *W. B. Yeats and Irish Folklore* (Dublin, Gill and Macmillan, 1980).

Torgovnick, Marianna, *Gone Primitive, Savage Intellects, Modern Lives* (Chicago and London, University of Chicago Press, 1990).

Turner, Martha A., *Mechanism and the Novel: Science in the Narrative Process* (Cambridge University Press, 1993).

Vendler, Helen, *On Extended Wings: Wallace Stevens' Longer Poetry* (London and Oxford, Harvard University Press, 1969).

Vickery, John B., *The Literary Impact of The Golden Bough* (Princeton University Press, 1973).

   Myths and Texts: Strategies of Incorporation and Displacement (Baton Rouge and London, Louisiana State University Press, 1983).

Volney, *The Ruins, or a Survey of the Revolutions of Empires* (London, T. Allman, 1835).

Waugh, Patricia, *Practising Postmodernism, Reading Modernism* (London, Edward Arnold, 1992).

Webb, Barbara, *Myth and History in Caribbean Fiction* (Amherst, University of Massachusetts Press, 1992).

Wellmer, Albrecht, *The Persistence of Modernity: Essays on Aesthetics, Ethics and Postmodernism* trans. David Midgely (Oxford, Polity in association with Blackwell, 1991).

White, J. J., *Mythology in the Modern Novel:A Study of Prefigurative Techniques* (Princeton University Press 1971).

Williams, Bernard, *Ethics and the Limits of Philosophy* (Cambridge, MA, Harvard University Press, 1985).

Williams, Raymond, ed. Robin Gable *Resources of Hope* (London, Verso, 1989).

Williamson, Edwin, ed. *Cervantes and the Modernists: the Question of Influence* (London and Madrid, Tamesis, 1994).

Winckelmann, J. J. *Winckelmann: Writings on Art* sel. and ed. David Irwin (London, Phaidon Press, 1972).

Wittgenstein, Ludwig, *Philosophical Investigations* trans. G. E. M. Anscombe (Oxford, Blackwell, 1958).

   Tractatus Logico-Philosophicus trans. D. F. Pears and B. T. McGuiness (London, Routledge and Kegan Paul, 1961).

Wood, Jessie (née Chambers, E. T.), *A Personal Record* (London, Cape, 1935).

Woolf, Virginia, *The Common Reader* (London, Hogarth Presss, 1925).

Wordsworth, William, *The Poetical Works of William Wordsworth* rev. edn Ernest de Selincourt (London and New York, Oxford University Press, 1936).

Yeats, W. B., ed. Stephen Maxfield Parrish *Concordance to the Poems of W. B. Yeats* (Ithaca NY, Cornell University Press, 1963).

   Essays and Introductions (New York, Macmillan, 1961).

   Explorations (London, Macmillan, 1962).

Young, Robert, *Colonial Desire: Hybridity in Theory, Culture and Race* (London, Routledge, 1994).

   White Mythologies: Writing History and the West (London, Routledge, 1990).

Index

Index